Defining Print Culture
for Youth

Recent Titles in
the Beta Phi Mu Monograph Series

DEFINING PRINT CULTURE FOR YOUTH

The Cultural Work of Children's Literature

Edited by

Anne Lundin
and
Wayne A. Wiegand

LIBRARIES
U N L I M I T E D
A Member of the Greenwood Publishing Group

Westport, Connecticut • London

Library of Congress Cataloging-in-Publication Data

Defining print culture for youth : the cultural work of children's literature /
edited by Anne Lundin and Wayne Wiegand.
    p. cm.
Papers presented at a conference sponsored by the Center for the History of Print
Culture in Modern America.
ISBN 0-313-32177-9 (alk. paper)
    1. Children's literature—History and criticism—Congresses. I. Lundin, Anne H.,
1944- II. Wiegand, Wayne. III. Center for the History of Print Culture in Modern
America.
PN1008.3.D44 2003
809'.89282—dc21   2003003756

British Library Cataloging in Publication Data is available.

Library of Congress Catalog Card Number: 2003003756
ISBN: 0-313-32177-9

First published in 2003

Libraries Unlimited
A Member of Greenwood Publishing Group, Inc.
88 Post Road West, Westport, CT 06881
www.lu.com

Printed in the United States of America

The paper used in this book complies with the
Permanent Paper Standard issued by the National
Information Standards Organization (Z39.48–1984).

10 9 8 7 6 5 4 3 2 1

Copyright Acknowledgment

Research reprinted from Bonnie James Shaker, *Coloring Locals: Racial Formation in
Kate Chopin's Youth's Companion Stories,* 2003, courtesy of University of Iowa Press.

*To our colleagues
at
the University of Wisconsin-Madison
School of Library and Information Studies,
whose encouragement and support
make projects like this
so rewarding.*

CONTENTS

ACKNOWLEDGMENTS

At the October 1995 annual meeting of the Advisory Board of the Center for the History of Print Culture in Modern America, Board Chairman Paul Boyer moved to approve "Defining Print Culture for Youth" as the Center's second biennial conference. That autumn, Codirectors Wayne A. Wiegand and James P. Danky worked with me to draft a Call for Papers. In late 1996, paper proposals were carefully evaluated by a committee of Board members including Wayne Wiegand, James P. Danky, Rima Apple, Ginny Moore Kruse, Steve Vaughn, and Maureen Hady, the Center's Assistant Director. In May 1997, Maureen organized a flawless conference. Over two days, a most diverse group of scholars—from graduate students to senior faculty—shared their work and created new bonds. Maureen was ably assisted in her organizing efforts by a number of Wisconsin Historical Society staff members, including Carol Crossan, Amy Castle, Michael Edmonds, John Cherney, and J. Kevin Graffagnino.

This anthology consists of a series of essays selected by the committee members identified above from the papers presented at that conference. We greatly appreciate the support of James V. Carmichael, Editor of the Beta Phi Mu Monographs Series, and, at Libraries Unlimited, Ed Kurdyla and Martin Dillon, who kept this work on track and helped to produce a much better book. We are also indebted to Heather Daniels for constructing the index. The enthusiastic support of Michael Edmonds and Peter Gottlieb of the Wisconsin Historical Society was critical to the success of the conference. The "home" for the Center for the History of Print Culture in Modern America is the University of Wisconsin-Madison's School of Library and Information Studies, where it has been nurtured and supported by numerous colleagues, and we thank especially its director, Louise Robbins. To all these friends and colleagues who generously gave of their time and energy (and especially to Wayne Wiegand and Jim Danky for their assistance above and beyond the call of duty), my thanks.

Anne Lundin

INTRODUCTION

Anne Lundin

From the first cautionary advice by Dr. Spock, read by an anxious mother holding in her hand an anguished infant, to the giddy goose rhymes or "Pat-the-Bunnies" read at bedtime, to the cereal boxes of champions on the breakfast table, to the scout manuals memorized, the fugitive diaries, the Peanuts cartoons, and to those first chapter books, a child is raised by arms of print. Those who survive lessons in one-, two-, and three-syllable words travel beyond the rearing borders of home and street through the agency of literature, the fiction and nonfiction journey of the mind.

The culture of print for children and youth is so vast and unexplored a journey that it calls, in all of its fluidity, for definition and identification. The effects of such naming acquire ever more perplexing significations and demand critical elasticity when applied to youth and the palimpsest of print. Acts of definition are anywhere problematic, since the academic culture potentially can define, marginalize, and erase otherness. As Edmund Burke observed over two centuries ago, when we define, we risk circumscribing nature within the bounds of our own notions. Yet in defining the culture of print for youth—an area of innocence if not experience—where do we move beyond our own boundaries?

In defining print culture for youth, what is "print culture"? I will offer a brief survey of scholarship in the field and then look toward the specialized nature of a print culture of childhood and youth in the modern America of the last century. With a grounding in popular culture, reader response, and the history of the book, the study of print culture is a complex social, literary, and bibliographic discourse into the form and function of print in social history. "Print culture" is a wide net that includes extraliterary texts under the rubric "literature", and reads them in the same way as traditional literature. The opening of the literary canon to popular culture and the opening of literary criticism to postmodernism and the return of the reader allow for a broader study of diverse kinds of cultural work. This reader-centered cultural criticism argues that literary canons are social constructions, that literary texts are intertextually connected to other literary and extraliterary (rather than nonliterary) texts, and that readers relate to interpretive communities and the transformed products of a culture, through which cultural discourse happens and matters.[1] The particular "print culture" stance is distinguished by the emphasis on book history as a more empirical approach to these issues of reader response and canon formation. While book history in itself holds pride of place in literary studies, the new attention expands literary history to include other interdisciplinary slants on the agency and practice of reader and reading: who read what, when, and how.

Normatively, literary historians and critics tend to pursue textual matters in terms of what Raymond Williams calls a "selective tradition," a dominating set of perspectives and world views. This restrictive transmission of knowledge, history, and culture of only elite groups functions as a pragmatic instrument and powerful abstraction to ratify historical and cultural social order as a vital element of hegemonic culture. This "lived system of meaning and values" becomes "reality for most people in society."[2] This transmission of class culture as common culture has privileged the canon and silenced cultures of the Other. The discourse over canon in the last few decades extends from the center to the margins, from the absolutes to the contingencies. The concept of culture is now recognized as the structure of social relations within class, race, gender, and age relations of power. Literary culture is part and parcel of the larger arena, whose institutions and practices make literature happen or not. In the words of literary historian Cathy Davidson, book history "constantly moves between material, aesthetic, and ideological planes," which are constructions of a specific historical context.[3]

In its interdisciplinarity—its explorations of the relations of literacy, knowledge, technology, and power in cultural production—print culture history is revolutionary. The field draws from various approaches and types of discourse, categorized by Janice Radway as literacy studies, reader-response theory, ethnographies of reading, and a social history of books.[4] Scholars like Harvey Graff, Elizabeth Eisenstein, and Carl Kaestle view the evolution of literacy through multiple perspectives, including the effects of oral traditions, technology, and class structures and cultural capital. The breadth of their approaches can be contrasted against a work such as E. D. Hirsch's *Cultural Literacy,* which, in decontextualizing cultural heritage, reduces the complexities of literacy to a listing of 5,000 "essential names, phrases, dates, and concepts."[5]

Reader-response theories view the reader as a creative maker of meaning. The reader is as significant to literature as the writer; cultural contexts affect what authors write and how we read. Stanley Fish argues that all texts exist in the reader and within certain "interpretive communities."[6] Reading is not merely the transfer of information from author to reader, but also a dynamic process of making meaning. The search for meaning in a text is shaped by a "horizon of expectations," in Hans Robert Jauss's terms.[7] This framework of sociocultural contexts, both contemporary and historical, creates the interpretive communities that receive texts. Jane Tompkins's study of the reception of popular American fiction in the nineteenth century recovers the historical response of contemporary readers to "sensational designs," a desired social and political order, "not in relation to unchanging formal, psychological, or philosophical standards of complexity, or truth, or correctness."[8] Reading is both social practice and private experience. As Louise Rosenblatt so eloquently expresses, a text is a performance, a kind of poem composed of the reader's interaction with a particular literary work.[9] The role of the audience complicates assumptions about the hegemonic influence on autonomous readers, whether this is domination or resistance. The return of the reader overturns the position of text and context and shifts interest from literary studies to cultural studies.

Ethnographies of reading explore the social bases of reading within particular contexts, or, "historically specific conditions."[10] Janice Radway and John Fiske are notable for their studies of popular culture audiences, in which they argue that texts become popular by offering to readers constructions that appeal to their psychological and social needs. Fiske suggests that audiences make choices based on the textual appropriation of relevant contemporary images and issues. These texts are called "producerly" in their construction of familiar motifs and multiple meanings.[11] In her study of romance readers, Radway suggests that readers choose texts that offer ways of reading their own experiences. "By focusing on social process—that is, on what people do with texts and objects rather than on those texts and objects themselves," she argues, "we should begin to see that people do not ingest mass culture whole but often remake it into something they can use."[12]

This approach, which is receiving further attention through the volume *The Ethnography of Reading,* is often based on Clifford Geertz's work on symbolic anthropology, in the compiling of a "thick description," which emphasizes the need not just to describe the "meaning particular social actions have for the actors whose actions they are," but also for "stating, as explicitly as we can manage, what the knowledge thus attained demonstrates about the society in which it is found, and, beyond that, about social life as such." The society, the social life, the culture is "a complex web of significance," in which the meanings are embodied as artifacts and practices.[13]

The final category of approaches to the history of the book encompasses social histories of books, which are also called "print culture history." Drawing on these various approaches of literacy—reader-response and the ethnography of reading, among others—print culture historians explore the historical existence of authors and texts within a broad sociocultural understanding. As Cathy Davidson suggests, "literature is not simply words upon a page but a complex social, political, and material process of cultural production."[14] Moving from a traditional historiography or textual interpretation, scholars look for the agency of texts as material artifact and conveyor of meaning in a complex mediation of writers, readers, publishers, media, and institutional forces like schools and libraries: the art and commerce of literature, the traffic of texts.

Print culture scholars—by whatever name they are known—play upon a spacious landscape of written communication, including formats of books; manuscripts, periodicals, and ephemera; high culture texts and popular culture; schoolbooks; scrapbooks; and manuals. The subjects include areas related to reading, authorship, publishing, book arts, censorship, libraries, literacy, advertising, propaganda, and related uses of script and print in any medium and for any age group. Thus, print culture scholars have an enlarged and problematized interest in children's literature—literary and extraliterary—as cultural work.

Children's literature as a field of study is experiencing a renaissance in interdisciplinary interest. As higher education developed over the past century, the study of children's books was largely relegated to schools of education and library science, with criticism largely hagiography or pedagogy. Children's literature became associated with "popular culture," which until recently was not deemed worthy of studies of intellectual history, bibliography, or literary criticism. Criticism of children's books has been largely the province of a small enclave of writers and critics whose background is more in practice than in theory, whose interests are more of function than of form, of utility or of an ideal child, removed from the larger sociohistorical frame that confounds all categories. Much of the writing about children's books has worked within a particular elite tradition of fantasy and has, until recently, slighted the phenomenally popular fiction of Horatio Alger's capitalist tales in the nineteenth century, or the adventurous tales of Nancy Drew and the Hardy boys in the twentieth. The new interest in Nancy Drew, stimulated by the School of Journalism's conference at the University of Iowa in 1993, draws scholars interested in the series as text and as culture industry. Various publications demonstrate the multiplicity of approaches.[15] Uli Knoeflmacher, in the introduction to the Modern Language text on teaching children's literature, argues that the multiplicity of approaches to a children's text generates more perspectives than what may be accessible to a traditional adult text, thus inspiring a flourishing scholarship similar to the excitement of the feminist critics of the 1970s.[16]

This marked increase in the amount and variety of scholarly work on children's books and printed matter is influenced by new trends in higher education: a blurring of genres; an emphasis on new theoretical approaches of feminism, reader response, New Historicism, and the larger rubric of cultural studies; a greater respect for popular culture; interest in the history of childhood; debate on cultural literacy; heightened attention to women and minorities; and, as this volume attests, the prominence of print culture—how print-based culture is produced, distributed, and absorbed by readers. As disciplines open up, new opportunities exist to include the study of print culture for youth in diverse fields.

The essays in this volume address the larger issues of print culture for children and youth as consumers, citizens, and members of a community of readers. They join a cultural debate over the nature of childhood in specific historical periods as well as the very nature of what is a literature of childhood. The definitions of what constitutes "children's literature" remain ambiguous, although new boundaries expand perceptions. To Harvey Darton, who wrote the first definitive history in 1932, a child's book was one that sought to provide pleasure, however defined by the age. That privileging of imaginative literature tended to exclude nonfictional discourses. Contemporary critics revise that focus with a broader sense of "pleasure" and a larger context of cultural production. John Townsend describes the genre pragmatically as any book that a publisher promotes for children. Brian Alderson sees the literature as comprising a semi-didactic and semi-recreational character. Peter Hunt defines the book in terms of the reader rather than the intentions of the text or the author. Mitzi Myers views an integrated text and sociohistoric context and questions the contingency of standard historical notions of the child and of literature.[17]

Few scholars from outside the fields of English, education, or librarianship attempt acts of definition; they instead focus on the representations in perhaps the most ardent audience of literary practice. Children's literature, for the purposes of this collection, is defined as texts written or read by children from infancy through adolescence—not just books written for that audience, but all print materials that children are capable of reading. An inclusive definition extends the boundaries of "literature" to whatever discourse children are reading, by which the text of a book enters the text of their lives. Children's literature exists in the context of childhood and of literary experience—a shifting horizon of expectation.

While social values are commonly explored in studies of children's literature, recent developments in literary criticism place new value on the reader. In short, critics of language and literature have moved from a focus of study on the text to the reader's response. Reader-response criticism—the multiple ways a text can be read—is the most commonly practiced approach in the field. Critics like Peter Hunt, Margaret Meek, and Aidan Chambers argue that the experience of literary culture always begins with the real reader.[18] Many of the works of intimate value to young readers throughout history, which had been dismissed by educators and scholars as flotsam and jetsam, are now receiving attention as important players in the culture industry of past or present. Scholars are ever broadening the notion of what constitutes a "text" and consider any text in relation to its readers. Since many of the texts that exist in the world bear some relationship to childhood literature, the genre—as well as its readers—is increasingly studied in diverse fields that bring their own questions to the fore. Controversy over the canon subverts traditional notions that privilege classic works and opens up a much larger universe of literary experience. Instead of viewing literature as possessing intrinsic values that speak from one generation to the next, critics approach literature as a construct within a cultural environment. Meanings of texts are contingent on their history of reception, on how these works have been experienced by readers and fashioned in a sociohistorical process. Children's texts are now receiving attention in terms of their historical reception—their contemporary readership—and the construction of a children's "classic" as a social process in which literary reputations are made, not born.[19]

The purpose of this volume is to allow varied voices to speak on the literature of childhood: the cultural work of a disparate, yet interrelated, literature in which ideological, political, and material factors shape the reader's role. The ten essays in this collection cover a wide range of print culture, considered as a whole as "children's literature," "adolescent literature," "the literature of childhood," or "print culture for youth." Not only is the very nature of canonical children's books at issue, but also the wider field of "extraliterary" texts that call for similar considerations: manuals, schoolbooks, scrapbooks, comics, journals, and mass-market books. The central question that unites these essays asks what a more elastic and dynamic discourse—including multiple perspectives and formats as well as the long-standing traditions—means for the definition of children's literature. As literary study over the last few decades has been revolutionized through many a slant of light, so too has children's literature been transformed through perspectives of cultural studies, including perspectives of feminism, popular culture, reader response, New Historicism, and Afro-American studies, among others. These new explorations directed toward the history of reading and print culture complicate already discursive definitions of a literature of childhood. Historians from diverse academic fields offer for critical consideration a vast body of publications that have been largely overlooked. The scholars in this collection—from fields of English, history, education, library science, journalism, and communications, among others—speak to the interdisciplinarity of the study of children's books as cultural discourse. Their labors of homesteading, of breaking new ground on the landscape called "children's literature," examine vectors of power and subversion in both text and reader. Their paths pose questions of who are the readers, where are the borders, and what is the cultural work of this broad expanse of informative and recreational textuality of youth in the American print culture of the last century?

Definitions of childhood and its literature indeed differ culturally and over time. The problematic hermeneutics of both "childhood" and "literature" complicate its trajectory in the cultural history of post-1870s America. Rather than a teleological trail of "better and brighter," the condition of children and the condition of their literature are contingent on the ways the culture wishes to see itself, its political choices amid competing ideologies, the relations between children and adults, and hegemonic power structures. Understanding these conditions requires the depth of "thick description," the accumulated data that are constructed by cultural studies such as these essays, that address issues of textual and sociohistorical context, that lure us to leave rooms of our own to see what children's literature has to say about itself in the world outside. These may not be canonical children's literature studies, although they could be. Cultural studies do not require a repudiation of elite cultural forms, but seek the representation of what gives these particular forms agency in specific contexts. These particular papers offer pieces of print culture that may never have been considered together before as part of the literature of childhood. Each essay strives toward a new definition of print culture for youth and, by extension, of literature itself, by crossing boundaries and presenting unique challenges of interpretation that are themselves acts of definition. These literary practices are social actions, whereby social conditions, ideologies, rhetorical practices, interpretive strategies, and cultural factors of race, class, and gender intersect and, in so doing, reconceive the reader in the text. These essays examine the literature of youth in these terms—the cultural politics of race, class, and gender—in which meaning is made at the junctures of dominant, mass, and popular cultures. These three discourses lend internal pressure that defines divisions and disturbs the definition of American youth literature in its sociohistorical context.

Feminist cultural criticism brings to consciousness the construction of subjects. Female subjectivity is created, in part, by the readers who read resistantly or readily, who respond to texts with texts of their own making. Susan Tucker's essay, "Reading and Re-reading: The Scrapbooks of Girls Growing into Women, 1900–1930," enlarges the perception of text and reader to include the material culture of scrapbooks, with its closely linked developments in reading, writing, printing, and publishing, and its intimate, gendered reader response. Tucker documents how these allegiances and identities have varied in their representation and changed as society changed. The use of print culture as private archive is documented as an enclosed series of images and readings of the past, present, and the future.

Paul C. Mishler's essay, "Communism for Kids: Class, Race, and Gender in Communist Children's Books in the United States," explores a prolific body of literature that has been long unknown: radical literature for children and young adults. Mishler presents a number of stories dealing with gender, ethnic nationality, and class that accommodated traditional forms while they also contested and subverted them. The stories pioneer the kinds of "social problems" literature for youth common since the 1960s.

Louise S. Robbins's study, "Publishing Pride: The Jim Crow Series of Harlow Publishing Company," examines the existence of reading materials for and about African Americans that countered the prevailing stereotypes in textual content as well as illustration. Emma Akin and the Harlow Publishing Company managed somehow to publish for the South's segregated schools a series of basal readers that met all the criteria for positive books for African-American children.

Leslie R. Miller's related essay on race, "The Power of Black and White: African Americans in Late-Nineteenth-Century Children's Periodicals," views children's periodicals as a kind of racial education, a problematic social construction that shaped the realities of a multiracial society in the twentieth century. Her double-entendre title suggests the role of print culture in shaping subjectivity in complex and sometimes conflicting ideologies and traditions.

Carole J. Trone's contribution, "Defining Democracy for Youth through Textbooks: Controversy over the Rugg Social Studies Series in Prewar America," reveals the intellectual freedom battles around Rugg's progressive social studies textbooks, published in the 1930s and 1940s, which struggled with the "truth" of American patriotism, civics, and democracy, and shaped subsequent postwar attitudes of conformity. Trone's essay, like that of Paul C. Mishler, illustrates how pedagogical materials are embedded in the contested terrain of constructing national identity and ideology.

Kathleen Chamberlain's work on school series fiction intersects with related perspectives on the sociology of school knowledge and its effects on class, gender, and race. Her essay, "'Being Poor Doesn't Count': Class, Ethnicity, and Democracy in American Girls' School Series, 1900–1920," presents conflicting messages to contemporary readers: democratic values and new visions of girlhood, based largely on traditional class and gender roles. Girls' school fiction, directed primarily to a white middle-class audience, presented a print culture that modeled the attributes needed for girls' place in democratic American society, while also subverting these ideals through discursive practices that reinforced a selective tradition. Agency seemed predicated on the maintenance of traditional hierarchical standards, a lower class on which middle-class young women could practice tolerance, nurturance, and charity.

Catherine Van Horn's essay, "Turning Child Readers into Consumers: Children's Magazines and Advertising, 1900–1920," examines the same period of American history. The advertising industry discovered the youth market after World War I and capitalized on the close relationship between editors and readers to construct the notion of advertising as part of children's reading long before the culture industry followed. Van Horn's research uncovers an area long neglected in print culture: the effect of the material production and commerce in which "the readers consumed a publication whole."

Like advertising, other cultural institutions of this time were instrumental in the socialization of youth. Rima D. Apple's and Joanne Passet's essay, "Learning to Be a Woman: Lessons from Girl Scouting and Home Economics, 1920–1970," examines the texts and sociohistorical contexts of these two related institutions of the Girl Scouts and home economics course of instruction in terms of character training and formation of domesticity—meanings that were not fixed, and that functioned on several levels simultaneously. As the authors suggest, "changes in the rhetoric surrounding the image of educated girlhood" offer insight into the idealization of modern American womanhood.

The essays also explore specific literary texts in terms of their influence on literary practices of American print culture. Bonnie James Shaker's piece, "Kate Chopin and the Birth of Young Adult Fiction," reveals the intimate relationship between Kate Chopin and the *Youth's Companion,* which led to literary contributions of a mixed-audience appeal. This fiction appealed at large as "family reading," but gradually became more identified as "young adult" in its themes and readership. Chopin's magazine fiction helped to form both a literary representation of adolescence and a cultural construction of the adolescent.

The most recent text to be examined, and perhaps the most influential in the gendering of young adolescent girls, is the Nancy Drew series, one of the most popular (and suppressed) texts of twentieth-century print culture for youth. Radhika Parameswaran's "Reading Nancy Drew in Urban India: Gender, Postcolonialism, and Memories of Home" offers a unique window view: a reader response to the experience of American print culture in her own native India. For various reasons, Nancy Drew novels were encouraged in India rather than banned, the latter being largely the practice of American librarians. Nancy Drew's privileged status in terms of linguistics and class imparted an enhanced image of class mobility and literacy, thus reinforcing the importance of reading in English and implicit colonial values.

These various acts of definition of American print culture for youth explore landscapes of the classroom, the scout meeting, the scrapbook, the periodical, the textbook, the home, and private and shared peer reading. The cultural politics engage race, class, and gender. The shared province in these cultural struggles is the reader. Through their diversity of subject and approach, these essays challenge existing cultural ideologies of what defines "children's literature," beyond the canons of classical children's fiction and privileged imaginative works. The commonality in this colloquy between material and literary texts is a concern for how cultural institutions and their subjectivities are shaped by print formations. Children's literature is conceived by its agency, but is also meant for preservational purposes. Children's literature is cultural work, designed by adults and refashioned by children. Print culture for youth entails differences in the definition of audience, the construction of subject, and the larger epistemic and political practice by which texts of books enter texts of lives.

Defining Print Culture for Youth is a selected compilation of papers presented at a conference held at the University of Wisconsin-Madison in May of 1997. It is a companion volume to *Print Culture in a Diverse America,* edited by James P. Danky and Wayne A. Wiegand.[20] Both works are sponsored by the Center for the History of Print Culture in Modern America, an interdisciplinary scholarly organization devoted to scholarship in print culture in America from 1875 to the present. The Center is a collaboration between the University of Wisconsin-Madison and the Wisconsin Historical Society. Begun in 1992, the Center has sponsored three national conferences (1995, 1997, 2001) and an international conference of the Society for the History of Authorship, Reading, and Publishing (1999). Proceeds from the publication of the two volumes go to the work of the Center for the History of Print Culture in Modern America.

NOTES

1. Jane Tompkins, *Sensational Designs: The Cultural Work of American Fiction, 1790–1860* (Oxford: Oxford University Press, 1985); Stanley Fish, *Is There a Text in This Class? The Authority of Interpretive Communities* (Cambridge: Harvard University Press, 1980).

2. Raymond Williams, *Marxism and Literature* (London: Oxford University Press, 1977), 110.

3. Cathy N. Davidson, *Reading in America: Literature and Social History* (Baltimore: Johns Hopkins University Press, 1989), 2.

4. Janice Radway, "Beyond Mary Bailey and Old Maid Librarians: Reimaging Readers and Rethinking Reading," *Journal of Education for Library and Information Science* 35 (Fall 1994): 275–96.

5. Harvey Graff, *The Literacy Myth: Literacy and Social Structure in the Nineteenth-Century City* (New York: Academic Press, 1979); Elizabeth Eisenstein, *The Printing Press as an Agent of Change: Communications and Cultural Transformation in Early Modern Europe,* 2 vols. (Cambridge: Cambridge University Press, 1978); and Carl F. Kaestle et al., *Literacy in the United States: Readers and Reading since 1880* (New Haven, CT: Yale University Press, 1991). See also E.D. Hirsch, Jr., *Cultural Literacy: What Every American Needs to Know* (Boston: Houghton Mifflin, 1987).

6. Fish, 1980.

7. Hans Robert Jauss, *Toward an Aesthetic of Reception* (Minneapolis: University of Minnesota Press, 1982).

8. Tompkins, xviii.

9. Louise Rosenblatt, *Reading as Exploration* (New York: Appleton—Century, 1938).

10. James L. Machor (ed.), *Readers in History: Nineteenth-Century American Literature and the Contexts of Reading* (Baltimore: Johns Hopkins University Press, 1993), viii.

11. John Fiske, *Understanding Popular Culture* (New York: Unwin Hyman, 1989).

12. Janice A. Radway, "Reading is Not Eating: Mass-Produced Literature and the *Research Quarterly:* Theoretical, Methodological, and Political Consequences of a Metaphor," *Book* 2 (1986): 26.

13. Jonathan Boyarin (ed.), *The Ethnography of Reading* (Berkeley, CA: University of California Press, 1993); Clifford Geertz, *The Interpretation of Cultures* (New York: Basic Books, 1973), 27.

14. Cathy N. Davidson, *Revolution and the Word: The Rise of the Novel in America* (New York: Oxford University Press, 1986), viii.

15. Carolyn Stewart Dyer and Nancy Tillman Romalov (eds.), *Rediscovering Nancy Drew* (Iowa City, IA: University of Iowa Press, 1995).

16. Uli Knoeflmacher, "Introduction," in *Teaching Children's Literature: Issues, Pedagogy, Resources*, ed. Glenn Edward Sadler (New York: Modern Language Association, 1992), 1.

17. F. J. Harvey Darton, *Children's Books in England*, revised by Brian Alderson, 3rd ed. (Cambridge: Cambridge University Press, 1982); John Townsend, *Written for Children,* 4th ed. (New York: Harper Trophy, 1990); Brian Alderson, "Some Additional Notes on Victorian and Edwardian Times, Appendix 1," in *Children's Books in England*, 3rd ed. (Cambridge: Cambridge University Press, 1982); Peter Hunt, *An Introduction to Children's Literature* (Oxford: Oxford University Press, 1994); Mitzi Myers, "Missed Opportunities and Critical Malpractice: New Historicism and Children's Literature," *Children's Literature Association Quarterly* 13 (1988), 1:41–43.

18. Peter Hunt, *An Introduction to Children's Literature* (Oxford: Oxford University Press, 1994); Margaret Meek, *How Texts Teach What Readers Learn* (South Woochester, England: Thimble Press, 1988); Aidan Chambers, *Booktalk* (London: Bodley Head, 1985).

19. Anne Lundin, *Victorian Horizons: The Reception of the Picture Books of Walter Crane, Randolph Caldecott, and Kate Greenaway* (Lanham, MD: Scarecrow Press, 2001).

20. James P. Danky and Wayne A. Wiegand (eds.), *Print Culture in a Diverse America* (Urbana, IL: University of Illinois Press, 1998).

1

READING AND RE-READING:

THE SCRAPBOOKS OF GIRLS
GROWING INTO WOMEN, 1900–1930

Susan Tucker

Scrapbooks inhabit an uneasy place in the world of print. Unique artifacts created most often from mass-produced texts and images, they find no comfortable resting place in the private home, the shelves of libraries, or the boxes of archives. They are too humble to be collage (and thus are not afforded the status of art); too revealing to rest "beside the family Bible on the parlor table"[1] (and thus, are not regularly saved as a family document); and too concealing to be the tool of a researcher (and thus not high up on the conservation priorities of libraries and archives). They are at once too precious, too common, too unfinished, too much a world unto themselves. They are handicraft objects between two covers, both ephemeral and long remembered.

Yet, for much of the nineteenth and early twentieth centuries, generations of readers made such books. Walter Benjamin defined them as the "seeds of a collection of children's books which is growing steadily even today though no longer in my garden." Here he spoke of his mother's albums with "stick-in pictures" (probably the colorful products of chromolithography). Benjamin himself enjoyed and learned from her compilations. Later in life, as he unpacked his library, he came to these albums and recognized them as key remnants of her life and his own. They formed the beginning of his collecting habits, the first of his library, these books that do not, he wrote, "strictly speaking belong in a book case at all." From them, he had grown to love reading and collecting and to understand the link between both activities.[2]

My essay explores such "seeds" of reading, of books "not strictly speaking in the book case" created by girls in their mid- to late-teenage years and their early twenties. I do so through a study of some eighty scrapbooks made between 1900 and 1940, in Illinois, Alabama, Louisiana, Texas, Virginia, and New York by middle-class girls and young women, ages fourteen to twenty-three from Catholic, Protestant, and Jewish homes of European and African descent.[3] I call these scrapbook makers "girls" (rather than women) because the content given their scrapbooks so named them. The texts of their lives showed them as not yet women. These texts, the words and images they chose for their scrapbooks, were very much a part of a period in which youth culture expanded to include a definite stage of late girlhood.

Like Benjamin in his own youth, many of these girls also came of age at precisely the same time that a staggering transformation occurred in the amount of words and images available to all readers. Their mothers and grandmothers, like Benjamin's own, had witnessed the beginning of this textual, pictorial, and polychromatic revolution—a revolution built around changes in the publishing process, photography, and colored printing. But in the daughters' scrapbooks, we see also changes in a public world that now offered a small percentage of girls the education once reserved only for boys. Their scrapbooks thus provide an excellent overall "reading" for us about the types of educated girls and women projected to the American public, and the self-images educated American girls saw in these printed images.

In my own reading of their scrapbooks, I take into consideration the work of Marianne Hirsch and a number of other scholars who have written that any collection on the self—albums of photographs, collage, and other assemblages—is essentially a lie, a public face, and a partial story. All such compilations fall into the trap implicit within making an identity: even as one strives for both uniqueness and conformity, one molds oneself with the tools at hand, themselves limited and, therefore, limiting. On the other hand, as Hirsch and others also note, to abandon the making of a self or of an identity means not dealing with the politics that shape the world, and not using creative agency to show oneself a part of this world.[4]

Girls in their scrapbooks seem to me to act with some agency, to show in their choice of printed and visual objects both the false self and a partially revealed, more authentic self. Their books also reveal the larger text of changing technologies, products, and ideas left for their later perusal and our own. Their icons are paper markers of identity, and these markers pinpoint one place where the publishing world joined with the handicraft tradition. Below, I discuss how girls' representations of self in scrapbooks served to legitimate traditional choices and, at the same time, celebrated new visions.

At least from one vantage point, nineteenth-century scrapbook making that specifically included work with printed objects (with reading) was seen as a means to focus learning. "Gossipy reading"—which pedagogues had long feared particularly for female readers—"could be cured if we read for a purpose, look for something, and keep it when found, and in no other form can it be so well preserved as in the pages of a good scrapbook," wrote E. W. Gurley in *Scrap-books and How to Make Them.*[5]

In the late 1870s as Gurley wrote, scrapbooks made by girls usually contained poems, autographs, and, most prominently, the frilly images of scrap—die-cut colored paper rendered on sheets of hearts, flowers, baskets, tender love scenes, and the like. These sometimes embossed and selectively gilded relief papers, the "stick-in" pictures of Benjamin's mother, were also called chromos, and had begun to appear with the invention and perfection of chromolithography in the early nineteenth century. Initially popularized in Germany, the collecting and pasting of scrap became a craze across Europe and North America, and was often lamented in newspaper articles when an author wished to comment on the useless pastimes of girls and women. When true scrap was not available, girls (and many boys, though girls seem to have been the larger group among scrapbook makers) cut from illustrated magazine articles or collected labels, which also, of course, were products of improved printing techniques.[6]

"Pleasurable beholding," a phrase used by art historian Barbara Stafford in relation to her efforts to disestablish the view of cognition as dominantly and aggressively linguistic, is a good starting place to evoke the type of children, and even adults, who made scrapbooks of chromos.[7] Using scissors and paste, these scrapbook makers shaped images they wished to remember in vivid color, something they could not have done very easily before. For the first time in history, someone other than an artist manipulated the richness of the hue, tint, shade, and tone. No wonder working with chromos, and even pasting in printed illustrations, made for a craze noted disparagingly by conservative writers.[8]

This cutting and pasting, this "pleasurable beholding" made for a different type of individual, one Benjamin would have recognized as the more active reader, the collector of words and images. A child born in 1850, or even in the 1860s and 1870s (as Benjamin's mother would have been), was raised, for example, on Bible stories and heard perhaps the first idea of a collection centered on Noah's gathering of animals for his ark.[9] By

Scrapbook page created by an unknown compiler, ca. 1850. Newcomb College Archives. Newcomb Center for Research on Women, Tulane University.

1890, for many children, the story involved probably some seeing, perhaps a colorful chromolithograph. Almost as often, the child hearing such a tale at the end of the nineteenth century and the beginning of the twentieth would have been encouraged to cut pictures from magazines to illustrate his or her own version of the ark within a scrapbook.

The local newspapers, and a number of magazines, had special segments for such clipping work.[10] Middle-class children of the late nineteenth and early twentieth centuries, thus, were raised to think of themselves as compilers, and the words and images they chose were to reflect on themselves, however remotely. The contemplative and useful nature of such an activity was highly valued by parents and educators. To be able to sit and think with an activity right at hand meant that neither time nor materials were wasted. "The questions and discussions which would arise over each picture chosen would be of great educational value. Years afterward recalling the memories ... such Sunday afternoons will be cherished as the foundation building of right and wholesome thoughts and principles in the minds of many men and women."[11] Baby's first book could be created by an older child from "sheets of old muslin, and pasted pictures and letters on them," and this scrapbook introduced a respect for reading to both children.[12]

Nineteenth-century and early twentieth-century educators also promoted scrapbooks as means to teach art. An 1872 book called *The Happy Nursery* urged that children "be taught to value paper products as tokens of affection." Assembled into scrapbooks, these tokens spoke of all "the best and warmest" feelings learned within the home.[13] Plus, making a scrapbook taught "expertness in cutting out and fixing, and neatness...."[14] But most of all scrapbooks offered the chance to personalize the world of images: "in choosing pictures it is better to select only those that you really believe in and can find a reason for using. By choosing the pictures with this care you make the work more interesting and the book particularly your own."[15]

For many older girls, then, continued scrapbook making meant reenacting an activity learned in childhood and creating again an identity based upon printed text and images. In much the same way that reading the romance novel reinforced the learned social needs and psychological desires of readers studied by Janice Radway and Suzanne Juhasz, scrapbook making reinforced reading the self into acceptable but also personalized images and words provided by popular culture.[16] In girlhood from 1900 to 1940, these likes and dislikes could be hidden or displayed (depending on how the scrapbook was revealed to others) within three types of albums. The first was the scrapbook commercially or handmade from cheap paper and bound with a shoestring. The second was the scrapbook transformed from an album or ledger, also usually made by a local printer or stationer. The third, and the one whose conventions show most vividly the world of the girl in this period, was that of a blank book, with printed headings, created by major publishing houses.[17]

Together these three types of books embody the evolution of the scrapbook genre from the book of true scraps, to its joining with other traditions of assemblage, to a bound, durable, and prescriptive volume. Among these other traditions, the friendship album lent most to the scrapbooks of girls. This was a handmade or locally fabricated album, a reinvention of the commonplace book, such that poems, greetings, comments, and moral instructions were shared in a book that was passed between friends. These albums, popular especially in the early nineteenth century, were frequently criticized for their sentimentality,[18] but they allowed young people to put to use some of the learning that was coming their way through an improved and more universal school system.

All the scrapbooks, of course, but especially the scrapbook in the form of a published blank book, involved "the girl" herself as a subject. Adding printed headings, typeset calligraphy and illustrations in which to frame the experience of school, these at-the-time new types of scrapbooks also resembled in cover and design the fancy bindings of gift books, and, in turn, were often given as gifts.[19] Between 1900 and 1920, Dodd, Mead and Company, for example, every year published a blank book called *My Commencement,* which seemed to have been a favorite gift for graduation. Between its covers, one added responses to the New York firm's printed guidance. The final product overtly offered a joint creation of publisher, illustrator, editor (or author), scrapbook maker, and sometimes later readers (whether they be the scrapbook maker herself in later life or others to whom she gave access to the scrapbook, who added comments).[20] One could even argue that the gift giver entered into the text of these books.

Dodd, Mead's book and many other such scrapbooks were of a small book size (usually around eight by five inches) and were made available usually in different bindings (limp, cloth, and leather) so as to accommodate different types of buyers. They could be easily held in one hand. This size suggests a conscious departure from the marketing of the previous and larger albums to be filled with true scrap, autographs, and poetry; from the type of large ledger-like scrapbook patented by Mark Twain in the 1880s; and from the album handmade from boards and shoestrings.[21] These new products were books to be read. Looking like a schoolbook itself, Dodd, Mead's 1910 edition of *My Commencement* provided the subtitle, "being a record of the school, the faculty, commencement exercises, essays and orations, speeches, prizes, social events, subjects studied, the class motto, colors, flowers, yells, the class history, poems and prophecy, my classmates, reunions." These were the categories that divided memories of the time spent in school. These reminiscences were framed in images of sentimentality—green vines, red hearts, and peach roses can be found on almost each page in the 1910 edition. Other published scrapbooks were entitled

The College Girl's Record, Alma Mater, Alma Mater Days, My Senior Year, The Girl Graduate: Her Own Book, My College Days, College Days, Days at College; and these books also have printed title pages that bear the name of an author or compiler.[22] The author or illustrator clearly guided the placement and even the conformity of memories.

Part of the appeal of this type of "staying within the lines," this directed memory making, was that the books came into being in response to, or in tandem with, a time when uneasiness surrounded the meaning of girlhood, particularly those girlhoods involving education. Before this, girls had not had the opportunity of schooling, or of a life apart from the family. Considerable controversy surrounded this change. Despite the low percentage of girls in higher education, newspaper articles gave them a disproportionately large bit of attention not only visually but also in print. Journalists pondered over the health of girls subjected to nights studying Greek and Latin. Essayists writing well into the twentieth century still cited the work of retired Harvard Medical School professor Dr. Edward Clarke and his popular 1878 publication *Sex in Education* that urged women to save themselves for their biological function as mothers. Other writers worried that women would desex themselves in arduous work. Even administrators and parents of students at the northeastern women's colleges worried that communal life with other women would make women unfit for marriage.[23]

As Helen Horowitz and other historians have shown, various arrangements were then made for keeping female students free from some of "the dangers of education."[24] The conventions of all types of scrapbooks, especially those created with headings, were one of these arrangements. I suggest that publishers and buyers alike were responding to a need to show visible markers of femininity—of girlishness—to accompany a then nontraditional girl with a diploma into traditional womanhood. Certainly, writers and publishers provided the printed versions of what were thought of as attractive girls. The images in all the prefabricated scrapbooks were those of a demure personality (portrayed with downcast eyes), comely figure (rendered through depictions showing a small waist and proportionate, but generous breasts), and upswept Gibson girl hair. Even those scrapbooks with only a printed cover or end pages often showed images such as cherubs and clasped hands that suggest the type of activity and the same sweet but busy girl suggested by earlier books like Lydia Maria Child's *A Girl's Own Book*.[25]

Given the newness of the female scholar, this close resemblance between the design of gift books, earlier books such as Child's, and the scrapbook is not surprising, yet the reserved poses and the classically "pretty" faces of

Title page from *Alma Mater Days* (scrapbook compiled by Julia
Schwabacher Levy, 1912–1916). Designed and illustrated by
Harry B. Matthews, *Alma Mater Days* was published in New York
by G. W. Dillingham Co., 1907. Newcomb College Archives.
Newcomb Center for Research on Women, Tulane University.

the students does seem significant in any analysis of images chosen to represent this new type of girl. The same sort of images was prevalent in other
types of books, for example, in Mary Caroline Crawford's *The College Girl
of America and the Institutions Which Make Her What She Is,* a book that

Page from *The College Girl's Record* (scrapbook compiled by Beatrix Fortune, 1906). The printed title page of this scrapbook gives Virginia Woodson Frame as the illustrator and compiler, and lists Paul Elder (San Francisco) as publisher. No publication date appears on the copy in Newcomb College Archives. Newcomb Center for Research on Women, Tulane University.

otherwise promotes the seriousness of study.[26] Like the characters in popular novels such as Helen Brown's *Two College Girls,* the girl scholars of both the scrapbook and other forms of printed materials showed young women within a frame that made for sweetness, tidiness, and only the smallest experiment with a newfound freedom.[27]

To hope always implies a menace, novelist and journalist Margaret Deland warned, and nowhere would such hope be more perilous than for "restless" college girls. Best keep them safely wrapped in traditional garb and with more or less traditional expectations. In being guided in how to arrange acceptable printed and handwritten memories, photographs, and other memorabilia, they would have less chance of becoming the spinsters foretold by Edward Clarke, or the excited new women feared by Margaret Deland.[28]

In 1897, the New Orleans' *Times-Picayune* placed the scrapbook, the "Memory Book," precisely within this place of familiarity:

> A Memory Book is an interesting tablet for the girl of the present time to keep. It consists of a generous sized, nicely bound volume, in which a record is kept of all the occasions and incidents in the life of a girl which she specially desires to remember, occasions of importance and occasions of great happiness. For instance, her graduation day, her confirmation, her introduction into the social world and her wedding day. Clippings from the press, in this great day of journals, in which she may be mentioned are also kept and pasted into the memory book. One New Orleans girl who is famous for her beauty and favoritism in the social world, and who has many times been selected to take part in the most prominent social functions of the carnival season and other affairs, has a record of her social triumphs perpetuated in her memory book, as well as several very charming sketches of herself.... Among other things which add to the interest of this memory book also are signatures and poems dedicated to herself ... which will no doubt give the owner a great pleasure in the years to come when she will open its pages; reminders of a happy past.[29]

The scrapbook, then, as sociologists have shown about the family album, proved an acceptable female activity because of its link to traditional female concerns, in this case, social triumphs.[30] Girl students would have approved markers of maturity. Ample pages in all the published scrapbooks requested information on men, even if these books were designed by and for someone at one of the women's colleges. Girls would have a place for poems about romances with men or boys. Often enough, they followed this guidance. "A.B. means a boy," wrote one Randolph-Macon student scrapbook maker.[31]

As in the earlier albums, the scrapbooks of girl scholars often held autographs, greetings, listings of friends, comments, and wishes. Also, letters tucked away in envelopes replicated the dialogic reciprocity of the earlier friendship albums. The sweet girl remained, then, in the making of the early twentieth-century scrapbook.

Yet the image of the high school and college student during these years carried an important message of freedom and intellect, and these too are clearly seen in the scrapbooks. The girl, after all, does own her book: *The Girl Graduate: My Own Book.* Similarly it is her senior year: *My Senior Year.* Though in the years that I studied, only three to four percent of women ages sixteen to twenty-one attended college, the image of the girl scholar appealed because it offered a glimpse of a new type of choice.[32] As Sally Mitchell has shown in her study of the fictional world of girl students in England, the image of the new type of girl appealed because both high school and college provided a screen to project desires, a script with images, places, and situations where victories could be envisioned. School, thus imagined, was a vastly improved home with minimal supervision, congenial companions, private space, and individual self-development— without any corresponding adult burden.[33]

The publishing world responded to the presence of this new identity formed around school by printing more and more about the lives of girl scholars, thus providing more text and images for clipping. In general, as the publishing of all sorts of newspapers and magazines expanded, girls of the middle class also came to occupy a larger part of the printed communication network. Newspapers hired high school girls and college women to report on the news from their schools. Until this time, custom dictated that a female's name should appear in the newspaper only three times— when she was born, when she was married, and when she died.[34] Yet, by 1894, girls and young women began to appear increasingly, most often in notices of parties, plays, basketball games, and graduation exercises. The scrapbooks allowed girls to reset their images, and this limit upon their names in print, within respectability in which they, and those around them, were comfortable.

Newspaper clippings in all the scrapbooks of girls from 1900 to 1940 reflect this change, with clippings increasing especially in the scrapbooks created after 1910. Then printed images overwhelmingly showed girls in their social life with few devoted to athletic endeavors and still fewer to academic achievements. More so than not, however, girls' activities with boys were especially noteworthy in clippings. For example, Fannie Seiferth's 1912 Newcomb scrapbook began with the opening of the school year noted in six newspaper articles and then moved to extensive coverage of her appointment as the manager of the football team. This coverage came from local and collegiate newspapers from Kansas, Connecticut, New Jersey, and New York City. In the *Times Democrat* of New Orleans under "Baseball-Racing-Pugilism," notice of her new job was expressed in a seven-paragraph article under the title "Girl to Help Manage Tulane

Page from Fannie Seiferth Scrapbook, 1912. Newcomb College Archives. Newcomb Center for Research on Women, Tulane University.

Football Team." Appointed active assistant manager, Seiferth was hailed as "the only college girl holding such a position actively in America." The article also reported that part of the reason for involving Miss Seiferth is to awaken the women's college she attended (Newcomb) to "a realization of the responsibility that it should share in the ups and downs of the football team." They wanted her appointment "to foster the college spirit in the institutions to which Tulane is joined." This college girl thus read of herself as most noteworthy in connection to men.

Other newspaper articles in scrapbooks of this period discussed politics and various academic experiences, but placed the female student increasingly alongside her male counterpart. Alice Catherine Grant, Barnard Class of 1909, clipped articles on the Settlement House Association throughout her time at college, but only in her last year did she clip articles on various outings with male students from Columbia.[35] Mary Gladys Owen, a Randolph-Macon scrapbook maker, placed articles on suffrage in 1915 alongside invitations to dances at men's colleges.[36] The Newcomb students pasted in straw ballots, showing that while women could not vote in national elections, they partook of the mock campaigns, with their male counterparts, from 1912 onward.[37]

In most clippings, female students are described as "girls." Yet, when they were pictured with college boys, more often described as men, the girls became women. Marion Spencer Fay's 1915 Newcomb scrapbook, *The Girl Graduate,* exhibited this tendency vividly. In one page, two clippings from May 1915 showed the diversity of images in the local press. One title read "Newcomb Girls in Clever Stunt on College Lawn—Seniors Imitate and Burlesque Noted Lectures They Have Heard This Year." The other title read, students "Attend Baccalaureate Services Sunday—The men and women of tomorrow to do twice as much as we do today—." On the next page, excerpts from final exercises (held jointly and including all men and women) noted that colleges for women are no longer an "experiment . . . they have been tested in the past 100 years. . . . and women's places in the reforms of today, because of their sense of beauty and refinement, are assured."[38] In other words, beauty and refinement were necessary to societal acceptance of female scholars as learning beings, something rarely, if ever, demanded of male students.

None of the student scrapbook makers commented on this type of inequality in the printed word. Their scrapbooks do, however, reveal other divisions within their own communities. At Newcomb College, Lillian Friend, Class of 1911, in her two scrapbooks, recorded every single gift she received from both high school and college graduations. These presents numbered over 100 and ranged from books of poetry and flowers to a ruby necklace and $100. Other students scrimped to afford an occasional box of chocolates. One student kept a strict tally of the cost of making a dress.[39]

Other students gave revealing glimpses about the undercurrents of religious and social class divisions among students. Josephine Janvier, a high school student, had strong opinions when her edition of *My Commencement* asked for a description of each class member in 1908. While she disliked one of her classmates, finding her "a Jewess of the worst kind," Janvier commented upon another "as a very nice sensible broadminded Jewess. She is one of the nicest girls in my class and one of my best friends." Of all the scrapbook makers, possibly because she is among the youngest (fourteen at the time of making her book), Janvier also provided the most plentiful reflection upon her own family and their influence on her. "Ethel is very pleasant and we are good friends at school but Papa will not let me go and see her." Janvier seemingly assumed her father's prejudices, as well. About another classmate she wrote, "Louisa is just simply common. Her father is the captain of a dredge boat and they live in

Gulfport, Mississippi. I don't care for her and yet sometimes I am sorry for her because she has a stepmother."[40]

Discomforts with schoolmates and disappointments were also evident in the other scrapbooks. A draft of a letter of resignation to the Dormitory Council showed one Sweet Briar student's discontent with the pettiness of others who would, she wrote, not obey rules. This draft was folded inside her more curtailed resignation and pasted opposite her class schedule.[41] A New Orleans scrapbook maker expressed her dismay when college women made fun of high school seniors.[42] But, for the most part, the school communities were depicted as harmonious. The "girl scholar" made sure she would later read of this time. By clipping and pasting items that reflected on images of a culture that had been publicly closed to their mothers, girls prepared to remember. An education offered a small percentage of middle-class girls of this period unparalleled choices: most significantly, the possibility of supporting oneself outside of marriage or a life of the mind, at any rate, separate from marriage.

The types of images that seem to have represented the learning and lively self within this new type of community are found in a vast array of printed matter, often published by the schools or colleges themselves (including cuttings from brochures and bulletins, menus, invitations, true scrap, cards, labels, newsletters, and literary magazines). In choice of materials, the scrapbook maker emphasized the physical location of the schools and colleges—and the community of fellow students—usually within the first five pages of all but eleven of the books I studied. The scrapbook maker thus located herself away from her family of origin, and also away from traditional social gatherings with boys and men, especially so in the case of those scrapbook makers in girls' schools and women's colleges.

These printed descriptions of and from the school campuses allow today a reading of schools not available in other sources. For example, photos of mosquito netting over the beds reveal a part of the past often forgotten and not noted in other literature about boarding at Newcomb College: the real need to shield oneself from insects in an era still plagued with the lack of screens, yellow fever epidemics, and other inconveniences. In addition, photos, promotional material, and clippings in the scrapbooks tell of the size and design of dormitory rooms. Girls' fascination with describing their rooms made them add their own comments, such as "Beds were better used when pushed together." This comment, for example, gives us a hint of the intimacy as well as the spatial limitations of dormitory life. The same scrapbook maker also noted that the closets might hold two people squeezed tightly together. And, her photos show her walls decorated extensively with banners from other colleges and universities.[43] In the scrapbooks of college women at Sweet Briar, Randolph-Macon, and Texas Woman's University, the beauty of rural campuses is heavily emphasized with printed images devoted to the campuses in various seasons.[44]

Attention also was given through photographs, clippings from bulletins and newsletters and other materials to the care of the grounds, the buildings, and the students themselves. Bulletins from Newcomb College tell us that indeed a gardener and a lady-in-charge were employed, but only in the scrapbooks do we have photographs of these people and, in one case, a letter showing their own words.[45] Similarly, the scrapbooks at Sweet Briar College and Randolph-Macon provide printed menus from the school for holidays, lists showing the seating of the faculty at evening meals, handwritten memories of the cook who prepared the meals and the janitor who carried trunks.[46] These inclusions reveal an understanding not only of social hierarchy but also of how each person within the community entered the official history—printed or handwritten.

This preoccupation with community is made quite vivid if one looks for the families of origin in the scrapbooks today. They are not easily found. Indeed mothers were only mentioned in letters, closed to the casual viewer. Only eight references to fathers were found in the eighty-two scrapbooks—one found in a newspaper clipping describing the student as the daughter of a deceased merchant, six others in telegraphs from fathers traveling or living elsewhere, and one in a handwritten commentary where a student notes her father's displeasure with particular classmates. Sisters and brothers too appeared infrequently, though more often than mothers and fathers. This propensity to ignore the family of origin cut across most boundaries of religion and class and distinctions between boarding and day students. The one exception is in the scrapbooks of African-American students, where the parents and children generally are seen interacting in written descriptions and photographs of social gatherings.[47]

But even for these African-American students, the scrapbook is a place for demonstrating an overriding place of one's own. If anything, the scrapbooks show the creation of one's own "family of schoolmates." This family was rounded out often by the addition of children. Certain girls were described as the baby of the class in written descriptions and in captions under photographs. An official child or mascot, usually a four- or five-year-old relative of one of the classmates, was also shown in many photographs. The focus of the scrapbooks, then, was the girl growing away from her biological family and her formation, with other girls, of another type of community.

Page from Marion Spencer Fay Scrapbook, 1915. Newcomb College Archives. Newcomb Center for Research on Women, Tulane University.

In all but fifteen of the scrapbooks, basketball teams figured prominently in this configuration of friendships. The basketball clippings and photographs document a part of collegiate life central to women's education in the early twentieth century. In group shots, in team play, and posed alone with a basketball in hand, the students appear as serious ballplayers, rarely smiling into the camera. In addition, clippings from school papers tell of the importance of physical education, for example, noting the importance of unfettered physical movement. In the Newcomb scrapbooks, the compilers were uniformly fascinated by their instructor, Clara Baer, her education at the Possee Normal School in Boston, and her marketing of the rules for the game, Newcomb Ball.[48]

The scrapbooks let the students reflect upon this new world, their own world. Some even show a rejection of the status quo. Frances Dreyfuss, 1921, for example, pasted in a cigarette and told of an unapproved and unchaperoned outing. The first page of her album shows a newspaper clipping of two women kissing. The clipping's printed comment says, "Gee,

Jim sure hates her to leave home." To this, Dreyfuss has replied "But who in the D—is Jim?"[49]

Juanita Page, in her 1923 scrapbook about a Chicago high school, provided the most obvious defiance of the printed headings, and of the publisher's world. Although she filled her book with notes from fellow students when asked for such things as classes, gatherings, and parties, her photographs themselves show what immediately distinguishes her world from that of the publisher. Juanita Page's high school was predominantly African American and the photographs she chose show African Americans. Moreover, unlike the illustrations that show prim dresses and long hair on Caucasian girls and women, Page's girlfriends had bobbed hair. These friends wore tailored blouses and shorter skirts. And Page had a friend draw pictures of a flapper throughout the book. Page "became" a dancer in a short dress with fringes at the hem, in stark contrast to the modest scholar portrayed by the publisher's illustrator.[50] If Page was presenting a "lie" about her identity, it was her own lie, one of the 1920s and not that of the white culture of 1910, here clearly displayed within the publisher's headings and illustrations.

School was clearly these scholars' "own place and own time" and they were pleased to consider just how it was so. Learning itself was highly valued, and papers pasted into scrapbooks—grades, texts of speeches given and heard, drawings of protozoa, names of books read, topics of debates, lists of assignments—made up over one-quarter of all but eighteen scrapbooks. These were the papers truly too dearly gained to part with—those not asked for by the printed headings but kept at the back of the books. As one Talladega student noted on the top of a printed brochure, the library would inspire her "forever."[51]

The ending of the scrapbooks, in turn, often returned the girl scholar to her traditional path of romance. Final pages revealed many good-bye wishes, photographs of linked arms, or various other not always sentimental conclusions: "Out of School Life, Into Life's School" and "Finis" declared two of the publisher's headings. Over half of the scrapbooks contained among the last pages newspaper accounts about the number of engaged students at the time of graduation. Barnard student Frances Purdon Leavitt ended her 1905 scrapbook with an article entitled "A Rah for Matrimony." Another Barnard scrapbook maker included an article entitled "A Sighting of Brides at Barnard, Cupid's Class, Married Already, 12 Girls."[52]

Other newspaper clippings at the end of the books speak of the scholarly experience as yet another part of a girl's preparation for marriage. The sweet girl graduate and her status as bright, tender, and sweet was still desirable to men, the clippings say over and over. Commencement speakers, both those quoted in newspaper clippings and those whose remarks were copied out in longhand, stressed that girls who graduated from high school and young women from college made better wives. A number of other women ended their scrapbooks with newspaper clippings on what they might do with a college education, the marriage and health of college women, and the aspiration to higher things.[53]

Benjamin correctly saw his mother's scraps and the book in which she pasted them as part of a long tradition—collecting, reading, thinking— which for many people involves placing and replacing items in a book case. The icons that mother, son, and other scrapbook makers saved were part of the creative agency evoked to interpret and remember the self within the printed and visual worlds. The collection of memorabilia formed "seeds" for later understandings. That these icons, saved between the covers of a book, required the use of color, design, and image selection shows the matrix of craft, choice, and modern identity. "The craftsman's handiwork teaches us to die and hence teaches us to live," wrote Octavio Paz. "Handmade objects," Paz said, "are the heartbeat of human time, beautiful because they last a long time but also slowly age away ... resigned to so doing and can be replaced by another object that is similar but not identical."[54]

Certainly all children scrapbook makers of the late nineteenth and early twentieth centuries would have understood quite well this pronouncement. Perhaps, some of their books of childhood were passed on to younger children, disassembled and remade by pasting new pictures over old ones. "You will find easily among your store of loose pictures a horse and cart, or a dog or a man, or a giraffe, which when cut out will fit in amusingly somewhere in the old picture," Dorothy Canfield advised in her section called "Composite Scrapbooks" in the book *What Shall We Do Now?*[55] But girl scrapbook makers understood this remaking differently, it seems to me, for all but three of the eighty-two scrapbooks I studied were clearly kept intact, valued, and reread.

Certainly, many of the scrapbooks have torn pages from years of reflection. Yet few images were actually removed, a circumstance very rare when one looks at other types of scrapbooks, and a fact that suggests something about the functionality of the scrapbooks to educated women and their propensity to retain clues about their pasts.[56]

The conventions of scrapbook making were well suited for this functionality and were rooted in the private negotiation of memory, the semipublic journey of the growing self, and the semipublic aspects of the scrapbook itself. The scrapbook's form—whether with preprinted headings or with blank pages—allowed a sifting and layering of competing allegiances and identities. Memories of learning or of reading could "steadily grow," yet could do so side by side with other memories that acknowledged an uncertainty about the future. Girls could paste in a test score, a clipping about a speech, an invitation, a description of a party; and then tell as much or little as they wished about each object. In addition, the materials not pasted into scrapbooks, but merely kept at the back of the books, could continue the layers of this coded reading. A telegraph concerning the sickness of a relative, cards from rejected boyfriends, an article on a woman professor—these were saved as mnemonic clues, with evidence of rereading.

Thus one can discern that the scrapbook served well as a vehicle for holding the memories of the past. Reading and rereading these books today, one can see how the allegiances and identities of young women varied in their representation and changed as society changed. The newness of photography and an increased access to masses of printed material (and to oneself within these assorted cards, newspaper articles, and other paper) all made a very big difference in self-knowledge, identity formation, remembering, and collecting. But such change did not mean that societal expectations were not carefully observed; it did not mean, above all, that appearances did not count. In the scrapbooks, girls left clear evidence that they understood that ambition should be hidden, that education should be carefully displayed, and that the paths they would lead in leaving school would not be so different from the paths of their mothers and grandmothers.

What then did their access to learning (and to the scrapbooks as symbols of a time of learning) mean? *Educated in Romance* by Dorothy Holland and Margaret Eisenhart may be helpful in reading the scrapbooks today. Studying college women from the 1970s and the 1980s, Holland and Eisenhart found that women adjusted downward their expectations for careers as they negotiated silently the emphasis on finding a mate or on finding some other alternate route to adulthood.[57] There is every reason to believe that this private negotiation was even more prevalent in the early twentieth century. The scrapbook's montage was a way of making partially revealed statements about the guarded journey between girlhood and adulthood, between the learning selves afforded the curriculum of boys and men and the selves who would become wives, mothers, or single women. Such a time in the history of girlhood was one of a very gradual change, one that required a tentative self (at least at times) and a tentative document. The scrapbook itself, with its reputation for superficiality and its means of hiding texts within envelopes and coded images, would mask the power of education, perhaps even to some of the scrapbook makers themselves.

The scrapbooks of girls often enough, though, played with a resistance to dominant culture, and always served as a vehicle for a conscious encounter with the many printed words, the readings, that shape identity. Like the photographic album that Susan Sontag named "a kit of images that bears witness to its connectedness," the scrapbooks of schoolgirls linked not only images but also readings of the past, present, and the future.[58] Such a kit would be replaced, more or less, by other ways of remembering as the twentieth century progressed. The year 1940 ended the strong tradition of scrapbook making among high school girls and college women and ushered in a preoccupation with the yearbook. The yearbook, though known in the more affluent schools from the end of the nineteenth century, would spread to almost all schools and would become a weighty volume with individual and group photos, but little chance for adding or subtracting items that one had chosen, cut, and pasted; there was little chance indeed for complicating the lie of the public face. The scrapbook, though still present, became more and more ephemeral, made on highly acidic paper, seldom with a durable binding. Its resemblance to a real book, to one's own book, would become even more rare, and its pages became overfilled with more and varied types of items. Scrapbooks themselves would not regain popularity until the late twentieth century, when once again changing technology altered the process of keeping memory.

NOTES

1. "Editor's Table: Photography and Its Album," *Godey's Lady's Book* 68 (March 1864): 304.

2. Walter Benjamin, "Unpacking My Library," in *Illuminations*, ed. Hannah Arendt (New York: Harcourt, Brace, and World, 1968), 60.

3. These scrapbooks are housed in the Newcomb Archives, Newcomb College Center for Research on Women, Tulane University; the Historic New Orleans Collection; the Manuscript Department, Howard-Tilton Library, Tulane University; the Amistad Research Center at Tulane University; the University of New Orleans; Texas Woman's University Library; North Texas State University Library; Barnard College Library, Columbia University; New York Public Library; Teachers' College Library, Columbia University; the New-York Historical Society; Sweet Briar College Library; and Randolph-Macon Woman's College Library.

4. Marianne Hirsch, *Family Frames: Photography, Narrative and Postmemory* (Cambridge, MA: Harvard University Press, 1997); Marianne Hirsch, ed., *The*

Familial Gaze (Hanover, MA: University Press of New England, 1999); Francoise Lionnet, *Autobiographical Voices: Gender, Race and Self-Portraiture* (Ithaca, NY: Cornell University Press, 1989); bell hooks, "In Our Glory: Photography and Black Life," in *Picturing Us: African American Identity in Photography*, ed. Deborah Willis (New York: The New Press, 1994); and Jacqueline Rose, *Sexuality in the Field of Vision* (London: Verso, 1986).

5. E. W. Gurley, *Scrap-books and How to Make Them, containing full instructions for making a complete and systematic set of useful books* (New York: The Authors' Publishing Company, 1880), 13.

6. Starr Ockenga, *On Women and Friendship: A Collection of Victorian Keepsakes and Traditions* (New York: Steward, Tabori & Chang, 1993); Alistair Allen and Joan Hoverstadt, *The History of Printed Scraps* (London: New Cavendish Books, 1983); and Peter Marzio, *The Democratic Art, Chromolithography 1840–1900: Pictures for a 19th-Century America* (Boston: David R. Godine, 1979).

7. Barbara Maria Stafford, *Good Looking: Essays on the Virtue of Images* (Cambridge, MA: MIT Press, 1996), 5.

8. Speaking at the 1995 meeting of the Society of American Archivists, Jim Burant of the National Archives of Canada noted that the craze was condemned in *Le Fantasque* (Quebec: March 30, 1840) by one "albumphobe" who spoke of the real "abuse" of the practice of swapping books for thoughts and souvenirs.

9. The idea of Noah as the first collector has been noted by many people, but for ideas about this story and other collectors, I am grateful to John Elsner and Roger Cardinal in their introduction to *The Cultures of Collecting* (London: Reaktion Books, 1994), 1–6.

10. Many newspapers and magazines ran regular features specifically designed for cutting. For example, *Harper's Weekly* in the 1870s ran such sections and alongside them ads for *Shipment's Common Sense Binder*, *The Alexander Graham Bell Scrapbook*, and *The Ideal Patented Scrapbook*.

11. Maude Cushing Nash, *Children's Occupations* (New York: Houghton-Mifflin Co., 1920), 124–125.

12. Julia McNair Wright, *The Complete Home: An Encyclopedia of Domestic Life and Affairs* (Brantford, Ontario: Bradley, Garretson & Company, 1879), 195.

13. Ellis Davidson, *The Happy Nursery: A Book for Mothers, Governesses and Nurses containing Games, Amusements, and Employments for Boys and Girls* (London: Cassell, Petter, and Balpin, 1872), 65.

14. Eliza Leslie, *The American Girl's Book: or, Occupations for Play Hours* (New York: R. Worthington, 1879), 17.

15. Dorothy Canfield, et al., *What Shall We Do Now? Five Hundred Games and Pasttimes: A Book of Suggestions for Children's Games and Employments* (New York: Frederick A. Stokes Company, 1907), 276.

16. Janice Radway, *Reading the Romance: Women, Patriarchy, and Popular Culture* (Chapel Hill: University of North Carolina Press, 1984); Suzanne Juhasz, *Reading from the Heart: Women, Literature and the Search for True Love* (New York: Penguin Books, 1994).

17. These first two types are found today in most manuscript collections in the United States, and are the type of book most often meant when one speaks of scrapbooks. They sometimes contain an embossed cover added with the name of the scrapbook maker, or, in the case of schoolgirls or college women, the name of an institution. In addition, companies such as the Wharton Clay College Memory Book Company of Chicago printed books with varied insignia and other motifs related to specific schools throughout the United States. The third type of book, on the other hand, seems to be most prevalent in either urban collections (such as the Amistad Collection and the Newcomb Archives, both in New Orleans) or in the archives of the northeastern women's colleges. The largest collections of these types of books seem to be at Vassar and Smith—both of which have hundreds of these types, according to archivists. The presence or absence of these books in different collections today must have to do with the selling of the books to selected populations, and thus, to the standardization of an elite image prescribed for all school girls, and college women, across the United States that began first with Vassar College in 1855. I have not been able to locate any bookseller's records about such books.

18. See Martha Banta, *Imaging American Women, Ideas and Ideals in Cultural History* (New York: Columbia University Press, 1987).

19. Many of the books note the names of gift givers: "to Lillian, from Aunt Sarah," for example.

20. *Cumulative Book Index* and *The United States Catalog* are helpful in tracing some of these titles of prefabricated scrapbooks, or blank books. Still, other titles appear to have been considered too ephemeral to be listed at all.

21. Mark Twain's scrapbook contains gummed pages to facilitate easy pasting of clippings. An oversized book with a heavy cardboard cover, his book also contains a notice of a registered patent obtained in the United States first in 1873. He then perfected his pages and obtained other patents in 1878 and 1890. His scrapbooks were published by Daniel Slote and Company of New York. For a discussion of other types of album structures and scrapbook conventions, see Richard Horton, "Photo Album Structure, 1850–1960," *Guild of Book Workers Journal* 32 (Spring 1994): 32–43.

22. The publishers of such scrapbooks aside from Dodd, Mead included Paul Elder, G. W. Dillingham Company, J. P. Lippincott Company, W. L. Bacon, the College Memorabilia Company, W. C. Horn Brothers, Reilly and Lee Company, and C. R.Gibson.

23. The names and pictures of girls and women in the newspapers increased dramatically during the years 1880–1940, with much attention given to women scholars and girl students. To compare what girls clipped versus what they might have clipped for their scrapbooks, I compared stories from the New Orleans papers to clippings in Newcomb scrapbooks in the years 1886, 1905, and 1916 from the months of February and June. In June 1886, for example, text about and pictures of women in the newspapers were confined almost exclusively to those of actresses or criminals. Women's names alone were confined to society balls, benevolent organizations, and other progressive causes. By 1906, not only had

halftones been circulating in the presses of America for almost ten years, thus increasing the number of illustrations, but also the subject of illustrations had changed. Women now appeared as teachers, mothers, librarians, nurses, suffrage workers, settlement house workers, visiting professionals, and lecturers—all of whom had some connection to a higher education. Girls appeared as debaters, artists, and athletes, with connections to school life. At the same time, the articles continually ponder the fate of such women and hearken back to worries about their health or describe how they are "new women."

24. Helen Lefkowitz Horowitz, *Alma Mater: Design and Experience in the Women's Colleges from Their Nineteenth Century Beginnings to the 1930s*, 2nd ed. (Amherst, MA: University of Massachusetts Press, 1993). See also Barbara Miller Solomon, *In the Company of Educated Women: A History of Women and Higher Education in America* (New Haven, CT: Yale University Press, 1985).

25. Lydia Maria Child's *A Girl's Own Book* was seemingly endlessly popular and repeatedly reprinted. It brought to girls the housekeeping messages of Catherine Beecher, combined with other pedagogical lessons and craft traditions. It is its title that most clearly resembles the published scrapbook, but other conventions of design, in the borders, for example, also show similarities.

26. Mary Caroline Crawford, *The College Girl of America and the Institutions Which Make Her What She Is* (Boston: L. C. Page, 1905).

27. For a discussion of these novels, see Sherrie A. Inness, *Intimate Communities: Representation and Social Transformation in Women's College Fiction, 1895–1910* (Bowling Green, OH: Bowling Green State University Popular Press, 1995).

28. For a discussion of Deland's disquiet and her comments on the "new woman," see Banta, *Imaging American Women*.

29. *Times-Picayune*, June 13, 1897.

30. See, for example, Jaap Boerdam and Warna Martinius, "Family Photographs: A Sociological Approach," *The Netherlands Journal of Sociology* 16 (October 1980): 95–120; and Sandra Gardner, "Exploring the Family Album: Social Class Differences in Images of Family Life," *Sociological Inquiry* 1 (May 1991): 242–51.

31. Scrapbook, Mary Gladys Owen, 1915, College Archives, Lipscomb Library, Randolph-Macon Woman's College, Lynchburg, Virginia.

32. Solomon, 64.

33. Sally Mitchell, *The New Girl: Girls' Culture in England, 1880–1915* (New York: Columbia University Press, 1995), 50.

34. This often quoted maxim of women's lives is quoted in a number of oral history interviews, especially that of Laura Landry, in the Newcomb Archives, Newcomb College Center for Research on Women, Tulane University, New Orleans, Louisiana. See also Thomas C. Leonard, *News for All: America's Coming of Age with the Press* (New York: Oxford University Press, 1995).

35. Scrapbook, Alice Catherine Grant, 1909, Barnard Archives, Barnard College Library, New York, New York.

36. Scrapbook, Mary Gladys Owen, 1915, College Archives, Lipscomb Library, Randolph-Macon Woman's College, Lynchburg, Virginia.

37. The scrapbooks of Doris Joffrion (1913–19) and Julia Schwabacher Levy (1912–16), Newcomb Archives, Newcomb College Center for Research on Women, Tulane University, New Orleans, Louisiana.

38. Scrapbook, Marion Spencer Fay, 1915, Newcomb Archives, Newcomb College Center for Research on Women, Tulane University, New Orleans, Louisiana.

39. Scrapbooks of Lillian Friend (1907, 1911), Newcomb Archives, Newcomb College Center for Research on Women, Tulane University, New Orleans, Louisiana.

40. Scrapbook, Josephine Janvier, 1908, Newcomb Archives, Newcomb College Center for Research on Women, Tulane University, New Orleans, Louisiana.

41. Scrapbook, Marie Klooz, 1923, Sweet Briar College, Library, Sweet Briar, Virginia.

42. Scrapbooks of Lillian Friend (1907, 1911), Newcomb Archives, Newcomb College Center for Research on Women, Tulane University, New Orleans, Louisiana.

43. Two scrapbooks illustrate a pattern of a "thick description" devoted to the campus especially well, that of Lydia Frotscher (1904, Newcomb Archives, Newcomb College Center for Research on Women, Tulane University, New Orleans, Louisia) and Sophie Woodman (1907, Barnard Archives, Barnard College Library, New York, New York).

44. Scrapbooks of Frances Pennypacker, 1915, Sweet Briar College, Library, Sweet Briar, Virginia; Nellie Scott, 1917, Lipscomb Library, Randolph-Macon Woman's College; and Willie White, 1924, and Dorothy Whiteside, 1925, Woman's Collection, Texas Woman's University, Denton, Texas.

45. Scrapbooks of Lois Janvier, Josephine Janvier, Lydia Frotscher; Newcomb Archives, Newcomb College Center for Research on Women, Tulane University, New Orleans, Louisiana.

46. Scrapbooks of Mary Gladys Owen, 1915, College Archives, Lipscomb Library, Randolph-Macon Woman's College, Lynchburg, Virginia; and Frances Pennypacker, 1915, Sweet Briar College, Library, Sweet Briar, Virginia.

47. Scrapbooks of Juanita Page Johnson, 1922–24, Ophelia Taylor Pinkard, 1935, and Gertrude Geddes, 1929, Amistad Research Center at Tulane University, New Orleans, Louisiana.

48. The Newcomb, Barnard, and Texas Woman's University scrapbooks contain more clippings on basketball and other games than do the scrapbooks in other collections that I studied. For information on Clara Baer, see the scrapbooks of Lydia Frotscher, 1904, Doris Joffrion, 1913–19, Marion Spencer Fay, 1915, and Helen Lowe, 1916–17, Newcomb Archives, Newcomb College Center for Research on Women, Tulane University.

49. Scrapbook, Frances Dreyfuss, 1921, Newcomb Archives, Newcomb College Center for Research on Women, Tulane University, New Orleans, Louisiana.

50. Scrapbook, Juanita Page Johnson, 1922–24, Amistad Research Center at Tulane University, New Orleans, Louisiana.

51. Scrapbook, Ophelia Pinkard Taylor, 1935, Amistad Research Center at Tulane University, New Orleans, Louisiana.

52. Scrapbooks of Frances Purdon Leavitt (1905) and an unidentified student (1908–1910), Barnard Archives, Barnard College Library, New York, New York.

53. Within the various collections, see the scrapbooks of Janet Sandworth (Sweet Briar), Marion Spencer Fay (Newcomb), Lucyle Hook (Texas Woman's University), and Alice Catherine Grant (Barnard), among others.

54. Octavio Paz, "Use and Contemplation" in *The Philosophy of the Visual Arts*, ed. Philip Alperson (New York: Oxford University Press, 1992), 402, 408.

55. Canfield, 276.

56. Most scrapbooks are disassembled and the images, scraps, photographs, postcards, and other items are sold separately.

57. Dorothy C. Holland and Margaret A. Eisenhart. *Educated in Romance: Women, Achievement and College Culture* (Chicago: University of Chicago Press, 1990).

58. Susan Sontag, *On Photography* (New York: Anchor Books, 1990), 14.

2

COMMUNISM FOR KIDS:

CLASS, RACE, AND GENDER IN
COMMUNIST CHILDREN'S BOOKS
IN THE UNITED STATES[1]

Paul C. Mishler

In March of 1999 the National Endowment for the Arts (NEA) rescinded its $15,000 grant to the Cinco Puntos Press of El Paso, Texas. While Americans have become used to controversy over federal arts grants, this money was to be for a project that contained no sexual images, nor did it poke fun at organized religion. Cinco Puntos was publishing a children's book, *The Story of Colors,* a retelling of an indigenous Mexican folktale. The grant was to translate the book from Spanish to English. The controversy arose after the book had already been printed, when a reporter brought to the attention of the NEA that the author was Subcommandant Marcos of the Zapatista movement. Marcos was well known throughout the world as the masked exponent of the radical movement of the indigenous peoples of Chiapas, Mexico. This book for children, however, was not overtly political; it did not attempt to persuade its young readers to join the guerrilla movement, nor did it explicitly criticize the existing social and political order. Yet Marcos' photograph on the back cover in battle fatigues and ski mask was enough to frighten the NEA.[2] Much of the controversy focused, predictably, on the absurdity of seeing political danger in a children's book. Most commentators contrasted the innocence of the book with the political position of the author. Yet was this concern truly absurd? Was this a politically innocent book? The reviewer in the Marxist journal *Monthly Review* believed that behind the seemingly innocuous fable about the emergence of color in a black-and-white world was the story of revolutionary transformation. The first part of the story, in which the world exists only in black and white, represents the "old class society (of owners and their captive workers) and modern global capitalism."[3] The colorful "joyous, diverse world at the end of the tale represents the whole world after the revolution."[4] No wonder the NEA withdrew the grant.

Children's literature has always been didactic and ideological; most of it attempts to inculcate the dominant values of the society in which it is produced. Recent political analysis of children's literature has focused on rereading even overtly nonpolitical children's books and stories to find the pervasive support for the social and political status quo that lies behind most traditional children's literature. Most important in the development of this framework has been Ariel Dorfman's work on reading the Babar and Donald Duck stories, and Jack Zipes' analysis of the Brothers Grimm fairy tales. Both Dorfman and Zipes have shown how traditional fairy tales and their modern equivalents represent values that support existing power relations—modern imperialism and early modern Europe, respectively.[5]

If the ideology of children's literature has been generally oriented toward supporting the status quo, is there a literature for children that contests those values and promotes alternative or oppositional ones? In the recent period, the struggles of the 1960s and 1970s have promoted a greater diversity of children's, and especially young adult, literature. In particular, the demands on the part of African Americans, Latinos, and women for new images of themselves have made themselves felt in the field.[6] There has been an increase in books dealing with workers' issues from an explicitly pro-labor perspective.[7] Not only are there numerous nonfictional historical accounts about the civil rights, women's rights, and labor movements, but these movements are the setting for many works of historical fiction, especially for young adults. Furthermore, there is now more complex fiction that places characters from previously marginalized groups at the center of its narratives.

If this children's literature seems to be breaking new ground, it is largely because earlier efforts in this area are largely unknown. Reaching its widest audience during the 1930s, the radical movement, which had the Communist Party at its center, attracted artists and writers, actors and dancers, all of whom attempted to put their talents at the service of the movement.[8] As part of these cultural efforts, the Communist Party itself published books for children and young adults. Writers sympathetic to the Communist Party during the 1930s created an enormous body of literature for adults. The period's novels, short stories, poems, and plays have been the subject of extensive discussion by historians and literary critics; indeed, the development of "proletarian literature" under the aegis of the Communist Party through journals such as the *New Masses* and the *Anvil* is considered one of the most striking aspects of the decade's literary creation. Similar efforts in the field of children's and young adult literature have received virtually no attention.[9] Alan Wald mentions that a number of radical writers of the 1930s also wrote children's books, but does not mention the books themselves.[10]

Histories of children's literature show a similar neglect. In fact, only English author Geoffrey Trease, who, after writing a number of radical historical novels for young people, went on to become prominent as an author of more mainstream fiction for young adults, is mentioned in the standard work in the field of children's literature. Even here, however, most of Trease's radical novels from the early 1930s are ignored.[11] Before he became the preeminent English author of mainstream young adult historical fiction, Trease began his career with a Marxist retelling of the Robin Hood story, *Bows Against the Barons*. This was followed by two more explicitly Marxist books, *Comrades for the Charter* (1934) and *Call to Arms* (1935). All three were published in the United States by the Communist publishing house, International Publishers, as well as in England. Trease claimed he gave up "propaganda" after 1936 but remained interested in the social perspective of young adult fiction. Referring to British young adult historical fiction in his autobiography, *Tales Told out of School* (1949), Trease writes: "more must be demanded of them in terms of social consciousness" and argued against the pro-aristocratic bias in most boys' adventure stories.[12] The radical children's literature produced in Europe has received greater attention. *Phaedrus,* an international journal of children's literature, published a number of studies in this area during the 1980s.[13] More recently, Jack Zipes has looked at Weimar left-wing writers of children's literature and their work while in exile.[14]

The marginal position of radicalism in the history of the United States, both in literary and political life, has further obscured the issue of radical children's literature. This has begun to open up as scholars have started to look at children's literature by writers who were more known in the field of adult literature. As Alan Wald has mentioned, the literary blacklist did not affect the children's publishing world, and a number of Communist or left-wing writers were able to have their children's books published by mainstream presses during the 1950s.[15] Julia Mickenberg has written about the children's books published by Communist author Meridel LeSueur during this period.[16] LeSueur's four novels for children attempt to frame "traditional American" folk or historical figures such as Davy Crockett, Johnny Appleseed, and Nancy Hanks Lincoln (Abe's mother) to reflect the prairie populist radicalism she had grown up with. As Mickenberg points out, this

required smoothing out the politically uncomfortable but historically prob-
able features such as Davy Crockett's racism.[17] LeSueur's writing during
this period reflects how American Communists tried to merge a developed
Marxist perspective on U.S. capitalism with native radicalism. Yet because
of the time during which they were written, these works do not reflect a
more organized approach for using literature for alternative or oppositional
socialization.

In this essay I examine a number of children's books published by the
Communist Party between the 1920s and the 1940s. In particular, I show
how the presentation of class, race, and gender diverged from or mirrored
the mainstream values, and look at some of the problems that the forms
available for children's literature presented to radical authors during this
period. Between 1925 and 1950 the Communist Party published almost
forty books for children and young adults. Most were published by International Publishers, the Communist Party publishing house, but a few
were also published by the Young Pioneers of America,[18] the International
Workers Order (IWO), other allied organizations, and individual authors.
These books were written and published for use in the activities organized
by the Communist Party and allied organizations during this period, and
were part of a project that included such activities as children's organizations, afterschool programs, and a network of children's summer
camps.[19] I will not, therefore, include in this discussion mainstream children's books written by radical writers, since these were not written as part
of this political project. They were also distributed through the network of
Communist bookstores and organizations. Both the form and content varied widely, and the books included fairy tales for young children, novels
for adolescents, science books, a song book, and a collection of plays.
Although two of the forty books in this study were first published in German, two in Russian, and at least four first appeared in England, most were
the work of American authors.[20]

Like the "proletarian" literature of the 1920s and early 1930s, and literature produced during the late 1930s and 1940s by writers associated with
the Communist Party, the children's literature focused on themes that
reflected the political concerns of the Communist left during this period. In
the discussions that took place in the pages of the *New Masses* and in the
American Writer's Congress, both writers and critics were concerned with
distinguishing propaganda from literature. However, the children's literature was more unabashedly propagandistic. The point of this literature was
to educate children in the ideology of the Communist movement.

Max Bedacht, General Secretary of the IWO, described the purpose of these books in his introduction to the *New Pioneer Story Book,* a compilation of stories that had first appeared in the *New Pioneer* magazine. He emphasized that the stories in the *New Pioneer Story Book* would help children gain a greater understanding of the world around them and, thus, in standard Marxist reasoning, increase their ability to change it. He directly addressed young readers:

> What you are learning in school now and what you read outside of school, in newspapers and books and magazines, is determining what you will do when you grow up. The rich people who own this country know that. That is why they want the government to control education. These rich men, the capitalists, also control the literature you read. American literature is rich in children's books and stories and magazines. But these books were not written to give you pleasure. They are written in order to give you certain ideas that the rich men want you to have.... Reading these stories will help you understand the life about you. As you learn to understand life, you will learn to shape your own lives. You will not merely be pawns kicked around by destiny; you will become masters of your own destiny. You will not only be part of history, but you will become makers of history.[21]

The authors of Communist children's literature contested the conventions of children's literature. Most mainstream children's literature was directed toward socializing children in the dominant values of the society. Communist children's literature was designed to teach children to reject those values and conventions. The question was, however, which of those values and conventions were to be contested. Was it possible to use the forms developed in children's literature, for example fairy tales or adventure stories, to teach radical ideas?

There were two fundamental lessons Communists wanted to teach through their children's literature. First was the existence of class exploitation as a significant facet of the lives of children. In the Communist perspective, most books written for children presented a false view of the social world especially because the lives of working-class children were rarely presented.[22] They were especially concerned with contesting a sentimental, idealized presentation of childhood, which they saw as prevalent in "bourgeois" children's literature. Secondly, Communists wanted to encourage children to become active politically. Particularly during the 1920s and early 1930s, Communists believed children could become activists, even at a very young age.

The first children's book published by the Communist Party was *Fairy Tales for Workers' Children* (1925) by Herminia zur Mühlen, which was originally published in German. The book contains four stories with revolutionary morals. All four of the stories are written as traditional fairy tales in which animals or plants are personified to teach lessons about the reasons for poverty, inequality, and exploitation. For example, the first story, "The Rose Bush," concerns the evils of private property and the right of workers to the proceeds of their labor. In the story, a rose bush speaks to the gardener who tends her, and offers him some of her flowers. He refuses, explaining that the flowers belong to the woman who employs him. The rose bush is horrified, and protests that in the natural world each gets the benefits of what he or she produces. In her disbelief, she asks the wind whether what the gardener has told her is true. The wind affirms that it is. The rose bush decides to refuse to bloom for the rich anymore. When the wealthy lady comes to pick her flowers, the rose bush pricks her with thorns. Finally, she refuses all water until she dries up and is thrown out. The gardener can then take her home, where she blooms once more to bring cheer to the poor. When Communist critic Mike Gold reviewed the book for the Communist journal *The Worker's Monthly* in 1925, he criticized what he called the "atmosphere of slave wistfulness, depression and yearning" about the stories and argued that "the proletariat must grow away from the mood of Christian slave-revolt" traditionally reflected in the fairy-tale form. Instead, Gold said, children's stories should reflect truly proletarian ideology by showing the real conditions of real workers.[23]

The books written by American authors did contain more realistic stories, in line with Gold's proposals, as well as fables and fairy tales. *Battle in the Barnyard* (1932) by Helen Kay was written as a sequel to *Fairy Tales for Workers' Children* and like zur Mühlen's book, it was directed at younger children. The stories in *Battle in the Barnyard* concern children's responses to the Depression. The first story, "Bread," begins:

> Jane put her head on the desk. It felt heavy and dull. She was weak and sick. Her stomach was empty. It seemed to gnaw and cry, "Please put some bread and butter into me. If you don't I'll keep being empty and I'll gnaw and gnaw, and make your head ache until you do."[24]

Jane is told by her teacher to leave school until she can concentrate on her lessons. On her way home, feeling dejected as well as hungry, she meets Cora, her friend. Cora brings her to a Young Pioneer demonstration where Pioneers are picketing the school and demanding free lunches for the children of the unemployed. In the demonstration Jane is arrested, but is no longer despondent because she knows that the solution to her problems lies in struggle.

Labor organization is the subject of many children's stories during this period, and it is through the presentation of children learning about labor conflict that lessons about class struggle are depicted. In "Strike Secret," another story in *Battle in the Barnyard,* Johnnie is the son of a striking miner. His friends accuse him of being the son of a scab, and Johnnie fights to defend his father's reputation. He returns home feeling ashamed and humiliated and asks his father whether it was true that he went to work that day. His father replies that he did go into the mine, and Johnnie, ashamed, runs away to the woods. When his father comes to find him, he explains that he is working for the union, trying to get working miners to join the strike. Yet this is a secret that Johnnie must tell no one. The next day Johnnie is expelled from his "gang," but he does not disclose that his father is really not a scab. When the strike is over, Johnnie explains to his friends that his father was working for the union.

The 1929 Communist-led textile strike in Gastonia, North Carolina, was the subject of a number of adult novels by left-wing writers during this period, including Fielding Burke's *Call Home the Heart* and Bea Lumpkin's *To Make My Bread.* Communist author Myra Page, whose novel *Gathering Storm* was also set during the Gastonia strike, wrote a story for the *New Pioneer Story Book,* "Pickets and Slippery Sticks," in which black and white children learn how to play together when white parents overcome their racist attitudes during a textile strike.

In the latter part of the 1930s, the stark depiction of class struggle shifts to reflect the emphases of the Popular Front Against Fascism. This change marked the end of "proletarian literature" in the adult literature.[25] One aspect of this shift was toward the depiction of "progressive" features in American history. At the same time a more general pro-labor viewpoint replaced the depiction of revolutionary class struggle that had characterized the earlier "proletarian" literature. Literature for children and young people also reflected this change.

The strategy of the Popular Front Against Fascism represented a significant change in the Communist perspective on American society.[26] Previously the Communists had staked out a place for themselves as complete opponents of the "democratic" values of American society, seeing those values as only the velvet glove masking the iron fist of capitalist oppression. The Communist attempt to adopt national values and to then frame them in a "progressive" way represented a shift that had both local and international origins. In the United States, the Communist Party had been a party of immigrants and had struggled to find a way to be "American." This effort preceded the Popular Front and was reflected in the valorization of the struggles of "American" workers in Gastonia and in the National Miners Union strikes of 1929. Internationally, the Popular Front drew from Georgi Dimitrov's report to the 7th Congress of the Communist International, which in turn influenced the cultural policies of all Communist parties.[27] Dimitrov argued that Communists should become representatives of the democratic traditions of their countries and ally with all political forces to fight against fascism. In the arts, this led Communists to pay greater attention to the national cultural traditions of each country instead of looking for a universal, non-national revolutionary culture.[28]

In Eric Lucas' *Corky: Adventure Stories for Young People* (1938), two stories reflect the new search for a "usable past" in American history on the part of American Communists. "Buckhorn Valley Tales" was purportedly based on a story of Abraham Lincoln's youth, and "Swamp Fox" features guerrilla soldiers during the American Revolution. "Swamp Fox" was later expanded by Lucas into a full-length historical novel for young people, *The Swamp Fox Brigade* (1945). The attempt by the Communists to relate to the American tradition was further expanded by the Midwestern Communist writer Meridel LeSueur, who wrote four children's books in the post–World War II period with themes drawn from the American tradition: *Little Brother of the Wilderness: The Story of Johnny Appleseed* (1947); *Nancy Hanks of Wilderness Road: A Story of Abraham Lincoln's Mother* (1949); *Sparrow Hawk* (1950); and *Chanticleer of Wilderness Road: A Story of Davy Crockett* (1951). In addition, in 1946, International Publishers brought out an edition of the poetry of Walt Whitman with an introduction written by Langston Hughes.

The attention to the working class characteristic of the pre–Popular Front children's literature was not entirely abandoned in the post-1936 books. However, there is an increased complexity of presentation (and perhaps a softening of class perspective, depending on one's point of view). In Lucas' *Corky,* a number of stories refer to the labor movement. In "Salty Steers His Course" and "Rusty," the main character is drawn into political struggle by his father's union activities. In the former, Salty is the son of a fisherman who is trying to organize a union. He helps defeat vigilantes organized by the ship owners who are out to break the strike. In the latter, Rusty is involved in a lumberman's strike in the Hudson Valley.

The Communists' belief in the importance of the struggles of African Americans was also reflected in the children's literature throughout the period. The presentation of African-American children in children's literature became a major issue in the context of the Civil Rights movement of the 1960s. Along with the Brownie Books published by W. E. B. DuBois and the National Association for the Advancement of Colored People, Communist literature pioneered in the presentation of stories with African-American characters thirty years before.[29] Even *Fairy Tales for Workers' Children* had one story in it that dealt with a black child escaping from slavery. This continues though the 1930s and 1940s. Martha Campion's *New Pioneer Story Book* (1934) contained "Picket-Lines and Slippery Sticks" by Myra Page. In *Battle in the Barnyard*, black children are the subjects of two of the stories. In "Us Alley Kids," Willie, a black child living in the South, climbs over a wall into the garden of a large estate. The weather is very hot and Willie wants to cool himself in the shade of the trees in the garden. Yet he is chased out by the groundskeeper and the owners, who tell him that because he is poor and black he has no right to enjoy the garden.

In "A Night's Adventure" a group of four black and four white Young Pioneers go out leafleting at night in Washington, D.C. The "adventure" occurs when some go into a black church and hand out leaflets to the congregation over the objections of the preacher. In Martha Campion's *Who Are the Young Pioneers* (1934), Leslie is a sharecropper's child in the South who helps in the organization of the sharecroppers' union.[30] When the sharecroppers host a union meeting, it is Leslie and his fellow Pioneers who are the guards, watching the roads and paths. They are supposed to warn the "croppers if they hear horses hoofs [*sic*] or the motor of a car or other such sign that the sheriff or the Ku Klux have found out about the meeting and are on their way to break it up or shoot it up."[31] This was written as a recruiting pamphlet for the Young Pioneers of America and the author claims that all the stories in it were true. In Eric Lucas' *Voyage Thirteen,* which dealt with merchant sailors on the Liberty Ships during World War II, one of the main adult characters is an African-American cook who teaches a young white seaman (the main character) about the importance of fighting racism.

Communist children's literature also dealt with ethnic and racial minorities other than African Americans. In the *New Pioneer Story Book,* Malcolm Kirkland's story "Siksika" is about Native Americans and the oppression they face. Good Man is an Indian worker in a salmon cannery in the Pacific Northwest. He is fired for his militancy during a strike. The employers attempt to frame him on a murder charge and he is killed by white vigilantes who come to his village to find him. Before he dies, however, he explains to his two children, Black Hair and Lone Star, how the

Indian people are exploited by the capitalists who own the canneries, and how his plight—rather than being an issue of whites versus Indians—is a conflict between all workers and their bosses. His last words implore his children to carry on the struggle. Although the point of this story seems to be that Indians are no longer the people of a romanticized West and no longer "primitives," some aspects of the story read like a Western movie. The Indians call automobiles "fire wagons" and liquor is referred to as "fire water."

Ethnic conflict was a critical part of the longer novels for older children and adolescents published during the 1930s and 1940s. Geoffrey Trease's novel *Comrades for the Charter* is set in Wales during the Chartist agitation of the early nineteenth century. A Welsh boy, Owen, and an English boy, Tom, meet while they are wandering the Welsh countryside looking for work. They are employed by a Chartist agitator masquerading as a patent medicine salesman. He draws both boys into the work of organizing for the Charter. The struggle to overcome Welsh-English ethnic antagonism and the ways that coal mining is beginning to destroy the natural beauty of the Welsh countryside are central themes in the story.

Jean Karsavina's *Tree by the Waters* (1948) is set in a western Massachusetts industrial town. In this strike novel the main character has to confront the prejudice of her New England Yankee family against the Polish immigrant workers. This is one of the few novels written about the Polish-American community in the Connecticut River valley. International Publishers also published *Eddie and the Gypsy* (1935) by the German Communist writer Alex Wedding. A German working-class boy in Berlin during the 1930s confronts the hardships of his father's unemployment with the help of the son of Communists and a Gypsy girl. The novel criticizes the common prejudice against Gypsies, as well as details German working class life during the period of the rise of Nazism.

The presentation of gender was more complicated in these children's books for a number of reasons. In the first place, unlike class and race, gender was not an accepted political category in Communist political ideology during this period. In particular, their conception of class was especially masculinized. The valorization of an ideally masculine male worker was emphasized in much of the "proletarian literature" for adults as both Barbara Foley and Paula Rabinowitz have pointed out. This was expressed in children's literature by having male adults, particularly fathers, serve as models of working-class activism and the almost complete absence of mothers. On the other hand, the socialist movement did have a tradition of support for what they termed "women's emancipation." As Rabinowitz has noted, in this tradition women had "both institutional and rhetorical avenues for organizing (or complaining) as women."[32]

Nonetheless, girls play an active role in a number of the children's books published in this period. In *New Pioneer Story Book,* the main characters are brother-and-sister pairs in Malcolm Kirkland's "Siksika," Vivian Dahl's "Don't Cry Over Spilt Milk," and Myra Page's "Pickets and Slippery Sticks." Geoffrey Trease's *Call to Arms* (1935)[33] is set in a Central American country (very much like Nicaragua) where three young people are drawn into the revolutionary movement. The main character and key revolutionary organizer is Nita, a young woman. In Jean Karsavina's *Tree by the Water* the main character is Abby Chapin, also a young woman. Karsavina's *Reunion in Poland* (1945),[34] also with a girl as the main character, is the story of a Polish girl who has spent the years in exile with her father in Moscow during World War II. When the war ends, she returns to Poland with her father to help build socialism and to perhaps find her mother and her adopted brother. She learns her mother had been killed by Nazis, but does find her brother, who had been a partisan.

The Communist children's literature of the 1920s through the 1940s was directed toward providing an alternative to mainstream children's literature that would help inculcate the Communist worldview in children. For the most part the children who read these books were children of Communists.[35] While the writers of these books often attempted to fit the political goals of the stories into conventional children's literature forms (e.g., fairy tales, adventure stories, etc.), the stories often contested those forms at the same time. While conventional children's literature tended to present the world of family and society as unproblematic, and children's activities were about succeeding in those worlds, the Communist children's literature criticized society, and often explicitly criticized the world of adults. Furthermore, in the presentation of class and racial oppression, the Communists pioneered the kinds of "social problems" literature for children that have become more common since the 1960s.

Even today, when there is a wide range of "social problems" literature for children and young adults from biographies of activist men and women to novels about the Holocaust and slavery, the framework of these books most often reflects the general values of U.S. society—people conquer adversity, whether individually based or socially caused, through individual spunk and hard work. The Communists believed that people succeeded together and rose as a group. This remains, therefore, a critical children's literature.

NOTES

1. An expanded treatment of this subject, along with a bibliography of Communist children's books can be found in my book, *Raising Reds: Young Pioneers, Radical Summer Camps and Communist Political Culture in the United States* (New York: Columbia University Press, 1999).

2. Julia Preston, "Dr. Seuss He's Not," *New York Times*, 14 March 1999, sec. 4, p. 2.

3. Jack Weston, "A Revolutionary Tale from the Mayans of the Lacadon," *Monthly Review* 5 (October 1999): 62.

4. Ibid.

5. See Ariel Dorfman and Armand Mattelart, *How to Read Donald Duck: Imperialist Ideology in the Disney Comic* (New York: International General, 1991); Ariel Dorfman, *The Empire's Old Clothes: What the Lone Ranger, Babar, and Other Innocent Heroes Do to Our Minds* (New York: Pantheon Books, 1983); and Jack Zipes, *The Brothers Grimm: From Enchanted Forests to the Modern World* (New York: Routledge, 1988).

6. The Council on Interracial Books for Children and its journal have been in the forefront of these efforts for many years.

7. See Ann Sparanese, *Selected Bibliography for a Public Library Labor Studies Collection* (Englewood, NJ: Englewood Public Library, 1999).

8. See Michael Denning, *The Cultural Front* (London: Verso, 1996) for a full discussion of these cultural movements.

9. The standard history of radical literature in the United States—Walter B. Rideout's *The Radical Novel in the United States* (Cambridge, MA: Harvard University Press, 1956)—contains no mention at all of radical books for children. There is also no mention of these books in Barbara Foley, *Radical Representations* (Durham, NC: Duke University Press, 1993), or in Paula Rabinowitz, *Labor and Desire: Women's Revolutionary Fiction in Depression America* (Chapel Hill, NC: University of North Carolina Press, 1991).

10. Alan Wald, *Writing from the Left: New Essays in Radical Culture and Politics* (London: Verso, 1994), 104.

11. For example, in Cornelia Miegs (et al.), *A Critical History of Children's Literature* (New York: Macmillan, 1969), 503; Geoffrey Trease, *Bows Against the Barons* (New York: International Publishers, 1934); *Comrades for Charter* (New York: International Publishers, 1934); and *Call to Arms* (New York: International Publishers, 1935). Although Geoffrey Trease is the only radical author mentioned, the entry states that the first of his books published in the United States was *Cue for Treason* (1940) when, in fact, International Publishers had brought out his *Bows Against the Barons* and *Comrades for the Charter* in 1934 and *Call to Arms* in 1935.

12. Quoted in Suzanne Rauh. " 'It Would Be Awful Not to Know Greek': Rediscovering Geoffrey Trease," *The Lion and the Unicorn* 14 (June, 1990): 35.

13. See Joachim Schmidt, "The Issue of Youth Literature and Socialism," *Phaedrus: An International Annual of Children's Literature Research* 8 (1981): 1–6; Carlo Poesia and Pino Boero, "Gianni Rodari: An Appreciation," ibid., 20–22; and James Fraser, "Walter Crane and His Socialist Children's Book Illustrations," ibid., 6–11. See also Thomas S. Hansen, "Emil and the Émigrés," ibid., 11 (1985), 6–13.

14. Jack Zipes (ed.), *Fairy Tales and Fables from Weimar Days* (Hanover, MA: University Press of New England, 1989).

15. Wald, 104.

16. Julia Mickenberg, "Communist in a Coonskin Hat? Meridel LeSueur's Books for Children and the Reformulation of America's Cold War Frontier Epic," *The Lion and the Unicorn* 21 (January 1997): 59–85.

17. Ibid., 69–71.

18. The Young Pioneers of America (1922–1934) was organized for children between the ages of seven and fourteen, after which the Pioneers were expected to graduate to the Young Communist League. The International Workers Order was a federation of Communist-led fraternal benefit societies organized on an ethnic basis.

19. The 1938 Massachusetts State Investigation into Communist Activities included a report about Young Pioneer activity earlier in the decade in Quincy where there were two reading groups: one reading Campion's *Who Are the Young Pioneers* and the other reading William Montgomery Brown's *Science and History for Boys and Girls*. Massachusetts, Commonwealth of, House. *Special Commission to Investigate Activities within Massachusetts of Communistic, Fascist, Nazi and other Subversive Organizations*, House report no. 2100 (1938), 147.

20. The sources for my compilation of titles of children's books are advertisements in the radical press, the archives of International Publishers, my personal collection, and the personal collection of Ernest Rymer, director of the Young Pioneers during the 1920s.

21. Martha Campion (ed.), *New Pioneer Story Book* (New York: New Pioneer Publishing Co., 1935), i.

22. This is not to say that most children's literature accurately represented the lives of middle-class children. The privileged lives of the children presented in most books were not only alienating for working-class children, but nefarious, as well.

23. Mike Gold, "Review of Fairy Tales for Workers' Children," *Worker's Monthly* 4 (October 1925): 572.

24. Helen Kay, *Battle in the Barnyard* (New York: Workers Library Publishers, 1932), 9.

25. Foley, 121–122.

26. Most historians of American Communism have noted the importance of the change in political perspective from the "Third Period" or "leftist" perspectives held by Communists from 1928 to 1936 to the Popular Front Against Fascism. The cultural effects of this change are just being studied. See the previously cited Foley and Denning.

27. Georgi Dimitrov, *The United Front Against Fascism and War* (New York: Workers Library Publishers, 1935), 74. On similar transformations in the culture of the Communist Party of Great Britain, see Michele Weinroth, *Reclaiming William Morris: Englishness, Sublimity, and the Rhetoric of Dissent* (Montreal: McGill-Queen's University Press, 1996), chapter 6.

28. The international cultural significance of this perspective can be seen by recounting the large number of Communist writers whose work came to define a national and democratic culture in their countries and in the development of world culture (e.g., Pablo Neruda in Chile; Yannis Ritsos in Greece; Nazim Hikmet in Turkey; and Hugh MacDiarmid in Scotland).

29. There were earlier anti-racist children's books. American abolitionists produced anti-slavery children's literature, like *The Child's Anti-Slavery Book* (New York: Carleton and Porter, 1859).

30. See Robin D. G. Kelley, *Hammer and Hoe* (Chapel Hill, NC: University of North Carolina Press, 1990) on the history of the Communist-led Sharecroppers Union.

31. Martha Campion, *Who Are the Young Pioneers* (New York: New Pioneer Publishing Co., 1934), 13.

32. Rabinowitz, 46.

33. Geoffrey Trease, *Call to Arms* (New York: International Publishers, 1935).

34. Jean Karsavina, *Reunion in Poland* (New York: International Publishers, 1945).

35. Personal communication with Amy Swerdlow, October 19, 1996. Richard Levins, the Marxist agronomist, recalled that he was introduced to the link between science and history when his grandfather read to him from the Communist defrocked Episcopal bishop William Montgomery Brown's *Science and History for Boys and Girls* when he was a child. See Richard Levins, "A Science of Our Own: Marxism and Nature," *Monthly Review* 38 (July–August 1986): 3.

3

PUBLISHING PRIDE:

THE JIM CROW SERIES OF
HARLOW PUBLISHING COMPANY

Louise S. Robbins

"Excellent readers in the *Negro American Series,* designed to be used with Negro children, to give them a pride in their race and to inspire them to become good American citizens. Brief biographical information about outstanding colored people of yesterday and today has been skillfully worked into the text. Photographs and silhouettes are used as illustrations. Large type."[1] So read the review of Emma E. Akin's four graded readers in the American Library Association's *Booklist,* a tool used by librarians across the United States to make selections for their collections.

The books—*Negro Boys and Girls, Gifts, A Booker T. Washington School,* and *Ideals and Adventures*—were unusual in the book world in 1938. First, they were designed and published specifically for African-American students. Second, their author, Emma E. Akin, supervisor of elementary grades for the Drumright, Oklahoma School District, was white. Third, the books were published by the Harlow Publishing Company of Oklahoma City, a firm closely associated with Oklahoma's white political establishment, owned and operated by Victor E. Harlow. What were the books' explicit and implicit messages? How widely known and used were they? Why did Akin labor to write and Harlow choose to publish books designed to instill pride in African-American children in segregated schools? While the evidence yields answers perhaps as fragile as the books' now brittle pages, the books' anomalous character makes the questions worth exploring.

At the beginning of each book, Akin explains "Why This Book Was Made." In language that differs only slightly from title to title, she explains: "[T]his book was made to help you learn more about your own people. You will enjoy seeing the real pictures of Negro children and Negro leaders." She continues: "You will be proud of the Negro race and of the many fine things your people are doing." Recalling Booker T. Washington as a model, she says that the book will tell children "what it means to be a good American citizen." Finally, "You will like the stories of friendship between black and white people. You will learn that even a small child can do much for his race."[2] Both Akin's distance from her subject—"your people"—and her ideology, an ideology of assimilation and accommodation advocated by Booker T. Washington, emerge from this brief statement. But more radical and oppositional messages emerge as well, those of racial pride and accomplishment, of rejection of stereotypes, and of racial uplift.

In her 1942 *We Build Together: A Reader's Guide to Negro Life and Literature for Elementary and High School Use,* African-American Chicago Public Library children's librarian Charlemae Rollins established criteria for illustrations, language, and theme to use when evaluating children's materials about African Americans.[3] Rollins' criteria, which contrast the usual treatment with the desired treatment of African-American subjects in books for children, reveal how different Akin's books were from others published at that time.

The first reader, *Negro Boys and Girls,* for example, introduces three six-year-olds in their first year at Dunbar School. The photographs, by the Oklahoma City photography firm That Man Stone, depict Clara, Harold, and Rosa Lee as "typical" African-American children from happy, middle-class homes, not as "ragged, barefoot, thick-lipped … child[ren] of a shiftless father," as Rollins described the usual depiction, and thus they meet her first criterion of realistic, rather than stereotypic, visual depiction of African Americans.[4] Their mother and teacher are both presented as attractive, even elegant women, in sharp contrast with other textbook depictions of African-American women as "Mammies." The photograph of Johnnie Mae waking up in her tidy, attractive bedroom, which appears on the very first page of *Gifts* (the second reader) reinforces the comfortable, warm images established in the first reader. Pictures of schoolrooms reveal neat, clean, orderly facilities populated by neat, clean, orderly children eager to be about the business of learning. Parents are shown to be involved with their children's education, with John Henry's father discussing a lesson with him, for example. Although women are more in evidence in both pictures and text, at least two fathers and the principal, Mr. Johnson, are depicted. In a story about poet Paul Laurence Dunbar, silhouettes realistically suggest the historical characters. The same is true of the depiction of poet Phillis Wheatley, artist Edmonia Lewis, the Fisk University Jubilee

Clara.

Singers, Booker T. Washington, and others throughout the volumes. At times the photographs amplify the text message, as when a passage about Dunbar's—and the children's—politeness is illustrated by a photograph of one of the children holding the door for the others. John Henry washing his hands accompanies a text about cleanliness.

Another of Rollins' major criteria for evaluating books about African Americans concerned language. Most often books designed for consumption by the white majority were written in dialect or used derogatory terms to describe African Americans. Dialect not only made books harder for children to read, Rollins said, but it was unfamiliar to children, most

The teacher.

of whom had never heard it spoken. In addition, it was "a kind of fraud perpetrated upon the reader," she asserted, since it gave white children the impression that African-American children spoke in dialect. More-over, derogatory names "infuriate and humiliate every Negro who reads them," she stated strongly.[5] The kinds of language to which she objected are illustrated by a 1937 schoolbook, *Life in Alabama.* While less deroga-tory than many books of the time and place, nevertheless its most concentrated discussion of African Americans dealt with antebellum

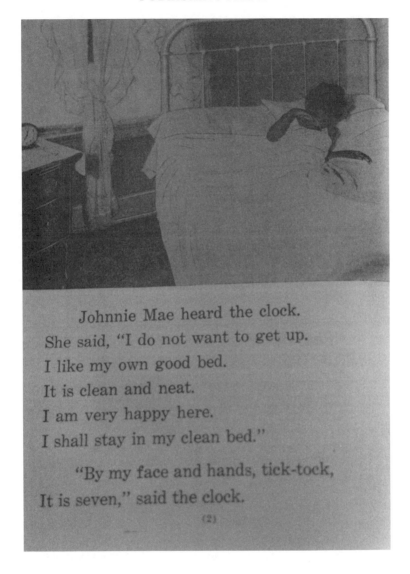

Johnnie Mae heard the clock.
She said, "I do not want to get up.
I like my own good bed.
It is clean and neat.
I am very happy here.
I shall stay in my clean bed."

"By my face and hands, tick-tock,
It is seven," said the clock.

(2)

"Awake, Awake!"

plantation life. In a portion called "Christmas in the Quarters," for example, the author referred to putting sorghum candy "into the pickaninnies' stockings."[6] A "Plantation Play" in the same book—the most extensive African-American dialogue—is written in dialect and contains many demeaning images and words.[7] These qualities of language contrast sharply with the careful use of terms in *The Negro American Series*.

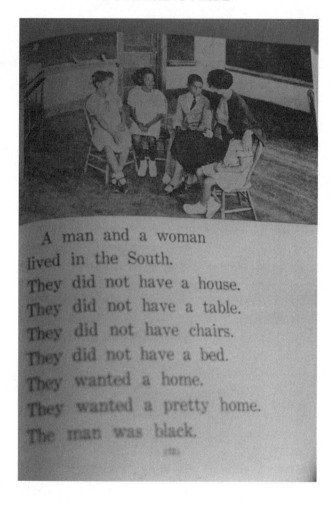

A man and a woman
lived in the South.
They did not have a house.
They did not have a table.
They did not have chairs.
They did not have a bed.
They wanted a home.
They wanted a pretty home.
The man was black.

Children at school.

"Negro," "colored," "black," and "brown" are the only racial terms used. Dialect is nowhere in evidence.

Theme or content was Rollins' third criterion for evaluating books about African Americans for children. Rollins decried the usual characterization of African Americans as, at best, menials or, at worst, buffoons. When shown in stories with whites, African Americans were always depicted as a lower class. African Americans were chiefly visible in many southern textbooks as slaves on pre–Civil War plantations. The author of *Life in Alabama,* for example, described African-American slaves as if they were

Paul Laurence Dunbar and his mother.

children—or puppies: "They were affectionate, dependent people and, if treated kindly, loved and looked up to their 'white folks'.... A good master understood this. He was fond of his people and felt it his duty to take care of them."[8] Whippings—"a punishment that everyone everywhere thought proper"—were meted out to slaves who were "saucy, lazy, or stubborn," as well as for more grievous offenses such as theft or "stir[ring] up trouble."[9] The slaves, according to the author, found freedom as much threat as promise. Some wanted to "see how it felt to be idle," but, ignorant of the ways of the world, "many of them got into trouble," while "others gradually sobered down, worked as servants or at their trades, and became good citizens."[10] While five pages of *Life in Alabama* are devoted to the accomplishments of Booker T. Washington and George Washington Carver, for the most part its message, like that of other texts, was largely silent on African-American contributions to the culture and reinforced the negative stereotypes *The Negro American Series* opposed. In short, the messages African-American children gleaned from the books to which they had access were likely to be detrimental. Rollins called for books

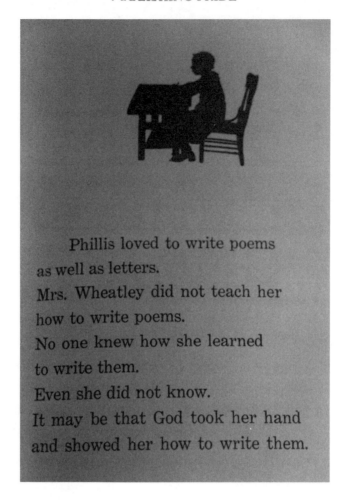

Phillis loved to write poems
as well as letters.
Mrs. Wheatley did not teach her
how to write poems.
No one knew how she learned
to write them.
Even she did not know.
It may be that God took her hand
and showed her how to write them.

Phillis Wheatley.

that, in the words of Langston Hughes, would give "America's Negro children ... back their own souls."[11]

The Negro American Series cut against the prevailing stereotypes in textual theme and content as it did in its illustrations. Each volume includes information on the accomplishments of at least one notable African American, from Paul Laurence Dunbar to Roland Hayes to Phillis Wheatley, to lesser-known figures as well. Farm children and children who live in town are treated with equal respect. Families are described as loving and concerned. Class differences are never mentioned; African Americans are depicted as solidly middle or working class. Neither children nor adults are depicted as menials or buffoons, although, in the spirit of Booker T. Washington, the dignity of all types of work, including the menial, is emphasized, as are the virtues of cleanliness, politeness, and good citizenship.

Race progress and race uplift are constant themes in the books, linked with those virtues of cleanliness, politeness, and good citizenship. In *A Booker T. Washington School,* for example, the children choose a good citizen each day to be the color bearer during the pledge of allegiance. When John Henry tells his parents he has been chosen, his father tells him to be a "color bearer for the race" to lead his people "toward better schools, better homes, better working conditions, and greater friendship with the white race." He valorizes Booker T. Washington's attitudes of patience and gradualism.[12]

Akin extols the progress the race has made, thanks to both African-American and white predecessors. For example, in *Gifts,* as Johnnie Mae and Floyd walk to the school bus that will take them to Wheatley School, their father tells them about his schooling: the abbreviated school year for African Americans; the distance he had to walk; and the poor conditions of the log school. He urges the children to "appreciate" Wheatley School, a school made possible through the generosity of Julius Rosenwald. And while their father never identifies Rosenwald as white in his conversation, Rosenwald's full-page picture accompanies the text.[13]

Friendship with whites is depicted as important, and white benefactors figure significantly in all the books. Rosenwald's establishment of schools, the legacy of Anna Jeanes in providing for the funding of Jeanes' teachers (who promoted the kinds of vocational education advocated by Washington), the help given Washington by his white mentor at Hampton Institute, and the contributions of the white founder of the Fisk University Jubilee Singers are among the stories highlighted. The books imply that African Americans' success is in some measure dependent upon the help of whites. Akin's text counsels gradual improvement of the status and conditions of African Americans through "friendship" with the white race.[14]

Only once does Akin abandon her moderate standpoint. In "Black Sambo and Li'l Hannibal," young Betty falls asleep while reading and dreams that the two children's book characters come alive, "crying as if their hearts would break" over their stereotypical depictions. Sambo is upset over his clothes: "Look at me! Just look at me! They have dressed me in these silly blue trousers. That was not enough, so they put on this awful red coat. Take a look at these shoes! Who ever heard of a real boy

that wore red shoes?" He continues, and is joined by a tearful Li'l Hannibal, who asks him what is wrong. "I know I look like a clown. But this is
not a play. They are sending me on a long journey. I will meet many boys
and girls. They will think I am really like this all the time. They will look
at me and laugh at me day after day." Hannibal protests that *his* problems
are worse than Sambo's: "It is my character, not my clothes that I am worried about. All the boys and girls will think I am a lazy, good-for-nothing
person. Oh, the disgrace! I am so ashamed! All they ever hear about me is
that I ran away from home because I did not want to work!" In fact, he had
been tired of "fetchin' and totin'." Awakened by the school bell, Betty
reflects on Sambo and Hannibal. She fears that they are right; no one
would want to be friends with clowns and lazy good-for-nothings.[15]

In "Black Sambo and Li'l Hannibal" Akin presents, within the dream
framework, the images against which her texts were written. The photographs of African-American children, their families, and teachers found
in *The Negro American Series* are powerfully oppositional to the prevailing popular depictions of African Americans. The narratives also, in presenting African-American men and women of achievement, as well as
solid, loving families, provide positive models for African-American
school children fortunate enough to read them. While the texts implicitly
and explicitly urge an accommodationist approach, they nevertheless—
through a combination of content, language, and illustration—present a
radically subversive vision of possibility for African-American children.[16] How many children might have had the opportunity to read these
books or books like them? Although contemporary newspaper accounts
indicated—without specifics—that *The Negro American Series* was sold
throughout the South, other evidence suggests that the market for the
book was not extensive, and that therefore relatively few children would
have been exposed to its carefully moderated opposition.[17]

First, the conditions of segregated education in the South, the market for
which the books were obviously intended, were notoriously poor. All
education was underfunded; the education of African Americans was desperately so. Only 11.7 percent of education funding went to African-
American children in the South in 1929–30, far below their proportional
representation. In 1930, the Julius Rosenwald Fund, which worked
(among other things) to improve schooling for African Americans in the
South, calculated that the average annual educational expenditure per
child in the United States was $99.00, whereas for whites in the South the
average was $44.31, and for African Americans only $12.57.[18] In the
1929–30 school year, Oklahoma expended $20.83 per African-American

child as compared to $40.48 per white child.[19] According to Henry Allen Bullock's *A History of Negro Education in the South,* in 1928 "over half the rural Negro school population was without the simplest materials of instruction."[20] The situation changed little in the succeeding ten years. In fact, in 1938, Willie Mae Simmons, a Muskogee, Oklahoma, African-American woman, sued to prevent issuance of school bonds to finance new white schools. She did not want to end segregation, she said, but to "end discrimination in administration of school finances."[21] Simmons sought to "show by testimony at the trial that facilities for Negro pupils at Muskogee are wholly inadequate and grossly inferior to those for white students."[22]

The lack of reading materials for African-American children was so pronounced that in the early 1930s, the Rosenwald Fund began to assist libraries in rural Negro schools by providing subsidized low-cost books, and to make simply written books available to elementary pupils of limited reading ability but of all ages. By the time the Rosenwald Fund ended its library program in 1948, more than half a million books had been distributed in 12,000 sets to schools in southern states.[23] The Rosenwald books were the first library books one Florida school had had, and a Tennessee teacher reported her pupils consuming the books like hungry birds.[24] In spite of the Rosenwald Fund's efforts, however, many African-American school children received at best only books discarded by white school children. As Ruth Bean Hicks, a graduate of Bartlesville, Oklahoma's segregated Douglass School said, "Before Brown v. the Board of Education we got the old books, the old typewriters, old band uniforms.... We never got new books; we got the old books, ... whatever they [the white school] used. [Until the Court decision] I'd never seen a brand new book in all my years of school and I was in the tenth grade."[25]

With rare exceptions, then, texts to which African-American children had access imparted a message about African Americans that was compatible with the ideology of the white power structure and denigrated them, their families, and their history. State-adopted texts in the South—particularly histories—had to pass the scrutiny of organized groups, such as the United Daughters of the Confederacy (UDC). For decades the UDC in many southern states exercised vigilance to ensure that United States and state histories depicted the "truth" about the South and the institution of slavery.[26]

The estimate—based on the circumscribed condition of African-American education in the Jim Crow South—that few African-American children had access to this series is substantiated by what little is known about the publishing history of the series. Although recommended in

Booklist and listed in the H. W. Wilson Company's *Children's Catalog* as recommended for elementary library collections[27]—albeit just for African-American children rather than for all children—nevertheless the series had only one edition. Since Harlow Publishing Company specialized in publishing textbooks (and one of many editions of Harlow's *Oklahoma History* was still in use in classes across the state in the late 1970s), had there been a market, Harlow would have capitalized on it and issued subsequent editions or printings.

Remaining evidence about the series' distribution is sketchy and only marginally helpful, since it is difficult to tell when titles in the series were acquired by libraries that now hold them, and I have to date been unable to locate Oklahoma's state-adopted textbook lists for 1938.[28] However, *The National Union Catalog: Pre-1956 Imprints* shows that by its 1968 publication date one or more titles in the series was held by a diverse group of libraries: the Free Library of Philadelphia, the Denver Public Library, the Brooklyn Public Library, and the libraries of the University of Virginia, Duke University, Hampton (VA) Institute, the University of Utah, and the Iliff School of Theology in Denver.[29] The printed catalogs of the Teachers College of Columbia University, the Jesse E. Moorland Collection of Negro Life and History of Howard University, and the Schomburg Collection of Negro Life and History of the New York Public Library indicate that all held copies at the time these catalogs were published, between 1962 and 1970.[30]

More important, Charlemae Rollins knew of the series in Chicago and included them in her list of recommended books about African Americans.[31] Akin's *A Booker T. Washington School* remained many years later on Augusta Baker's *Books about Negro Life for Children,* published by the New York Public Library in 1961.[32] They did not, however, appear on other selection lists, such as the American Library Association's (ALA) 1938 *Inexpensive Books for Boys and Girls* or John Day Company's 1942 *The Right Book for the Right Child: A Graded Buying List of Children's Books,* compiled by a subcommittee of ALA's Board on Library Service to Children and Young People, both of which would have been influential among professional librarians making selections for school and public libraries in both the South and the North. Those lists did, however, include *Little Black Sambo* and similar titles,[33] indicating that librarians—whom Rollins had faulted in 1942 for the demeaning language found in some of their reviews—participated in sustaining the "selective tradition" in literature that reinforced the dominance of white majority culture and the subordinate status of African Americans.[34]

A
BOOKER T. WASHINGTON SCHOOL
EMMA E. AKIN

Textbook cover.

Given their oppositional nature and the uncertain market for *The Negro American Series,* why did Emma Akin write, and Victor Harlow publish, these books? There are a few hints as to Akin's motivation. An elementary supervisor in a school district between Oklahoma City and Tulsa, Akin had attended college in Oklahoma beginning in 1904 and had taught in several small schools before settling in Drumright. When she retired in 1953, she had been in the district for thirty-two years, according to her employment record.[35] A friend said she simply thought that the African-American children under her supervision deserved more than they were getting.[36] Violet J. Harris indicates that Akin belonged at some time to the National

Association for the Advancement of Colored People (NAACP),[37] and the acknowledgments in the books thank Roscoe Dunjee, editor of the state's leading African-American newspaper, the Oklahoma *Black Dispatch,* and an active member of both the state and national NAACP, for "constructive criticism, advice, and inspirational insight."[38]

The books resembled in purpose and content NAACP founder W. E. B. DuBois' periodical *The Brownie's Book,* which was also created to give African-American children an alternative to demeaning literature about themselves. DuBois and Jessie Fauset, the periodical's prime movers, outlined understandings they wished children to gain that were very similar to those articulated by Akin: that their color is beautiful; that others of their race have accomplished great things; that their race has a rich history; that they have a responsibility to be productive and intelligent citizens and to work for racial uplift and progress.[39] Like *The Brownie's Book,* Akin's texts avoided dialect, depicted African Americans of accomplishment, and held up desirable behaviors and attitudes for children. In addition, the periodical used photographs and realistic artwork to present a positive picture of African-American children to African-American children, as did Akin's schoolbooks.[40] Akin's reading books, while embracing the accommodationist philosophy of Booker T. Washington (which DuBois clearly did not) still opposed the selective tradition in children's literature in much the same way as *The Brownie's Book.*

It is likely that Victor E. Harlow, president of Harlow Publishing Company, rather than having any particular sense that African-American children had been cheated, decided that changing conditions in the South in general and Oklahoma in particular had created a new market that a company like Harlow Publishing would be wise to try to fill. The Rosenwald Fund's efforts for African-American education in the South were contemporaneous with the Depression and the New Deal. In Oklahoma, as in the rest of the South, the Depression was not only a time of hardship for African Americans, but was also a time of hope and welcome change. Franklin Roosevelt's New Deal, while aiming to improve the economic lot of all Americans, shook up old political and economic relationships, leaving the door open for greater participation by African Americans. Dunjee's *Black Dispatch* highlighted the administration's racial liberalism and the activities of such groups as the NAACP, which met in Oklahoma in 1934—the first time it had met in the South since 1921.[41]

Harlow would have been well aware of these changes. From 1912 until 1942 he edited and published *Harlow's Weekly: A Journal of Comment & Current Events,* referred to by Oklahoma historian Arrell Morgan Gibson as the "mother lode of information on Oklahoma politics as well as social, economic, and cultural developments."[42] Harlow recorded the state's battles over enabling legislation for New Deal programs such as the Civilian Conservation Corps and the Works Progress Administration, both of which came later to Oklahoma than to other states thanks to the obstructionism of anti–New Deal Governor William "Alfalfa Bill" Murray. He closely watched Murray's successor, Governor E. W. Marland, who won the allegiance of African Americans in part through his support of the New Deal, as he went down to defeat in a race for a Senate seat in 1936. Just after the August Democrat primary, in which Marland was defeated, Harlow reproduced in full "the most important editorial" written after the election—Roscoe Dunjee's "Marland and the Negro Vote" from the *Black Dispatch*.[43]

Dunjee pointed to the nearly solid vote for Marland from Oklahoma's African Americans and noted, "Men who run for office in this state hereafter now know that faithful performance in office will cause Negroes to stick by them...." Their vote was growing and becoming more intelligent, Dunjee said. "Uncle Tom" leadership had lost control, and African Americans were no longer "political pocket change for Republicans." African Americans now constituted "the one positive, permanent bloc in state politics," he claimed.[44] Harlow recognized that the changing political climate brought increased power to African Americans. "Are you adjusted to the idea that by unifying his vote and making it independent the Negro may move into the seats of power in Oklahoma?" Harlow asked rhetorically. "It is in the minds of Negroes like Dunjee and it is within the limits of possibility," he asserted.[45] Two years later, in 1938, *Harlow's Weekly* commented on a "changed attitude [toward African Americans] in Oklahoma, brought about largely through the agencies of the New Deal." African Americans were now seated in the front row—not at the back—at conventions, and allowed to work in the Democratic party, in spite of that party's early insistence that Oklahoma be a "white man's state."[46]

Harlow had long paid attention to Oklahoma's African Americans. More than twenty years before, he had asked Dunjee to write an article for *Harlow's Weekly* about African Americans' response to a proposed amendment to the Oklahoma constitution requiring a literacy test for voters, the effect of which would be to disenfranchise many African Americans. Harlow wrote that "those most affected by the proposed law ought to be heard from."[47] Harlow's relationship with Dunjee was a long and seemingly respectful one.

But the respect Harlow felt for Dunjee would have been unlikely to provide sufficient motivation for his commitment of significant expenditures for *The Negro American Series*. It is more likely that, as the state's African Americans gained a measure of political power, Harlow decided that helping to educate Oklahoma's young African-American citizens into the ideology of Booker T. Washington was to the advantage of the majority, and that those who purchased textbooks for African-American schools would share his viewpoint. To the degree that the books' images, both verbal and visual, are "culturally authentic,"[48] they reflect the growing power and status of African Americans in New Deal Oklahoma. That the positive, liberating images are carefully set within a frame of politeness, good citizenship, and dependence upon whites suggests that perhaps neither author nor publisher was entirely comfortable with the images' radical potential and sought to diffuse or control it, just as they perhaps sought to use education to create the kinds of citizens they felt would not challenge too strongly the power structure. Or it may suggest, simply, that books for children in segregated schools could not be too subversive of prevailing majority views if they expected to find buyers among white school administrators.

It appears that Harlow may, in fact, have overestimated the willingness of school administrators to purchase the books, which, according to Akin, were "under construction" for six years.[49] Or he may have published the series speculating that he would find a market through the Rosenwald Fund (mentioned prominently in more than one book) and its purchases for school libraries throughout the South. In March 1938, Harlow sent a copy of *A Booker T. Washington School* to Edwin R. Embree, president of the Fund, with the explanation that the book was intended as a "supplementary reader in Negro Schools everywhere."[50] It was one of four already published in a planned series of eight, one for each grade. He asked Embree to evaluate the book. "If in any way it fits into your plans and can be used in any operation or project under your direction, we shall be glad to supply your needs."[51] Although the Fund expressed admiration for the book, they told Harlow that they could not use it in their libraries.[52] Harlow was obviously disappointed and hoped for a change of heart. "We have been very hopeful that this series would be included in your library plans," he wrote, "and still hope that at some future time this may be possible." Having the Fund use the books would be "the most substantial assistance possible," Harlow concluded.[53] Two months later he sent another of the books in the series—now under consideration, he said, for adoption in four states—to Embree "for such comment as it may arouse in you and for such cooperation in securing its use as you may see fit to give it."[54] When Embree wrote in response that the book was "a joy" and expressed hope that the book would find "wide acceptance in southern schools," Harlow asked permission to use Embree's endorsement of the book for promotional purposes.[55]

Whether or not Embree's letter was used to promote the *Negro American Series,* there was apparently insufficient market for the books, and plans for the last four volumes in the series were abandoned. Nevertheless, in the four small volumes that did appear, Akin and the Harlow Publishing Company managed to publish for the South's segregated schools a remarkable series of supplementary basal readers that met all the criteria for positive books for African-American children. Through realistic illustrations, respectful and dialect-free language, and themes of caring families, the importance of schooling, the accomplishments of African Americans, and racial uplift, the *Negro American Series* provided a healthy alternative to the many denigrating messages African-American children received from their surroundings and from other children's books. They did, perhaps in spite of themselves, publish pride.

NOTES

1. [Review], *The Booklist* 35 (June 1, 1939): 334.

2. Emma E. Akin, *A Booker T. Washington School* (Oklahoma City: Harlow Publishing Company, 1938): n.p.

3. Charlemae Rollins, *We Build Together: A Reader's Guide to Negro Life and Literature for Elementary and High School Use* (Chicago: National Council of Teachers of English, [1942]), 4–19.

4. Rollins, 5.

5. Rollins, 7.

6. Susan Kirkman Vaughn, *Life in Alabama* (Montgomery, AL: Dixie Book Company, Inc., 1937), 140.

7. Vaughn, 142–148.

8. Vaughn, 137.

9. Vaughn, 135–136.

10. Vaughn, 217–218.

11. Rollins, 9–10.

12. Akin, 102.

13. Emma E. Akin, *Gifts* (Oklahoma City: Harlow Publishing Company, 1938), 15–20.

14. Violet J. Harris, "Historic Readers for African-American Children (1868–1944): Uncovering and Reclaiming a Tradition of Opposition," in *Too Much Schooling, Too Little Education: Paradox of Black Life in White Societies*, ed. Mwalimu J. Shujaa (Trenton, NJ: Africa World Press, 1994), 164–165.

15. Akin, *A Booker T. Washington School,* 151–154.

16. See Harris for a discussion of the selective tradition in children's literature that emerges from the hegemonic role of literature as a cultural artifact.

17. Harris, 163.

18. Louis R. Wilson and Edward A. Wight, *County Library Service in the South: A Study of the Rosenwald County Library Demonstration* (Chicago: University of Chicago Press, 1935), 16.

19. Henry Allen Bullock, *A History of Negro Education in the South from 1619 to the Present* (Cambridge, MA: Harvard University Press, 1967), 179–180.

20. Bullock, 141.

21. "Race Issue Raised on Two State Fronts," *Harlow's Weekly* (October 8, 1938), 3.

22. "Negro-white School Case to United States Supreme Court," *Harlow's Weekly* (October 15, 1938), 4.

23. Bullock, 140–141.

24. G. W. Hampton to Julius Rosenwald Fund, April 22, 1939, and Nellie H. Mead to Julius Rosenwald Fund, April 21, 1939, Folder 4, Box 285, Julius Rosenwald Fund Archives, Special Collections, Fisk University Library, Nashville, TN (hereafter JRFA).

25. Ruth Bean Hicks, in a group interview by author with DouglassAires Group, graduates of Bartlesville's Douglass High School, at the Westside Community Center, Bartlesville, Oklahoma, July 22, 1994.

26. Fred A. Bailey, "The Textbooks of the 'Lost Cause': Censorship and the Creation of Southern State Histories," *Georgia Historical Quarterly* 75 (Fall 1991): 507–533.

27. *Children's Catalog: A Dictionary Catalog of 4200 Books with Analytical Entries for 910 Books and a Classified List Indicating Subject Headings*, 6th ed. revised (New York: H. W. Wilson Company, 1941), 12. The series appears also in the 1946 edition, but not in the 1951 edition. *Little Black Sambo*, however, appears in all three editions in several versions. The classic version, published by Lippincott, appears with a double star, indicating it is highly recommended for purchase. According to Wilson's *Cumulative Book Index* for 1939, Wilson also printed catalog cards to be sold and distributed with the books listed in *Children's Catalog*, a feature that was supposed to make processing a book easier for librarians.

28. Linscheid Library, East Central University, Ada, Oklahoma, for example, acquired the books—as did other Oklahoma colleges—when Harlow went out of business in 1978. Other libraries may have acquired the texts for their research collections because of their oppositional quality.

29. *The National Union Catalog: Pre-1956 Imprints,* Vol. 6 (London: Mansell Information Publishing, 1968), 360.

30. *Dictionary Catalog of the Schomburg Collection of Negro Life and History, New York Public Library,* vol. 1 (Boston: G. K. Hall, 1962), 400; *Dictionary Catalog of the Jesse E. Moorland Collection of Negro Life and History, Howard*

University Library, Washington, D.C., vol. 1 (Boston: G.K. Hall, 1970), 350; *Columbia University Dictionary Catalog of the Teachers College Library,* vol. 1 (Boston: G.K. Hall, 1970), 532.

31. Rollins, 20.

32. Augusta Baker, *Books about Negro Life for Children,* revised ed. (New York: The Public Library, 1961), 9.

33. Book Evaluation Committee of the Section for Library Work for Children of the American Library Association (comp.), *Inexpensive Books for Boys and Girls* (Chicago: American Library Association, 1938); American Library Association Board on Library Service to Children and Young People (comp.), *The Right Book for the Right Child: A Graded Buying List of Children's Books* (New York: John Day Company, 1942).

34. Harris, 152–154, discusses the "selective tradition" in more detail.

35. Telephone conversation with Barbara Burditt, April 16, 1997.

36. Telephone conversation with Lucile Anderson, April 20, 1997.

37. Harris, 162.

38. Akin, *A Booker T. Washington School,* Acknowledgments.

39. Violet J. Harris, *The Brownie's Book: Challenge to the Selective Tradition in Literature* (Athens, GA: University of Georgia Press, 1986), 3–4.

40. Harris, *The Brownie's Book,* 3–4.

41. Patricia Sullivan, *Days of Hope: Race and Democracy in the New Deal Era* (Chapel Hill, NC: University of North Carolina Press, 1996), 87.

42. Arrell Morgan Gibson, "Indian Pioneer Legacy: A Guide to Oklahoma Literature," *Chronicles of Oklahoma* 56 (Spring 1978), 6.

43. Victor E. Harlow, "The Negro in Oklahoma," *Harlow's Weekly* (August 8, 1936), 3.

44. Harlow, 3.

45. Harlow, 4.

46. "Oklahoma Develops New Race Attitude," *Harlow's Weekly* (November 26, 1938), 3.

47. "The Election Controversy from Four Viewpoints," *Harlow's Weekly* (April 8, 1916), 9.

48. Harris, *The Brownie's Book,* 156.

49. Akin, *A Booker T. Washington School,* Acknowledgments.

50. Victor E. Harlow to Edwin R. Embree, March 9, 1953, Folder 3, Box 285, JRFA.

51. Harlow to Embree, March 9, 1953, Folder 3, Box 285, JRFA.

52. Margaret S. Simon to Victor E. Harlow, March 25, 1938, Folder 3, Box 285, JRFA.

53. Harlow to Simon, March 31, 1938, Folder 3, Box 285, JRFA.

54. Harlow to Embree, May 20, 1938, Folder 3, Box 285, JRFA.

55. Embree to Harlow, May 24, 1938 and Harlow to Embree, May 27, 1938, both Folder 3, Box 285, JRFA.

4

THE POWER OF BLACK AND WHITE:

AFRICAN AMERICANS IN LATE-NINETEENTH-CENTURY CHILDREN'S PERIODICALS

Leslie R. Miller

With any effort to define print culture for youth, scholars must recognize its powerful influence in teaching American values to children. The portrayal of African Americans in late-nineteenth-century children's periodicals demonstrates how popular culture, such as children's literature, helped shape social relations in the United States. During the nineteenth century, American children's literature achieved a wide readership in both the North and the South as a source of both informal education and entertainment.[1] Anne Scott MacLeod argues that the study of children's literature, which usually represents the "broadly accepted attitudes of its period," offers scholars the opportunity to understand better one of the more elusive yet important parts of history: how people thought about and understood their world.[2] One such nineteenth-century American attitude was the assumption that nonwhite people were inferior.

Although children learned this attitude from a variety of sources, children's literature played a significant role in children's racial education.[3] As one instrument of nineteenth-century child rearing that has survived, children's literature offers an opportunity to trace the crucial transmission of racial ideologies to new generations.[4] The predominance of children's literature made written material as important in teaching values in the nineteenth century as the ubiquitous television and films are today. Cultural influences upon the young continue to be important sources for understanding the continually changing (but also invariably existing) racism in American society.

An important venue of children's literature in the nineteenth century was the magazine.[5] Two of the most significant children's periodicals during the late nineteenth century were the *Youth's Companion* and *St. Nicholas*. These magazines, as well as the vast majority of all written material for children, were created for a white audience. In her introduction to this anthology, Anne Lundin underlines the importance of addressing the issue of readership by suggesting that scholars have to be wary of equating "class culture" with "common culture." Because of the cost of magazines, upper-middle-class children had easiest access to most magazines. But with the changing nature of the production of periodicals, magazines such as the *Youth's Companion* did reach a much larger audience. These sources are significant to study because of the power in shaping their readers' understanding of the world—readers who would later shape American society. In the preceding essay, Louise Robbins demonstrates the recognition of this power by those in the publishing world in her discussion of the efforts of the Harlow Publishing Company to provide a counterimage of African Americans for at least some black children. Decades would pass before books for the larger community of children would be revised (of course, this process is still not finished).

These youth magazines were not limited to a single region. Judging from letters written by the young readers to the magazines, the publications reached the homes of children all over the country, including the South and the West.[6] The *Youth's Companion* enjoyed unmatched longevity and the largest audience of all American children's periodicals.[7] This weekly magazine's circulation eventually passed the half million mark in the 1890s, making it one of the five top-selling magazines in the United States.[8] The *Youth's Companion* not only provided stories of scientific, geographic, and historical interest, but also demonstrated a consistent commitment to moral ideals.[9]

St. Nicholas: Scribner's Illustrated Magazine for Girls and Boys offered the highest quality material available in a children's magazine during the nineteenth century.[10] Its circulation reached approximately 70,000 copies per issue soon after it first appeared in 1873.[11] *St. Nicholas* offered forty-eight and eventually ninety-six pages of entertaining and value-laden literature monthly. In addition to the fictional entries, the magazine carried stories covering travel, biography, history, and science. *St. Nicholas* also featured a correspondence page as well as numerous puzzles and games. The editors of these periodicals typically exercised tight control over the contents of their magazines.[12] One source described *St. Nicholas* editor Mary Mapes Dodge's control as so complete that she regulated "not only what was said, but how it was said."[13] Daniel Ford, the editor of the *Youth's Companion,* offered tightly constructed guidelines for stories published in his magazine in a pamphlet sent to all interested story writers entitled "The *Youth's Companion* Story."[14] Since the editors crafted each page of their magazines so carefully, the portrayal of African Americans proved no accident.

Many of the characterizations of African Americans were based on stereotypes. Most humans, past and present, stereotype people who are different, in order, as Sander L. Gilman has said, to "control our world."[15] Humans simplify reality in order to process it better. Racism further warps these stereotypes. Racial prejudice adds to their "rigidity, error, and hostility."[16] Thus, despite the fact that stereotypes were often based on untruths, people often accepted these untruths as fact. Once again, Sander L. Gilman's own words best explain the significance of the stereotypes people create: "Our internal, mental representations of the world [often shared by those around us] become the world. We act as if this world were real, external to ourselves...."[17] White Americans utilized racial stereotypes to understand African-American people. Of course, they not only stereotyped African Americans but also many other groups of people, including Native Americans, Mexican Americans, and Asian Americans.

While white Americans did not understand the concept of race in the same way, they shared several assumptions.[18] Americans had constructed a racial hierarchy that exalted white people and devalued black people.[19] Race defined one's intellectual and spiritual qualities, as well as one's physical attributes. Consequently, it was assumed that African Americans lacked responsibility, industry, and initiative, the very characteristics associated with success in an industrial age.[20] Accordingly, black Americans could not succeed in American society. Children memorized the characteristics and rank of each race from their geography books. Their schoolbooks reinforced these concepts of race by asking study questions such as "Which is the most intelligent race?" at the end of chapters.[21] The assumed inferiority of all nonwhite peoples increasingly shaped and limited almost all discussions of race. This created a mentality in which very few people would even think an egalitarian multiracial society was possible.[22]

Many creators of culture incorporated assumptions of the inferiority of black people into their works, buttressing the belief in the "scientific" inferiority of African Americans. Popular culture as an important source for shaping society's values and beliefs has a long and unfortunately rich history of perpetuating black stereotypes.[23] Authors and artists most commonly utilized the Sambo figure—a happy, childlike, entertaining, unconditionally loyal, and incompetent character—as the universal representation of African Americans.[24] The Sambo character flourished on the plantations in the South and on the minstrel stage in the North. The Sambo stereotype infiltrated the national consciousness and appeared everywhere, including books, magazines, and advertisements, long after the end of slavery. Many white Americans held onto the Sambo stereotype throughout the nineteenth century and beyond; the internalized stereotype continued to shape how white people understood black people in the twentieth century.

While racial prejudice "bent" following the Civil War, and northerners "allowed" black Americans to enjoy political, civil, and social advances in status that they had sought, the reality for most northern blacks continued to be a life in urban poverty.[25] As demonstrated by a number of northern states' efforts to keep black Americans out of their state altogether in the antebellum period, most northerners were not comfortable or interested in living in a multiracial democracy. While black Americans had fought successfully for the Union cause, their actions did not earn them a right to equal treatment. Instead, white Americans interpreted their service in the war effort, which was under white officers, as proof of their docility; they followed orders well, but they were not self-reliant.[26] In the South during Reconstruction, a group of white people expressed surprise at the economic and educational progress black Americans had made since the Civil War. But most white southerners had no interest in watching black southerners succeed and pressed for a renewed commitment to using racial, economic, and social controls to oppress black people.[27] During Reconstruction, white southerners were best able to control black advancement through restricting their economic well-being by instituting a crop lien system, which left many African Americans in virtually permanent debt.

As northerners became more interested in their economic condition as well as in reuniting the country, they "returned" the South to white southerners during the 1870s.[28] Historian Nina Silber explains that northerners, as they increasingly desired reconciliation between North and South, viewed the white planter class with "pity and respect" while they came to understand black southerners as "pathetic and entertaining." Thus the Sambo stereotype proved more powerful than the humanity of African Americans. Instead of welcoming African Americans as deserving citizens into the union in the years following the Civil War, they instead became a "picturesque" element of the South. Black southerners in the eyes of many northerners were loyal servants in the "mythical south of great plantations." This is the South that tourists "saw" when they visited. It also became the South that appeared in plays, minstrel shows, and other cultural creations.[29]

Following the end of federal Reconstruction, white southerners reasserted control over ex-slaves. While they had diverse interests and backgrounds, many white southerners united behind a program of dismantling Reconstruction governments, reducing black political power through disfranchisement, reshaping the South's legal statutes to formalize racial subordination as well as labor control, and using terroristic violence when desired. This process was not identical throughout the South. Race relations continued in a state of flux for several more years, and the political and social options of blacks narrowed during this time.[30] Stereotypical, derogatory, and inaccurate representations of African Americans in popular culture only presented more difficulty for black Americans to overcome the racial oppression of the late nineteenth century.

A pervasive and significant stereotype in children's magazines was the idea that the proper and ideal relationship between white people and black people was that of the benevolent white master/mistress and the loyal black servant. The end of slavery was the most profound change in the status of African Americans in the nineteenth century. That change of status of African-American lives, however, shaped their image in children's magazines only in limited ways. While the magazines' attitudes toward slavery shifted several times during the nineteenth century, their advocacy of an idealized relationship between white and black people did not. Magazines usually depicted African-American characters as servants, whether slave or free. Moreover, often they presented black people as contented servants. The magazines' consistent portrayal of a successful relationship between the paternalistic white character and the inferior but usually happy-to-serve black character through the 1890s suggested to readers that these were the ideal relationships and the ideal social roles for white and black Americans.[31]

This mythical relationship rang true for both northerners and southerners into the final decades of the nineteenth century. Silber explains that southerners accepted the loss of the Civil War, in part, by turning the South into a "land of idyllic plantation settings" that included the memory of slavery as a "happy and beneficial arrangement." Many northerners accepted this myth because it provided an escape from the class conflict and ethnic strife in their increasingly industrialized world.[32] These "soothing images" came at the long-term expense of African-American integrity.[33]

So the institution of slavery did not disappear from the pages of the magazines after the Civil War years. Nor was it altogether condemned. For example, an 1878 *Youth's Companion* story suggested that the relationship between white people and black people was a positive aspect of slavery as it used to exist. The author wrote:

There were two sides to even the story of slavery. The Northern people knew little of the strong, warm relations between a faithful master and slaves who had been part of his family for generations. On the part of the slaves, too, the sense of loyalty to their owners led often to acts of self-sacrifice, finely human and noble.[34]

Authors utilizing the slavery era in their stories for the rest of the century focused on the paternalist-servant relationship between white and black people. Scenes of happy, carefree days on plantations occupied a number of pages of the children's magazines from the 1870s through the 1890s. The magazines almost completely ignored the increasing oppression of African Americans throughout the country.

Black characters in stories about slavery published in the last quarter of the nineteenth century did not necessarily demonstrate a desire to be free, and they seemed to need white leadership. In this manner, the magazines portrayed slavery as rather benign. In the 1890s serialized *St. Nicholas* story "The Sole Survivors," "Shanti's" owner offered him his freedom in exchange for saving his son's life. However, the slave declined, "Shanti no wish to be free ... What he do widout a massa to take care ob him?" When his owner offered to pay him wages, Shanti was again unimpressed, believing he had everything he would ever want. "What Shanti want wid wages, massa? He got clothes, he got food, he got ebery t'ink dat he wants. Shanti have no use for money."[35] When the son grew up and owned slaves, the author suggested that the slaves should feel blessed to be owned by such a man. He ended the series with the phrase: "they had reason to congratulate themselves on having fallen into the hands of the kindest and best master in the colony."[36]

Even slave characters that desperately desired freedom remained determined to serve their former masters. In an 1893 *Youth's Companion* story, five-year-old Wesley, a slave, became the body-servant for his master's infant son, Sidney. Despite the "liberties" Wesley enjoyed as a body-servant, he still longed for freedom. After he saved his young master's life, his owner granted Wesley and his mother their freedom. Though both expressed great joy, they turned down the chance to move North in favor of spending the rest of their days working for their former master on the plantation. The story concluded: "Wesley is, after thirty years, still on the old plantation, earning good wages and enjoyment as the little master's body-servant and trusty friend."[37] While this story explicitly acknowledged a desire within black people for freedom, it also implied that they were satisfied to serve their former masters and that the closest bond they had was with the white people they served. Ignoring the context of African-American reality, these stories set in the slavery era with messages of black service and loyalty to white people offered powerful messages of "proper" black-white interaction.

Magazines even reinforced with humor their messages of African Americans' supposed propensity for loyalty and respect for whites. In an 1895 *Youth's Companion* story, a master and his slave played the violin together. Once, after they finished, the master exclaimed, "You handle the bow pretty well, Ned, but you are always a bar or so behind. Why is that?" "'Out ob deference to you, colonel,'" said Uncle Ned."[38] The author suggested that the respect and loyalty the slave displayed pointed to his inferiority. His loyalty was not honorable. Instead, it indicated a reflexive servility that was a "natural" and inferior African-American characteristic.

Not all African-American servants in the children's stories presented model servant behavior. Some authors presented black servants who acted in a rather lazy and selfish manner. This characterization contributed, as did the happy-to-serve characterization, to the propriety of the inferior-superior relationship between black and white people. For example, Mrs. Burton Harrison's 1896 reminiscence of her childhood days in Virginia, recounted in the *Youth's Companion,* pointed to a realization that slavery was wrong as an institution. However, as a child looking at the black people around her, Harrison saw their relationship with the family as the best situation for them. She wrote about life in the years before the Civil War up through Lincoln's assassination. While her family chose to free its slaves, they still hired slaves from a nearby slaveowner to replace their lost servants.

As a child, Harrison had obtained a copy of *Uncle Tom's Cabin* and read it secretly as part of an effort to decide whether slavery was evil. Upon completing the novel, she "looked from one to the other of the placid black or yellow faces that surrounded [her], and wondered if such tragedies ... could be in existence among their race."[39] She studied the servants to try to surmise an answer based on their lives. Harrison decided that although slavery was wrong, the African Americans immediately around her were happy and content as slaves and even had an easy existence. The pantry-maid Fanny sang all day long as she worked and the coachman Abram whistled and "did not hesitate to object if the ladies of the family called upon to harness his horses at an inconvenient time." The cook must have been in "seventh heaven" because she "did almost exactly as she pleased." And then there was Susan who "forgot her own people in her devotion to us."[40] This story left the distinct impression that while slavery was morally wrong, black people themselves were childlike in their need to be watched.

While in reality African Americans contributed significantly to the economy of the South through their labor in the fields and elsewhere, in children's magazines they were depicted primarily as waiting on white people through their work as household servants.[41] African-American female characters were almost exclusively servants who were cooks, cleaners, and/or mammy figures who happily took care of the children.[42] The mammy was overwhelmingly loyal and served "her" people well. Old male black servants and young black children also existed, in the stories, to be ready at all times to aid white people in their daily lives.[43] For example, white children took their servants along on their adventures. Older black servants, usually referred to with the title "Uncle," frequently accompanied white boys on fishing trips.[44]

The magazines reinforced black people's prescribed roles as servants with illustrations. Most of the illustrations of black characters in the magazines, in fact, showed them as servile characters.[45] A number of them portrayed black men as "shuffling" old servants standing in the yard or by the river with their white charges. Magazine illustrators almost always drew black women as overweight people who wore a long dress, an apron, and a head turban. Widely printed advertisements in the children's magazines also strengthened these stereotypes, such as a smiling Aunt Jemima who sold pancake flour to the world and a happy black male cook who sold Cream of Wheat.[46] The pictures of the "smiling servant" powerfully reinforced the stereotype that black people were pleased to serve white people.[47]

While throughout the nineteenth century stories and illustrations repeatedly presented idealized relationships between white people and black people, relationships among black characters were portrayed as flimsy and fraught with difficulties, especially between family members. In children's magazines, black women put all of their energies into caring for the white families and did not properly care for their own family. In such portrayals, the magazines overlooked the reality that black women did not ignore their children because they cared less for them, but because of their long hours of work.

Authors also presented African Americans as needing parental help. White mistresses often had to correct the women on how properly to discipline or love their children. For example, an 1898 *St. Nicholas* story highlighted a relationship between a white mistress and her servant's child. The mistress discovered that "Jim Crow's" mother had not provided him with a sufficient wardrobe or training in proper manners, so she did. The white mistress also served as his comforter and protector. After neighborhood white kids called him a "nigger" and stopped playing with him, the mistress bought him special clothes to cheer him up. She then acted to prevent his sister from taking and selling them. When the white family was finally forced to fire "Jim Crow's" mother and sister, his affection and loyalty were clearly to the white mistress and he was devastated to leave her. The author fails to point out that the white mistress is able to devote time to the child because his mother is the one taking care of her house.[48] Such magazine stories emphasized a special relationship between white people and black people instead of identifying the "superior" white characters as the ones guilty of devaluing black family bonds.

Altogether the images of African Americans in late-nineteenth-century children's periodicals created a distorted picture. The periodicals repeatedly portrayed black characters as eager servants, not as people trapped in a menial position because of a lack of opportunity in American society. Their continual portrayal of black house servants meant that they ignored black contributions to the economy of the South. In addition, because racial occupancy of social roles is one of the instruments by which children develop racial attitudes, the images of black servants in the magazines would have further solidified the idea of African-American inferiority in their minds.[49] The servant role also reinforced an inferior-superior relationship between black and white people. Since Americans tended to idealize first the slave-master and then the servant-employer relationship, many white Americans also imagined themselves as good caretakers of black people.[50] Racist images thrived not just in children's magazines, but throughout American society. Everywhere the black image, as interpreted by white fantasy, appeared. It sold products for advertisers, told stories on stage, peered from books and magazines, and smiled from every imaginable knickknack. By 1900, everywhere a middle-class person saw a black image, as Henry Louis Gates Jr. has stated, "that image would be negative."[51]

Examining the widespread distorted images of black people in white culture is crucial to understanding race relations in the nineteenth century because these white-constructed images of African Americans shaped social relations. Race was not a physical fact but a social construction of the nineteenth century, meaning it was "artificially formed."[52] But even though it was not concrete it was still a powerful force. Assumptions about race, created within the social context of nineteenth-century America, shaped social reality. For example, although many white Southerners interacted with blacks on a regular basis, their mental construction of African Americans in general shaped how they perceived black people.

This construction was reinforced and also shaped by images from culture, including children's magazines.

Thus, because the magazines continually used stereotypical African-American servant characters in stories, black people interacted with a white society who believed and treated them as if they enjoyed serving white people. Black people, of course, did not have a special affinity for serving white people, but did so because it was an economic necessity. However, the perception that African Americans were eager and happy to serve became the social reality for many white Americans. People, as historian Ronald G. Walters has explained, "see what their values, attitudes, and preconceptions prepare them to see."[53] Because white children were taught that African Americans were inferior to them and were happy to serve white people, one can not be surprised that they believed this.

For example, Theodore Roosevelt grew up reading the magazine *Our Young Folks* that presented happy and loyal black servants in their stories.[54] Years later, he recalled that the black servants in his childhood home acted just like the servants in *Our Young Folks*. Roosevelt more likely than not perceived this, since the likelihood that all of his family's servants acted the same way as all of the servants in the magazines was very small. This perception, however untrue, was the social reality for Roosevelt and he acted on it and others. Roosevelt's perceptions held long-term consequences for more than the African Americans he interacted with personally, since he helped to create American public policy as well as shape the racial assumptions of other white Americans through his popular writings on race.[55]

African Americans themselves recognized the power of white peoples' social construction of them and felt compelled to create a counter-construction in the late nineteenth century. African Americans comprehended that "to manipulate the image of the black was, in a sense, to manipulate reality."[56] They hoped to improve their reality by improving their image. At the turn of the century they "advertised" their new image, which they titled the "New Negro," in literature and in art. For example, many images of well-dressed, dignified-looking African-American men and women graced the pages of magazines and books.[57] Their need to develop a counter-construction demonstrated the power and hegemony of the racism of the cultural elite. The lack of financial resources prevented the African-American community from providing sustained counter images for their children as demonstrated by the excellent but short-lived magazine by W. E. B. DuBois called *The Brownies' Book*. Even the efforts of white publishing companies such as that of the Harlow Publishing

Company in Oklahoma City in 1938 that Robbins discusses in the previous essay met with limited success. A lot of progress has been made in the last few decades as opportunities in the publishing world have expanded. However, deep concern for the portrayal of African Americans in print culture continues today, as demonstrated by the outcry over the use of the book *Nappy Hair* by a white teacher in New York.[58]

Children's magazines in general served two purposes: to help children understand the world around them, and to provide entertainment. With their portrayal of African Americans at the end of the nineteenth century, children's magazines provided neither an accurate representation of the black experience, nor innocent or harmless entertaining images. Their presentation of African Americans contributed in a larger sense to the racial education of young white Americans who helped to shape the nature of the multiracial society in the twentieth century. Children's material also contributed to the further obscuring of the reality for most African Americans—not only a reality of poverty, but also one of violence. This did not play out for that generation alone. Disturbing portrayals of Americans with a multitude of differences still plague society today.

NOTES

1. Marjory Lang, "Childhood's Champions: Mid-Victorian Children's Periodicals and the Critics," *Victorian Periodicals Review* 8 (Spring and Summer 1980): 26; R. Gordon Kelly (ed.), *Children's Periodicals of the United States* (Westport, CT: Greenwood Press, 1984), xv.

2. Anne Scott MacLeod, "Education for Freedom: Children's Fiction in Jacksonian America," *Harvard Educational Review* 46 (August 1976): 428.

3. Researchers have found that children learn racial attitudes around the age of three or four from interaction with their families and from listening to grown-ups discuss racial issues. In addition, they learn racial attitudes at school, from reading materials, from value-laden words such as white and black, and by association with "racial occupancy of social roles." Judith D. R. Porter, *Black Child, White Child: The Development of Racial Attitudes* (Cambridge, MA: Harvard University Press, 1971), 14–19.

4. R. Gordon Kelly, *Mother Was a Lady: Self and Society in Selected American Children's Periodicals, 1865–1890* (Westport, CT: Greenwood Press, 1974), xvi.

5. Although a huge and successful enterprise with many loyal readers by the end of the nineteenth century, the magazine industry still had to overcome obstacles. The publishers had to maneuver their wares into middle-class leisure time. As magazines grew in popularity and the economics of the business improved,

writers of high stature began to contribute to magazines, including children's periodicals. Magazines, including children's periodicals, enjoyed unprecedented success during the last quarter of the nineteenth century because of technological innovations in publishing, the use of advertising, and improvements in the postal delivery system. Frank Luther Mott, *A History of American Magazines,* 5 vols. (Cambridge, MA: Harvard University Press, 1938–1968).

6. In one issue *St. Nicholas* published letters from California, New Jersey, North Carolina, New York, Pennsylvania, Missouri, Virginia, and Tennessee. "The Letter-Box," *St. Nicholas* 19 (March 1892): 396–98.

7. Kelly, *Children's Periodicals,* xiii.

8. Frank Luther Mott, *A History of American Magazines,* vol. 4: 16, 266, 268.

9. David L. Greene, "The Youth's Companion," in Kelly, *Children's Periodicals,* 508–509.

10. Mott, 16.

11. Fred Erisman, "St. Nicholas," in Kelly, *Children's Periodicals,* 378.

12. Lang, "Childhood's Champions," 379; Kelly, *Mother Was a Lady,* 14.

13. Erisman, 379.

14. Kelly, *Mother Was a Lady,* 33.

15. Sander L. Gilman, *Difference and Pathology: Stereotypes of Sexuality, Race, and Madness* (Ithaca, NY: Cornell University Press, 1985), 12.

16. Porter, 9.

17. Gilman, 240.

18. For an excellent discussion about different understandings among a variety of people regarding race over time, see Barbara Jeanne Fields, "Ideology and Race in American History," in *Region, Race, and Reconstruction: Essays in Honor of C. Vann Woodward,* ed. J. Morgan Kousser and James M. McPherson (New York: Oxford University Press, 1982), 143–176; and "Slavery, Race and Ideology in the United States of America," *New Left Review* 181 (May/June 1990): 95–128.

19. Russel Blaine Nye, *Society and Culture in America 1830–1860* (New York: Harper & Row, 1974), 199–200.

20. W. E. Marsden, "Rooting Racism into the Educational Experience of Childhood and Youth in the Nineteenth and Twentieth Centuries," *History of Education* 19 (December 1990): 333; Ruth Miller Elson, *Guardians of Tradition: American Schoolbooks of the Nineteenth Century* (Lincoln, NE: University of Nebraska Press, 1964), 66.

21. Elson, 66–67.

22. George M. Fredrickson, *The Black Image in the White Mind: The Debate on Afro-American Character and Destiny, 1817–1914* (New York: Harper & Row, 1971), 321, 97, xiii.

23. Christopher D. Geist and Jack Nachbar (ed.), *The Popular Culture Reader,* (Bowling Green, OH: Bowling Green University Popular Press, 1983), 3–11. See, for example, Christopher D. Geist and Angela M. S. Nelson, "From the Plantation

to Bel-Air: A Brief History of Black Stereotypes," in *Popular Culture: An Introductory Text*, ed. Jack Nachbar and Kevin Lause (Bowling Green, OH: Bowling Green State University Popular Press, 1992); William L. Van Deburg, *Slavery & Race in American Popular Culture* (Madison: University of Wisconsin Press, 1984).

24. Joseph Boskin, *The Rise and Demise of an American Jester* (New York: Oxford University Press, 1986), 16.

25. Eric Foner, *Reconstruction: America's Unfinished Revolution, 1863–1877* (New York: Harper & Row, 1988), 28, 472.

26. Fredrickson, 170, 169.

27. Ibid., 207.

28. For more complete accounts of the Reconstruction era, see Laura F. Edwards, *Gendered Strife and Confusion: The Political Culture of Reconstruction* (Urbana, IL: University of Illinois Press, 1997); Eric Foner, *Nothing but Freedom: Emancipation and Its Legacy* (Baton Rouge, LA: Louisiana State University Press, 1983); and Kenneth M. Stampp and Leon F. Litwack, *Reconstruction: An Anthology of Revisionist Writings* (Baton Rouge, LA: Louisiana State University Press, 1969).

29. Nina Silber, *The Romance of Reunion: Northerners and the South, 1865–1900* (Chapel Hill, NC: The University of North Carolina Press, 1993), 6, 78, 130.

30. Foner, *Reconstruction*, 588, 592. For more detailed summaries of post-Reconstruction America, see Edward L. Ayers, *The Promise of the New South: Life After Reconstruction* (New York: Oxford University Press, 1992); Fitzhugh W. Brundage, *Lynching in the New South: Georgia and Virginia, 1880–1930* (Urbana, IL: University of Illinois Press, 1993); Glenda Elizabeth Gilmore, *Gender and Jim Crow: Women and the Politics of White Supremacy in North Carolina, 1896–1920* (Chapel Hill, NC: University of North Carolina Press, 1996); Grace Elizabeth Hale, *Making Whiteness: The Culture of Segregation in the South, 1890–1940* (New York: Pantheon Books, 1998); C. Vann Woodward, *Origins of the New South, 1877–1913* (Baton Rouge, LA: Louisiana State University Press, 1951); C. Vann Woodward, *The Strange Career of Jim Crow* (New York: Oxford University Press, 1974); Joel Williamson, *The Crucible of Race: Black-White Relations in the American South Since Emancipation* (New York: Oxford University Press, 1984).

31. While qualities associated with a paternalistic relationship, such as obedience, loyalty, and submission, would have been desired qualities to inculcate in the young white readers of the magazines, one should note that these traits were expected of African-American adults as well as children in the stories.

32. Silber, 4, 82, 85.

33. Thomas C. Holt, "Marking: Race, Race-making, and the Writing of History," *American Historical Review* 100 (February 1995): 16.

34. "A Slave's Devotion," *The Youth's Companion* 51 (October 3, 1878): 320.

35. George A. Henty, "The Sole Survivors," *St. Nicholas* 26 (November 1898): 23.

36. George A. Henty, "The Sole Survivors," *St. Nicholas* 26 (April 1899): 484.

37. Sarah Winter Kellogg, "Sidney's Body-Servant," *The Youth's Companion* 66 (December 21, 1893): 652.

38. "Too Respectful," *The Youth's Companion* 69 (March 14, 1895): 134.

39. Mrs. Burton Harrison, "A Girlhood in Virginia," *The Youth's Companion* 70 (December 24, 1896): 687.

40. Ibid.

41. I am not suggesting that domestic labor was not also significant to the economy of the South. This labor was and continues to be undervalued.

42. See, for example, "Pleasant-Spoken," *St. Nicholas* 2 (May 1875): 411–415; Sargent Flint, "Christmas at Number One, Crawlin Place," *St. Nicholas* 7 (December 1879): 114–116; Edwin Lassetter Bynner, "Our Special Artist," *St. Nicholas* 10 (August 1883): 744–745; Jessie C. Glasier, "Ole Mammy Prissy," *St. Nicholas* 14 (July 1887): 916–921; Edward A. Oldham, "Mammy's Bed-Time Song," *St. Nicholas* 18 (September 1891): 882–884; "Mammy's Disappointment," *The Youth's Companion* 70 (December 24, 1896): 704.

43. See, for example, Lizzie W. Champney, "How Persimmons Took Cah Ob Der Baby," *St. Nicholas* 1 (May 1874): 420–422; Rebecca Harding Davis, "The Races at Shark Bay," *St. Nicholas* 3 (September 1876): 710–713; Susan Archer Weiss, "Nellie in the Light-House," *St. Nicholas* 4 (July 1877): 577–580; Mary Norwest, "A Mississippi Chowder," *St. Nicholas* 6 (August 1879): 635–639; Helene J. Hicks, "Becky's Surprise Day," *St. Nicholas* 6 (August 1879): 658–661; Maurice Thompson, "Marvin and His Boy Hunters," *St. Nicholas* 11 (July 1884): 702–711; and (October 1884): 953–958.

44. See, for example, "Dab Kinzer," "Mr. Carothers' Secret," *St. Nicholas* 6 (October 1879): 786–791.

45. See, for example, "An Errand at Midnight," *The Youth's Companion* 49 (November 30, 1876): 405; J. T. Trowbridge, "His Own Master," *St. Nicholas* 14 (October 1877): 809; Mary Hartwell Catherwood, "The American Mardi-Gras," *St. Nicholas* 6 (March 1879): 337; Jessie C. Glasier, "Ole Mammy Prissy," *St. Nicholas* 14 (October 1887): 917; Louise Herrick, "How the Yankees Came to Blackwood," *St. Nicholas* 15 (January 1888): 210–215; "'Me 'N' Pearline," *The Youth's Companion* 63 (April 10, 1890): 202; Eudora S. Bumstead, "A Year with Dolly," *St. Nicholas* 19 (January 1892): 224.

46. Advertisements, *The Youth's Companion* 70 (October 29, 1896): 588, 598.

47. *Ethnic Notions*, produced and directed by Marlon Riggs, 58 min., California Newsreel, 1986, videocassette.

48. Clara Morris, "My Little Jim Crow," *St. Nicholas* 26 (December 1898): 148–158. See also Jessie C. Glasier, "A Gunpowder Plot," *St. Nicholas* 14 (July 1887): 664–671.

49. Porter, *Black Child, White Child*, 19.

50. See for example Richard Malcolm Johnston, "Little Ike Templin," *St. Nicholas* 15, (August 1888): 749–752; and (October 1888): 833–837; Clara Morris, "My Little Jim Crow," *St. Nicholas* 26 (December 1898): 158.

51. Henry Louis Gates Jr., "Trope of a New Negro and the Reconstruction of the Image of the Black," *Representations* 24 (Fall 1988): 150.

52. Ibid., 130.

53. Ronald G. Walters, *The Antislavery Appeal: American Abolitionism After 1830* (Baltimore: Johns Hopkins University Press, 1976), xv.

54. *Our Young Folks* handled a circulation of 75,000 between the years 1865 and 1873 when they sold their subscription list to Scribner & Co., who converted many of those readers to fans of *St. Nicholas.*

55. Thomas G. Dyer, *Theodore Roosevelt and the Idea of Race* (Baton Rouge, LA: Louisiana State University Press, 1980), 3, 19.

56. Gates, 136.

57. Ibid., 143.

58. Carolivia Herron, *Nappy Hair* (New York: Knopf, 1997).

5

DEFINING DEMOCRACY FOR YOUTH THROUGH TEXTBOOKS:

CONTROVERSY OVER THE RUGG SOCIAL STUDIES SERIES IN PREWAR AMERICA

Carole J. Trone

On the eve of America's entry into the Second World War, Teachers College professor Harold Rugg responded to the increasingly vitriolic attacks on his social studies textbook series with a 355-page defense of his patriotism and his educational purposes. "I believe that to guarantee maximum understanding, the very foundation of education must be the study of the actual problems and controversial issues of our people," he wrote. "Consent based upon knowledge of only one aspect or side of a problem, upon the avoidance of controversy, is a travesty of both knowledge and democracy. To keep issues out of the school, therefore, is to keep thought out of it; it is to keep life out of it."[1] Rugg's phenomenally successful textbook series, used by thousands of teachers in schools across the country for over a decade, was in 1941 being labeled by war-anxious Americans as undemocratic, un-American, godless, and Communistic. Perhaps even more surprising to the educator was the wide range of attack: Rugg's chief accusers included the millionaire Bertie Forbes, members of the Advertising Federation of America (AFA), the National Association of Manufacturers, and the American Legion. Significantly, not included among these initial critics were the vast majority of teachers, principals, and school board members who over the years had selected and used the Rugg textbooks.

The debate revolved around whether it was more important to show the righteousness of the American way, or whether responsible Americanism came from understanding the multiple perspectives surrounding controversial issues in American society. Indeed, the very definition of democracy was at stake, and the battles that ensued in these pre–World War II days garnered national attention. This controversy was not the first case of censorship or red-baiting in the schools, nor would it be the last. At least since Noah Webster's 1783 speller established distinctly American words and meanings, public school textbooks have represented powerful symbols of American culture and values. In the decades before and after the Civil War, southern legislators and their patriotic committees continually campaigned for textbooks that portrayed their culture and institutions sympathetically. Patriotic fervor during World War I inspired renewed critical scrutiny on history textbooks by David Muzzey and other historians trained along the ascendant German university research model for their supposedly pro-German and European perspective. Textbooks in more recent years have been attacked for their lack of ethnic and racial diversity. Whether the offensive book in question happened to be a textbook, or in later years *Catcher in the Rye,* parents have reacted swiftly to accusations of corruption in their children's classrooms. In the politicized world of public education, textbooks represent the key to the cultural values—or indoctrination—of the next generation of Americans.

This essay traces the development, use, and subsequent controversy over the Rugg textbook series. It is a history situated within the larger context of contemporary textbooks and the prevailing curriculum ideas that inspired an early generation of professional educational innovators. This essay attempts to demonstrate how the *Man and His Changing Society* series drew upon a complex interplay of curriculum principles with implications that were often at odds with each other. Scientific curriculum-making, social reconstruction, child-centeredness, and vocationalism in education meant different and often contradictory things to different individuals, as curriculum historian Herbert M. Kliebard has noted.[2] Harold Rugg is best remembered as a social reconstructionist, intent on improving society through the power of teachers and schools. He advanced many of the pedagogical ideas commonly associated with progressive education for the ways they nurtured children's interests in their studies. Like John Dewey, however, Rugg was alarmed at their tendency to focus exclusively on the child and ignore the more important relationship between the child, school, and society. Rugg believed that education should become more socially useful, and used his statistical expertise to itemize and quantify what that meant. His techniques of scientific curriculum-making, Rugg believed, could be used to legitimate the need for more curricular attention to music and the fine arts. By systematically identifying and then probing various issues of race, class, and gender through the pages of the series, Rugg believed he was providing the objective means for children to better understand and improve their society.

Wartime anxieties frequently mean little public tolerance for new or controversial ideas, particularly in a school textbook read by millions of American children. The controversy over Rugg's textbook series, however, was neither expected nor straightforward. The episode drew a diverse coalition of antagonists from business, advertising, and veterans groups, provoking a spirited and widely publicized defense from publishers, historians, and educators. The ideologically charged nature of the attack and the defense transcended the actual words of the textbooks and the detailed preparations that marked their development. This seemed inexplicable to Rugg, whose scientific and methodological approach surely seemed beyond the reproach of emotional accusations. The history of this series, and the subsequent controversy, serves as a powerful reminder of the complexity involved in attempting to define American values through textbooks. The power of textbooks, with their captive youthful audiences and didactic tones, resists straightforward definition.

There was little from Rugg's upbringing that foreshadowed such controversy. Rugg was part of the first generation of university experts in education. Like many of his peers, Harold Ordway Rugg was born to a family whose American heritage traced back many generations. He was born in Fitchburg, Massachusetts, in 1886 to a family of lower-middle-class means. Rugg later reflected that the austere surroundings, coupled with the grim life of the textile mills and his carpenter father's constant struggle to bring home enough food, shaped his vision for education as much as did his later friendships with the leading social critics of his day.[3] Years before blending into the culturally progressive social scene of New York, Rugg demonstrated an early interest in developing a scientifically sound approach to curriculum construction.

Fellow university educators were often eager to point out Rugg's formal training in the "hard" science of engineering that he gained from undergraduate study at Dartmouth. Rugg continued to teach engineering at the University of Illinois while working on his doctoral degree in education under William C. Bagley.[4] Rugg's 1915 dissertation, *The Experimental Determination of Mental Discipline in School Studies,* followed along the quantitative path of pioneering educational psychologist Edward Lee Thorndike. It was a statistical study of the effects that the various school subjects had on strengthening the mind for other mental tasks, in which he concluded that school subjects such as Latin had no direct effect on improving one's ability to learn other subjects. For Rugg, however, these findings suggested that the school curriculum should be as integrative and multifaceted as the modern world, an idea that reappears immediately after World War I in his pioneering development of a "social studies."

Rugg remained fascinated with the possibilities of a statistically oriented science of education, and regularly contributed articles and papers in educational journals and professional publications, hoping to encourage teachers to use statistics to improve their own work.[5]

Equally revealing of Rugg's later educational interests was an early study of history textbooks. "The Content of American History as Taught in the Seventh and Eighth Grades" was a collaborative study with mentor William C. Bagley, published in the 1916 University of Illinois School of Education *Bulletin*. Bagley and Rugg examined twenty-three history textbooks published since the Civil War that were used mostly in seventh and eighth grades. They determined "minimal essentials" in grade school geography and history by rating the frequency with which certain facts appeared in textbooks. A supplementary assessment of each fact's significance qualified each rating. Each book was examined according to historical epochs, such as the Civil War or "The Period of Discovery and Exploration." The survey found a prevalence of facts and names associated with political and military history, with a recent shift in the newer books to examining economic and industrial development. Certain names were mentioned so frequently that the sheer repetition, the authors believed, would contribute to students' ability to remember them. Rugg reveals a perspective in this early analysis that became significant in his later textbook construction: "It cannot be doubted that points of view, attitudes, and prejudices engendered at this time will tend to persist even if the detailed facts are largely forgotten. It is these enduring outcomes of the initial study of history that will form the perspective through which the next generation will view the problems of national life."[6]

Finally, the authors noted a recent shift towards emphasizing causal connections and the "problem" as a way of introducing history. While limiting their study principally to a compilation of the findings, Rugg and Bagley noted disparagingly the increasing emphasis upon nationalism and patriotism in the textbooks, perhaps all the more prevalent in their minds as American involvement in World War I seemed imminent. So long as the emphasis remained nationalism in these history textbooks, political and militaristic events would dominate, all featuring the same "Hall of Fame" individuals. If the focus could shift to other aspects of life—art, literature, industry, science—then the content could conceivably change as well. These early observations became instrumental in Rugg's own ambitious curriculum undertaking a decade later.

Rugg followed his Illinois graduate work with a faculty position at the University of Chicago. Earlier, Francis Wayland Parker and John Dewey invigorated educational study at Chicago with their dynamic experimental schools. Under Charles H. Judd's leadership, however, educational innovation was restrained into various quantified investigations of administrative issues. After spending a few years under this somewhat restrictive leadership, Rugg moved in 1920 to the cosmopolitan world of New York and a position at Teachers College. Rugg's growing interests in the avant-garde world of art and literature complemented his educational sympathies with pedagogical progressives such as George S. Counts and John Dewey. Methodologically, however, Rugg's writings in these years reveal a continued insistence on utilizing the most stringent scientific approaches to the new education.

Rugg's fascination with a science of education was by no means unique, although the extent to which he applied it to advance his own educational agenda was. Rugg lashed out at the illustrious committees of the American Historical Association, who gathered in the socially uncertain times following World War I to consider the proper formulation of social studies and its blending of geography, history, civics, and cultural concepts. They pursued their task in the theoretical manner fashioned in an earlier period by Harvard President Charles William Eliot and his scholarly Committee of Ten. This abstract approach to a very real dilemma provoked angry criticisms from Rugg, who couldn't understand how any valid curriculum reconstruction could be discussed without the necessary empirical data. His response to this abstract kind of curriculum reconstruction appeared in the National Society for the Study of Education (NSSE) yearbook, *Historical Outlook,* and many of the other leading educational forums of the day. In a critique written for *The Elementary School Journal,* Rugg wrote, "The most important task of the committee is to draw up a scientific program for curriculum-making."[7] That program had to promote material of acknowledged social worth, organized by units-of-understanding or units-of-experience, rather than by discrete subject matter that traditionalists argued were inherently logical or valuable.[8] Rugg had been contemplating his own social studies reconstruction at least since the earlier collaborative study with Bagley, and did not wait for the American Historical Association committee to adopt his views. By 1921, Rugg had already initiated the years of research and development that eventually culminated in a fourteen-volume textbook series.

The effort expended by Rugg and his research team over the years to construct the *Man and His Changing Society* series is impressive. As Rugg himself reflected in 1941: "Had I had the slightest prevision of the scope of the enterprise that was to develop out of the three-page mimeographed letter sent to my schoolmaster friends in the winter of 1921/22, I am confident that I would never have undertaken it."[9] The preface to each of Rugg's textbooks outlined this approach. Between 1921 and 1930, thirteen of Rugg's graduate assistants undertook an impressive range of quantitative studies, giving themselves dissertation topics while providing Rugg with the data he desired. One such study, *Children's Interpretations of Cartoons* by Laurance F. Shaffer, showed ten different political cartoons gathered from city newspapers across the country to approximately 2,700 girls and boys in grades four through twelve. He had grouped these children carefully by age and IQ, and dutifully recorded and tabulated their interpretations of the cartoons. The subjects of the cartoons represented a range of current political issues, from women's suffrage to immigration and school support. The wide range of incorrect impressions of each cartoon made it impossible for Shaffer to conclusively determine what precise remedies would improve the interpretations. Despite the children's unpredictable responses, the pedagogical possibilities of including cartoons in the textbooks for at least the older students proved appealing. The six-volume textbook series for junior high grades are filled with political cartoons, but often more simply drawn and accompanied by detailed, explanatory captions.[10]

Other research assistants chose less entertaining topics, though equally quantitative in keeping with their mentor's preferences. Research assistant John A. Hockett analyzed twenty-two contemporary books from significant social analysts—those whom Teachers College professor William Heard Kilpatrick labeled "frontier" thinkers—in order to tabulate and classify the predominant social problems they identified.[11] Student Neal Billings carried this research a step further by considering the specific applications of these generalizations to the construction of a social studies curriculum. Billings listed 888 generalizations culled from the writings of those "frontier" thinkers. The concept of "thought" ranked highest. Many of those generalizations (e.g., No. 580: "The suppression of free agitation invites revolution.") garnered only one mention by a single frontier thinker.[12]

These quantitative compilations were only a small contribution to the measurement mania that gripped the most prominent among science of education proponents of the day. In later years Rugg himself called it "one long orgy of tabulation."[13] Fellow scientific curriculum-maker John Franklin Bobbitt declared that the curriculum should strive for objectives that are "numerous, definite, and particularized."[14] So too, Rugg hoped to uncover those ideas that were scientifically proven to be most worth knowing. Curriculum efficiency experts Bobbitt, W. W. Charters, and

David Snedden, however, believed that modern education in a democracy meant preparation for each student according to each individual's social class and tested abilities. In contrast, Rugg applied a similar kind of quantitative approach towards a social studies curriculum with a radically more flexible interpretation of democracy and social roles.

The research findings by Rugg's doctoral students, though they may have proved inconclusive, fueled Rugg's efforts to isolate and identify the most important lessons that any social studies textbook should include. Ideas and events were sufficiently important to include in a social studies curriculum if they "enable prospective citizens to understand and think about the problems of the present dynamic society, and ... build meaning into the generalizations, themes, and concepts which make possible intelligent solution of these problems."[15] It is unclear whether Rugg was interested in or able to incorporate these generalizations into his textbooks in a similarly quantitative fashion.[16] If Rugg ever conducted such a quantitative study on his own work, the results remain buried. Even without such evidence, however, "intelligent solution of problems" was a goal that remained foremost in Rugg's textbooks.

Rugg combined this kind of educational research with the kind of practical resourcefulness that probably did more to ensure his textbook series' success. He gathered together names and addresses of previous students who had become administrators and teachers and petitioned them to try out three different test editions of the series. By the time the first textbook was published in 1929, over three hundred school systems had tested *Man and His Changing Society.* Between 1922 and 1929 Rugg distributed 600,000 copies of the third edition, the *Social Science Pamphlets.*[17] Equally vital to such a research program was the financial support from these former students; Rugg estimated that seven years of research cost $378,000, nearly all of which was covered by the sales of these experimental pamphlets.[18]

While the approach and the complexity of Rugg's efforts to reconstruct the social studies curriculum are certainly distinctive, his goals were well within the context of what many of his peers advocated. Frank M. McMurry of Teachers College summarized in the NSSE *Twenty-Second Yearbook* that Charles H. Judd (University of Chicago), Superintendent Carleton Washburne (Winnetka, Illinois, schools), A. S. Barr (Detroit public schools), and many others shared Rugg's view that a newly reformulated social studies curriculum could uniquely prepare students for future citizenship and modern American living. McMurry pointed out that all these proposals shared a "revolt against encyclopedic education; the acceptance of the 'problem' as the unit of subject matter; and the demand for activities or practice."[19] Proper training for citizenship was the unmistakable goal for all these curriculum reformers. While they were sensitive to attacks that they would be sacrificing scholarship in the process, Rugg and his contemporaries believed that structuring the information around its usefulness to good citizens would deepen student understanding of the material presented. Even the presentation of that material would be revised, since the scientific method demanded active inquiry rather than a passive absorption of textbook material. The NSSE yearbook showed broad consensus among these educators about what constituted a meaningful educational approach to learning. A decade later, a survey of civics and history textbooks revealed how many other curriculum-makers shared their ideas. "Problems of democracy" was a standard phrase educators used to describe this popular textbook strategy.[20] In 1930, Bessie Pierce of the University of Chicago conducted an exhaustive study of nearly four hundred textbooks then used by American schools. Including Rugg's preliminary *Social Science Pamphlets* in her survey, Pierce wrote, "Textbooks are permeated with a national or patriotic spirit.... None can be charged with disloyalty to American ideals.... Nor do textbooks fail to advocate a loyalty to the government of this country."[21]

The very idea of the "fusion" of courses, as Rugg's blending of history, civics, and geography into a unified social studies was labeled, represented an effort to reverse what many educators believed was an artificial separation of course material. John Dewey, Rugg's contemporary at Columbia, also believed that many of the divisions between school subjects were artificial and obscured the important interrelationships between knowledge and living. Although the conventional subject divisions into geography, history, or civics appeared to allow a larger presentation of facts, figures, and dates, Rugg noted that "in more than a hundred years of systematization of the national educational scheme, the materials of instruction have not only been largely aloof from, [but also] indeed foreign to, the institutions and culture of the American people; they have failed equally to provide for maximal child growth."[22] He argued that school subjects had little to do with everyday life, and believed he could make them relevant by reconstructing social studies. In 1920, this fairly new idea of a "social studies" drew criticism for simplifying content material and diluting strong disciplinary rigor. Indeed, the "fusion" approach had not replaced traditional textbook divisions of history, geography, and civics, thus obstructing important comparisons with Rugg's textbooks. By 1940, critics with little understanding of curriculum theory suspected that "fusion" was just another way of saying "collectivism." Rugg's social studies represented for these critics a sinister blend of complex socialistic ideology and subversive indoctrination.

Even within the genre of textbooks that shared Rugg's "problem" approach, however, Rugg's topics are notable. In a conventional 1934 high school textbook, problems of democracy include the threat to law and order from slums and the "breaking down of the home."[23] Yet another 1934 junior high civics textbook highlighted the problem of women entering the workforce and displacing men. "The home-making impulse is strong in girls. That is the career for which most of them are best fitted."[24] In contrast, a two-chapter section from Rugg's 1931 volume, *An Introduction to Problems in American Culture,* focused on "The Changing American Family." Here Rugg emphasized the varieties of wealth, size, occupation, and lifestyle by profiling several imaginary families. He closed each profile with the words, "This is an American home, and an American family lives in it." Changing lifestyles have not "displaced" men from the workforce, he argued. Instead, it offered a challenge to find new companionship between husbands and wives. The problem that Rugg presents here and in countless other passages throughout the series is that of broadening definitions of American living rather than safeguarding the predominant middle-class lifestyle.[25]

Indeed, so many of the chapters devoted to understanding America in the broadest sense are unique among textbooks of the period. Bessie Pierce's 1930 survey of four hundred textbooks found little mention of immigrants or black Americans, a startling omission given the tremendous influx of immigrants up to the 1920s and African Americans' "Great Migration" to northern cities during these years. Rugg's earliest experimental editions included "America and Her Immigrants." This 300-page "pamphlet" from 1926 asked questions such as, "Who Is an American?" and "Shall We Exclude Immigrants?" Congress had already answered that last question with its 1924 Immigration Restriction Act; Rugg's response reminded readers that all white Americans had once been immigrants.

In the same pamphlet, Rugg included several chapters on "Negro" migration with the prescient subheading, "The Problem of Two Races Living Side by Side." The problem, Rugg explains, comes from the combination of lynching, mob violence, the Negro's denied access to education, skills and resources, and northern white insistence on segregated and inferior housing.[26] A civics textbook of nearly two decades later indicates that Rugg's complex treatment did not soon generate many followers in the textbook industry. A caption for a photo of children playing reads:

"Allowed to express their natural gift for happy living, these Negro children are a few of the tenants in a housing project in Dayton, Ohio."[27] These examples may not initially speak to common definitions of democracy, but a broader conception of democracy, lived daily, was precisely Rugg's intention. Although the *Man and His Changing Society* series did not ignore conventional notions of civic duty, Rugg's chapter lessons continually refer back to responsible citizenship, the "march toward democracy," and the duties that come along with the privilege of being an American.

Harold Rugg left the University of Chicago in 1920 in large part to serve as educational psychologist for the experimental Lincoln School at Teachers College. Textbook critics of later years remained convinced that Rugg's call for collective solutions to America's problems was just another way of demonstrating his Communism. In fact, however, Rugg criticized American individualism from a pedagogical as well as an economic viewpoint. In 1928, after years of involvement with Lincoln, Rugg coauthored a book with Ann Shumaker called *The Child-Centered School.* Here they set out to assess the extent to which this and other child-centered schools promoted "tolerant understanding and creative self-expression—the two great aims of the new education."[28] Such progressive schools were certainly important and indispensable, they argued, but not without many egregious flaws. Overall, these schools were lacking in planning and preparation, and teachers revealed "extreme individualism," they argued. "Teachers have not become students—either of society, of child needs, or of curriculum construction."[29] Rugg and Shumaker argued that teachers had to acknowledge their much larger responsibility to educating American society.

School could be more meaningful, Rugg believed, if it was more relevant to everyday living. He applauded efforts at Lincoln to develop project activities stemming from the students' own interests. But in order to develop the educational benefit of these activities to their fullest, he argued, the teacher must expertly guide the scope and direction of the project. Meaning in a particular project or "unit of work" would not necessarily be self-evident, Rugg believed. It was the teacher's responsibility to draw those meanings and connections to the child's larger world. The teacher must make the problems of living both apparent and important: "the rise of industrial civilization, problems of immigration, municipal and national government, and economic imperialism" would not likely stir the student's interest of his own free will.[30] Rugg was highly critical of progressive schools for overlooking the importance of this guidance and emphasis.

This perspective became more carefully articulated in the educational movement known as "social reconstructionism." In his dramatic manifesto *Dare the School Build a New Social Order?* (1932), fellow Teachers College professor George S. Counts criticized capitalism and challenged teachers to overcome their fear of "the bogies of *imposition* and *indoctrination.*"[31] Though generally more moderate in his reconstructivist views, Harold Rugg was equally critical of the "epoch of laissez-faire" capitalism as described in his visionary 1933 book, *The Great Technology: Social Chaos and the Public Mind.* Chapters included "Plans for a Controlled Private Capitalism" along with "Education for the New Social Order."[32] Counts, Rugg, and other social reconstructionists believed that education was essential for American society to lead to an improved social order. More importantly, Rugg believed this new social order to be an important extension of America's democratic foundations.[33] Although Rugg never referred to arguments in *The Great Technology* during the long development of his textbook series, critics later found in these unrelated writings convincing evidence that these textbooks were un-American.

It is tempting to interpret Rugg's social studies series against the economic uncertainty of the 1930s. Certainly Rugg was intimately involved with the social reconstructionist movement in education and protested publicly when the editorial board summarily decided in late 1943 to close down the reconstructionist journal, *Frontiers of Democracy.*[34] But his broad conception of democracy is evident in his earliest interests in education. His dissertation work in 1916 with William C. Bagley targeted topics in current history textbooks as overly focused on war and patriotism. The content of these books, they declared, had little to do with the everyday problems of modern living. Subsequently, Rugg's efforts to improve the social studies curriculum immediately after World War I inspired his efforts throughout the economically robust 1920s to produce a more engaging social studies curriculum. Even as late as 1939, in *Democracy and the Curriculum,* Rugg stated: "Democratic government is government by the consent of the people and true consent can be given only by people who understand their conditions and their problems."[35] The phenomenal success of his textbook series throughout the 1930s indicates that in many ways American educators agreed with him.

Rugg published his first full textbook in 1929, after two earlier sets of experimental pamphlets led him to modify his approach. His careful curriculum research paid large dividends. Through the 1930s, Rugg published fourteen textbooks that sold nearly 300,000 copies yearly and were used in over 5,000 schools by 15,000 teachers across the country. "Everybody wanted the Rugg books," a sales representative for Ginn and Company recollected later.[36] In late 1939 Rugg prepared to add to his series with revised editions and new volumes for senior high schools, but this time controversy sidetracked his efforts.

Prior to 1939, the textbook series had largely escaped criticisms in any of the prominent educational or popular magazines.[37] After 1939, however, Rugg's critics emerged suddenly. An unlikely combination of civic organizations and business interests "discovered" what they thought was un-American in Rugg's writing. Among those most offended were millionaire Bertie Forbes and members of the Advertising Federation of America, the National Association of Manufacturers, and the American Legion. Their concerns originated from business and ideological interests, but together they mounted a nationwide campaign that transcended the content of the textbooks and became a debate over Americanism itself.

One of the earliest attacks came from the advertising industry. American consumerism and the advertising that fueled it had become for many the reason for the Great Depression. Such accusations rattled advertising's confidence. The AFA was keen to reassert its preeminence after a decade of bad press. Alfred T. Falk headed the AFA's Bureau of Research and Education, and in June 1939 criticized a chapter on advertising contained in one of Rugg's textbooks.

An Introduction to Problems of American Culture was the fifth volume of the junior high textbooks in the *Man and His Changing Society* series. The final unit included a thirty-page look at "Advertising and the Consumer," a topic overlooked by most civics textbooks.[38] In it Rugg included a lively combination of political cartoons, actual advertisements, tables, photographs, and illustrations. The section begins with a "dramatic episode," in which one man chooses to buy automobile oil because of its proven quality while a second individual purchases the most popularly advertised brand. The "scientific" buyer, Rugg tells the reader, is the one who is not merely influenced by advertising techniques. Americans are all consumers, he reminds his readers, and advertising constantly tells the American to "Buy, buy, buy!"[39] Indeed, Rugg points out, by 1927 advertising was a $1.5 billion industry that fueled interest in products, while at the same time adding to the cost of those goods. Modern advertising tactics not only informed the reader, he says, but also attempted to influence and persuade as well. Rugg spends only a few pages discussing the dangers of false testimonials and misrepresentation of goods, but balances that account by discussing some advertising agencies' efforts to eliminate misleading practices within the industry. Nearly a third of the chapter is devoted to ways in which the consumer can become more knowledgeable and careful: he compliments government agencies and private consumer research groups that help the consumer as the best ways to combat excesses encouraged by advertising.

The chapter's perspective clearly favored the consumer, a view that Falk could not condone. Reports in *Advertising Age* and the *New York Times* revealed advertisers' sensitivity to "dangers" emphasized in many consumer courses.[40] A "more-balanced" perspective, Falk argued, would point out how advertising saves the consumer money through the economies of mass production. He issued his report at the AFA annual convention in June, where sixty local affiliates were urged to scrutinize the textbooks in their own locations. In addition, copies of Falk's review—released under the guise of a major campaign to expose "anti-advertising propaganda"— was sent to every daily newspaper in the country and became part of AFA President Norman Rose's efforts to increase membership.[41]

Other defenders of Americanism soon carried on Falk's campaign with their own particular attacks. In contrast to the AFA, the American Legion had a much longer self-assumed mission of safeguarding "One Hundred Percent Americanism" in America's schools. Since it organized in 1919, the Legion had formed various committees to investigate the "subversive" element that may have crept into the schools through the efforts of Communists and other unnamed radicals. "Freedom ends where treason begins," announced a 1936 article in the *National Legionnaire.* Why protect the rights of individuals who would overturn the very system on which these rights are founded, the article asked.[42]

Rugg himself had assailed the Legion's demand for a loyalty oath from teachers at a 1935 Progressive Education Association conference, where he sparred with American Legion representative Abraham J. Rosenblum by shouting, "The American Legion has in the past twelve months conducted a devilish program against the American way of teaching."[43] The Legion had reason to suspect even greater "subversivism" at Teachers College in 1938, after William Gellerman, one of George Counts' students, wrote a scathing dissertation on American Legion educational activities. Angry Legionnaires demanded and got a meeting with Teachers College President William Russell, who managed to temporarily defuse the situation.[44]

But the trouble had only started. In 1940, the Legion's National Executive Committee ordered a study of civics and history textbooks. Amidst this scrutiny, a loyal Missouri Legionnaire named O. K. Armstrong published an article entitled "Treason in the Textbooks" in the September 1940 issue of *American Legion Magazine,* which he embellished with

lurid illustrations of teachers depicted with slime dripping out of their hands. Armstrong said he wrote the article as a concerned parent, alarmed by his son's question, "Daddy, was George Washington a big business man?" which Armstrong surmised emanated from chapter seven in *A History of American Government and Culture,* where Rugg commented on the authors of the American constitution. "The convention was made up chiefly of prominent leaders," he wrote, "from the more well-to-do and prosperous Americans." Rugg immediately follows that sentence with "It was a convention of intelligent, even brilliant, Americans" and elsewhere refers to Washington as "dignified,"[45] but Armstrong gives no indication that he had read those sentences. Instead, he proceeded to place the entire educational system on trial: teachers are condescending, prominent textbook writers are "radical and communistic," and schools across the coun-

This vivid illustration of a sinister teacher in the September 1940 issue of *American Legion Magazine* provoked strong reactions from both magazine readers and educators.

try have unwittingly been "taken for a ride by the most insidious attack of un-Americanism yet perfected by the Trojan horseman."[46]

Earlier in the year, fellow Legionnaire Augustin G. Rudd launched his own textbook investigation. Rudd cited Rugg's 1933 book, *The Great Technology,* instead of a textbook for his criticisms. Like Armstrong, however, Rudd embellished his criticisms with spectacular, large illustrations showing a Stalin-like teacher leading thousands of schoolchildren, all holding hammer-and-sickle textbooks in their hands, away from the quintessential American schoolhouse.[47] Rudd's complaint, while more subdued than Armstrong's wording, nevertheless reaffirmed the growing perception that dangerous and anti-business attitudes festered in all schools.

In 1941, the Legion's Americanism Committee published findings of its own textbook survey in three pocket-sized pamphlets. Called "Rugg

The "Frontier Thinkers" are trying to
sell our youth the idea that the American way of life has failed

This illustration from the September 1940 issue of *American
Legion Magazine* depicts textbook author Harold Rugg and
other "frontier thinkers" as a diabolical teacher in the classroom
placing dark glasses on alarmed students.

Philosophy Analyzed," the pamphlets largely misquoted excerpts from
The Great Technology with bold-faced topic headings such as "Revolution" or "Youth Indoctrinated." Although the pamphlets provided little
analysis, that proved no obstacle to detailing a clear plan of action. Properly concerned citizens and parents should be wary of all textbooks their
children used, and "social studies" textbooks were especially suspect,
since they often hid subversive material in coverage of history, civics, and
geography. Parents in every community must demand to see all textbooks. Even more, they should be aware that the Rugg textbooks had a
separate teacher's guide. "Demand to see the teacher's guides," one pamphlet concluded. The Legion passed thousands of these pamphlets to
local posts across the country. Although many Legionnaires had strongly

protested the broadside attack in Armstrong's article, many more anx-
iously crowded school meetings to monitor the patriotism of their children and their country. Over the next few years, school boards in San
Francisco, Philadelphia, Tampa, Yonkers and Binghamton (New York),
Cedar Rapids (Iowa), and countless communities in between debated
whether to ban the books.

One of the most remarkable debates occurred in Englewood, the New
Jersey home of millionaire Bertie Forbes. Public schools in Englewood, a
prosperous New York City suburb, had been using the *Man and His
Changing Society* series for six years when school board member Bertie
Forbes and a colleague revealed a three-year effort to uncover subversive
and radical elements in American schools. Their efforts brought them to
Teachers College and Union Theological Seminary as well as to the Engle-
wood public schools. After privately pressuring the school superintendent
to get rid of the Rugg textbooks in 1939, Forbes went public in his own
Forbes magazine and through a syndicated column in Hearst newspapers.
In articles entitled "Treacherous Teachings," Forbes called Rugg "vi-
ciously un-American." In a June 6, 1940, column, he taunted readers who
"supinely tolerate our children's minds being poisoned against America."
Rugg struck back by noting that Forbes' own children did not attend public schools where such poisoning was apparently occurring. But elsewhere
in New York, these kinds of pressures began to test the resolve of school
administrators. *Time* reported in its September 9, 1940, issue that Binghamton Superintendent Daniel J. Kelley had ordered the Rugg books off
the library shelves in response to demands by a few school board members
to burn the books. Kelley sighed, "Personally, I can see no harm in the
books. In fact, they are just the type of material I wish my children and
grandchildren to use."[48]

But Englewood's citizens were willing to challenge Forbes. Longtime
resident T. H. P. Sailer formed a Committee of Parents and Taxpayers to
examine what Forbes meant in his charges of un-Americanism. In late
November 1940, 300 residents attended a Parent-Teacher Association
meeting covered by the *New York Times* and many other publications to
hear Rugg personally defend himself against the charges brought by
Forbes and the American Legion. On January 14, 1941, the school board
voted to retain Rugg's books and to oust Forbes. Rugg considered it a
"victory for the true American democratic way."[49]

Few other communities followed Englewood's example, however.
Instead, a pattern emerged that made it increasingly difficult for Rugg to
respond. The textbooks were portrayed as part of a long and cleverly

hidden campaign—like a "Trojan horse"—to strike at youthful minds. This argument convinced alarmed readers that a tremendous and pervasive conspiracy existed in American schools. Although the attacks focused on Rugg's books alone, the AFA, American Legion, Guardians of American Education, Daughters of the American Revolution, and other interest groups presented each report as merely the start of a thorough investigation. As it did Rugg and his publisher, Ginn and Company, the vehemence of these charges seems to have caught teachers and administrators by surprise. In correspondence to the American Legion, H. C. Lucas of Ginn reported that "we do not have on file in any of our offices a single statement from any teacher, principal, or superintendent who indicated that these books were subversive or unpatriotic in the slightest degree."[50]

Despite the attacks, however, Rugg was confident he could demonstrate the merits of his textbook series. Perhaps he believed he could triumph and even benefit from so much publicity by exposing the irrational nature of the controversy. In May and June of 1940 he and his assistants collected a file of 240 published attacks and defenses of his textbook series, most of which had appeared in the past year. In June, Rugg circulated a twenty-nine-page "Confidential Analysis" to President William Russell at Teachers College, to his representatives at Ginn, and to anyone else whose support he thought would be crucial. Versions of this analysis later appeared in a variety of education journals, in the Alumni Magazine of his alma mater, Dartmouth, and finally in a book.[51]

Rugg's defenders included teachers and administrators who had used the textbook series, his Teachers College colleagues, distinguished historians, and observers who worried much more about free speech rights than whether Rugg should have been more flattering towards the Founding Fathers. Walter Wilson of the American Civil Liberties Union, who had already challenged the Legion's censorious practices in a September 1936 pamphlet, spoke sharply in Rugg's defense. In 1941, fourteen university professors headed by Columbia's Wesley C. Mitchell formed the five-member American Committee for Democracy and Intellectual Freedom. To promote "honest inquiry and to avoid acrimonious controversy that generates more heat than light" and to respond to a National Association of Manufacturers decision to "investigate" over six hundred current textbooks abstracted by conservative economist and Columbia professor Ralph W. Robey, the committee carefully reviewed Rugg's textbooks for their Americanism.[52] Although this activity might have elevated the intellectual level of the debates, it is unlikely that they influenced many American Legion post meetings. *Publisher's Weekly* followed the controversy carefully, and in its April 12, 1941, issue, ran a full-page editorial entitled,

"Rugg Serves Freedom of Education." Editor Frederic G. Melcher considered Rugg's ideals the noblest forms of liberal democracy.[53] Nonetheless, the controversy continued to fester.

In hindsight, Rugg's methodical defense of his books clearly overestimated the mental level of the debate. The emotional response provoked by unsubstantiated accusations of treason and Communism resonated with many anxious parents and businessmen as fascism and world war loomed. Rugg himself parodied the irrationality of those who initiated criticisms with the words, "I Haven't Read the Books But—!" Overwhelmed school administrators in Bradnor, Ohio, admitted to burning the offending textbooks simply because they did not have the fortitude to face the community's frenzy.[54] In 1940 alone, dozens of articles appeared in publications like *Time, Newsweek, Publisher's Weekly,* and the *New Republic.* For most reporters, the controversy represented another case of "red-baiting." But by 1944, the press had moved on to fresher news.

Ideologically charged battles often enable both sides to claim victory. The Legion's Americanism Commission claimed that its agitation caused the Rugg books to be dropped from acceptable lists in many school districts by 1943. Their efforts, by their own estimation, had revealed to many the hidden "poison."[55] By 1944, Rugg's textbooks sold only 21,000 copies, down ninety-three percent from six years earlier.[56] A later account from a Ginn and Company representative recalled that Rugg dropped plans to revise the textbooks in the 1940s after refusing to alter the sections the AFA and American Legion had found offensive. Rugg realized that a decade without a revised edition would discourage sales of any textbook. Although the *Man and His Changing Society* series had enjoyed a long tenure in America's schools, their disappearance in the 1940s may only reflect, as another Ginn representative speculated, that the series had become outdated.[57]

During the 1930s, Rugg himself counted more than 5,000 schools that used *That Men May Understand.* The tremendous popularity of the books suggests that Americans agreed with Rugg about the compelling issues of those times. The notoriety that the series gained by World War II provides a cautionary tale for future textbook developers, and also raises important questions about the possibilities of constructing generalizations or "basic questions" about a society that is increasingly complex and multifaceted. Rugg defined this battle as the right to foster more informed democratic living within the school curriculum. His defense against the demands of Bertie Forbes to remove his textbooks from the Englewood, New Jersey public schools was based on a deeply held belief that free and open discussion of important issues and problems of American culture was essential to democracy. Thoughtful commentary came from John Dewey in his 1937 article for *Frontiers of Democracy:* "The *problem* of education in its relation to direction of social change is all one with the *problem* of finding out what democracy means in its total range of concrete applications; economic, domestic, international, religious, cultural, economic, *and* political."[58] Democracy, Dewey reminded his readers, was itself a problem to be addressed in order to be carefully understood. Had Rugg shared Dewey's understanding of democracy, the attacks on the textbooks may not have seemed so inexplicable.

Why was the Rugg textbook series so popular for so long? Great Depression troubles led many Americans to take a critical look around themselves. Although relatively few teachers heeded George Counts' call to build a new social order through the schools, educators hoped that they could mark their enduring niche in a society that felt betrayed by many of its businesses and leaders.[59] America's social mood, however, can offer only a limited explanation for textbook trends in these years. The 1920s, a decade marked by isolationism and anti-immigrant feeling, was also the starting point for Rugg's experimental social science pamphlets. The first issue in this popular series was a 162-page look at "America and Her Immigrants." Indeed, only two of the fourteen-volume textbook series felt the brunt of the anti-American accusations that stirred nearly two decades later.

No other social science series of the time can compare with the breadth and variety of Rugg's series. Chapters were filled with lively illustrations and photographs alongside "dramatic episodes" that captured true-life accounts of "How Carlo and His Family Came to America" or "How Tony Acosta Became Naturalized." Teachers welcomed the detailed lesson outlines and discussion suggestions that filled their ample teacher guides. Small-town administrators may well have been flattered when their illustrious former professor at Teachers College solicited their support in developing the series. In an era of scientific curriculum-making, few if any textbook writers approached the level of detail that characterized the *Man and His Changing Society* series.

Once accusations of corruption tainted the Rugg series, however, a cadre of distinguished professors, generally supportive press, and even loyal teachers themselves could not save these books from being purged from many school systems. At the height of their popularity, the *Man and His Changing Society* series meshed with the economic and social upheaval of the Great Depression years. Rugg's textbooks probed the sensitive issues of class, race, and gender on the assumption that a strong democracy demanded an active and continually evolving self-examination. After sensationalistic journalism had largely undermined the series, social studies textbooks that replaced the Rugg series typically featured a patriotic, celebratory theme that dispensed with Rugg's probing "problem-solving" approach as well. This shift was surely connected to broader social changes within a more affluent and confidently capitalistic American society. A critical transformation had occurred alongside a war against the foes of democracy: Americans now equated capitalism with democracy, and patriotism with an uncritical acceptance of American society. In this new definition of democracy, Harold Rugg's textbooks became, as one attacker labeled them, "treason."

Within the educational world as well, the attack on the Rugg textbooks in 1940 and 1941 sent a clear message that schools should not challenge predominant social values. Schools and the textbooks they used served a much safer role in reaffirming the proudest images of Americanism and conventional living. In the wake of the Rugg textbook controversy, social studies and civics textbook writers ignored Rugg's efforts toward a more complex notion of democracy. School textbooks retreated from addressing issues of immigration, poverty, and diversity in the immediate postwar years, and portrayed instead an America of unity and consensus that belied the civil rights issues already stirring. Frances FitzGerald wrote, "Those of us who grew up in the fifties believed in the permanence of our American-history textbooks."[60] The closedmindedness that accompanied that sense of permanence proved stifling for Harold Rugg, who briefly challenged this narrow textbook orthodoxy, and for other visionaries like him.

NOTES

1. Harold Rugg, *That Men May Understand: An American in the Long Armistice* (New York: Doubleday, Doran and Company, 1941), xv.

2. Herbert M. Kliebard, *The Struggle for the American Curriculum, 1893–1958* (New York: Routledge, 1995).

3. Rugg, *That Men May Understand*, 172–177.

4. Elmer A. Winters, "Harold Rugg and Education for Social Reconstruction" (Ph.D. diss., University of Wisconsin, 1968), 8.

5. See Harold Rugg, *A Primer of Graphics and Statistics for Teachers* (Boston: Houghton Mifflin, 1925); and Harold Rugg, *Statistical Method Applied to Education* (New York: Houghton Mifflin, 1917). Rugg's dissertation was published as a monograph in 1916 as *The Experimental Determination of Mental Discipline in School Studies* (Baltimore: Warwick and York, 1916).

6. Harold O. Rugg and William C. Bagley, "The Content of American History as Taught in the Seventh and Eighth Grades: An Analysis of Typical Textbooks," in *University of Illinois Bulletin* 16 (Urbana, IL, 1916): 7.

7. Harold Rugg, "Needed Changes in the Committee Procedure of Recon-structing the Social Studies," *The Elementary School Journal* 21 (May 1921): 690.

8. Howard E. Wilson, *The Fusion of Social Studies in Junior High Schools: A Critical Analysis* (Cambridge, MA: Harvard University Press, 1933), 35.

9. Rugg, *That Men May Understand,* 36.

10. Laurance F. Shaffer, "Children's Interpretations of Cartoons: A Study of the Nature and Development of the Ability to Interpret Symbolic Drawings" (Ph.D. diss., Columbia University, Teachers College, 1930).

11. John A. Hockett, "A Determination of the Major Social Problems of Amer-ican Life" (Ph.D. diss., Columbia University, Teachers College, 1927).

12. Neal Billings, "A Determination of Generalizations Basic to the Social Studies Curriculum" (Ph.D. diss, Columbia University, Teachers College, 1929), 174.

13. Rugg, *That Men May Understand,* 182.

14. John Franklin Bobbitt, *The Curriculum* (Boston: Houghton Mifflin, 1918), 42.

15. Billings, 262.

16. The remaining statistical studies considered topics such as proper arrange-ment of materials according to grade, children's conceptual abilities, and map-reading abilities. Rugg counts twenty-two "thorough investigations" and lists most of them in his textbook prefaces.

17. Harold Rugg, *An Introduction to American Civilization: A Study of Eco-nomic Life in the United States* (Boston: Ginn and Company, 1929), vi–ix. This was the first volume in the *Man and His Changing Society* series.

18. Rugg, *That Men May Understand,* 41.

19. Frank M. McMurry, "A Critical Appraisement of Proposed Reorganiza-tions," in Guy M. Whipple (ed.), *Twenty-Second Yearbook of the National Society for the Study of Education* (Bloomington, IL: Public School Publishing Company, 1923), 294–96.

20. See for example, Wilbur F. Murra (et al.), *Bibliography of Textbooks in the Social Studies* (Cambridge, MA: National Council for the Social Studies, 1939). "Problems of Democracy" is listed as a category heading for textbooks.

21. Bessie Louise Pierce, *Civic Attitudes in American Social Textbooks* (Chicago: University of Chicago Press, 1930), 254–56.

22. Harold Rugg, "The Foundations and Technique of Curriculum-Construction," in *Twenty-Sixth Yearbook of the National Society for the Study of Education*, ed. Guy Montrose Whipple (Chicago: University of Chicago Press, 1926); reprinted as "The School Curriculum and the Drama of American Life," in *Cur-riculum-Making, Past and Present,* Harold Rugg et al. (New York: Arno Press, 1969), 3.

23. Frank Abbott Magruder, *American Government: A Consideration of the Problems of Democracy* (Boston: Allyn and Bacon, 1934), 666.

24. Louise I. Capen and D. Montfort Melchior, *My Worth to the World: Stud-ies in Citizenship* (New York: American Book Company, 1934), 401.

25. Harold Rugg, *An Introduction to Problems of American Culture* (Boston: Ginn and Company, 1931), 92–144.

26. Harold Rugg, "America and Her Immigrants," *Social Science Pamphlet Series* (New York: Teachers College Press, 1926): 172–185.

27. John Lincoln Williams and Palmer Peckham Howard, *Today's American Democracy* (Chicago: J. B. Lippincott Company, 1943), 173.

28. Harold Rugg and Ann Shumaker, *The Child-Centered School: An Appraisal of the New Education* (Yonkers-on-Hudson, NY: World Book Company, 1928), ix.

29. Rugg and Shumaker, 315.

30. Rugg and Shumaker, 108.

31. George S. Counts, *Dare the School Build a New Social Order?* (New York: John Day Company, 1932).

32. Harold Rugg, *The Great Technology: Social Chaos and the Public Mind* (New York: John Day Company, 1933).

33. For examples of these skirmishes, see C. A. Bowers, "Social Reconstructionism: Views from the Left and the Right, 1932–1942." *History of Education Quarterly* 10 (Spring 1970): 22–52.

34. This journal was called *Social Frontiers* until 1939. See Harold Rugg, "We Accept in Principle but Reject in Practice: Is This Leadership?" *Frontiers of Democracy* 9 (December 1943): 153–58.

35. Harold Rugg (ed.), *Democracy and the Curriculum: The Life and the Program of the American School* (New York: D. Appleton-Century Company, 1939), ix.

36. As quoted in E. A. Winters, "Man and His Changing Society: The Textbooks of Harold Rugg." *History of Education Quarterly* 7 (Winter 1967): 510.

37. Winters, "Harold Rugg and Education," 136–43.

38. Rugg, *Problems of American Culture,* 447–77.

39. Rugg, *Problems of American Culture,* 450.

40. See for example, "News and Notes of the Advertising Field," *New York Times,* 12 June 1939, sec. 1, p. 26; and W. H. Watt, "Eager Students Find Both Good and Bad in Advertising," *Advertising Age* 10 (July 10, 1939): 4–5.

41. "AFA Launches Drive Against 'Anti' Textbook in Schools," *Advertising Age* 10 (June 12, 1939): 2.

42. *National Legionnaire* 2 (January 1936): 5.

43. "Education Policy of Legion Scored," *New York Times,* 24 November 1935, sec. 2, 7.

44. William Pencak, *For God and Country: The American Legion, 1919–1941* (Boston: Northeastern University Press, 1989).

45. Harold Rugg, *A History of American Government and Culture: America's March Toward Democracy* (Boston: Ginn and Company, 1931), 131.

46. O. K. Armstrong, "Treason in the Textbooks." *American Legion Magazine* 29 (September 1940): 8–9ff.

47. Augustin G. Rudd, "Our 'Reconstructed' Educational System," *Nation's Business* 28 (April 1940): 27–28ff.

48. "Book Burnings," *Time* 36 (September 9, 1940): 64–5.

49. "Rugg Textbooks Restored in Englewood," *Publisher's Weekly* 139 (January 25, 1941): 434. Much of this account comes from "Englewood: A Case Study in Democracy" in Rugg, *That Men May Understand,* 20–35.

50. As quoted in Pencak, 273.

51. See for example, Harold Rugg, "That Men May Understand," *Dartmouth Alumni Magazine* 34 (January 1941): 101–3ff.; Harold Rugg, "Confidential Analysis of the Current (1939–1940) Attacks on the Rugg Social Science Series," May–June 1940, Harold Rugg folder, William F. Russell Papers, Box 58, Teachers College Special Collection; Harold Rugg, "This Has Happened Before," *Frontiers of Democracy* 7 (January 1941): 105–8; Rugg, "Study in Censorship: Good Concepts and Bad Words," *Social Education* 5 (March 1941): 176–81; Rugg, "Education and Social Hysteria," *Teachers College Record* 42 (March 1941): 493–505.

52. Dean George H. Sabine of Cornell, Arthur N. Holcombe of Harvard, Dean Carl Wittke of Oberlin, and Columbia faculty members Arthur W. Macmahon and Robert S. Lynd each reviewed one of the Rugg textbooks. Committee members hoped these thoughtful appraisals would provide a timely response to the superficial interpretations in Robey's brief abstracts. The twenty-eight-page pamphlet did not appear until 1942, however, and was overlooked amid wartime concerns. See American Committee for Democracy and Intellectual Freedom, "The Textbooks of Harold Rugg" (New York, 1942).

53. Frederic G. Melcher, "Editorial: Rugg Serves Freedom of Education," *Publisher's Weekly* 139 (April 12, 1941): 1533.

54. Rugg, *That Men May Understand,* 7.

55. Richard Seelye Jones, *A History of the American Legion* (Indianapolis: Bobbs-Merrill Company, 1946), 277.

56. Frances FitzGerald, *America Revised: History Schoolbooks in the Twentieth Century* (Boston: Little, Brown and Company, 1979), 37.

57. Winters, "Harold Rugg and Education for Social Reconstruction," 146.

58. John Dewey, "Education and Social Change," *Frontiers of Democracy* 3 (May 1937): 235–8.

59. See David Tyack, Robert Lowe, and Elisabeth Hansot, *Public Schools in Hard Times: The Great Depression and Recent Years* (Cambridge, MA: Harvard University Press, 1984), for a more detailed examination of the school's role and response to the economic crises of the 1930s.

60. FitzGerald, *America Revised,* 7.

6

"BEING POOR DOESN'T COUNT":

CLASS, ETHNICITY, AND DEMOCRACY IN
AMERICAN GIRLS' SCHOOL SERIES, 1900–1920

Kathleen Chamberlain

In the early 1920s, a couple named Mr. and Mrs. C. A. Walker purchased a copy of a mass-marketed juvenile series book entitled *The Girls of Central High Aiding the Red Cross.* The Walkers gave the volume as a gift to a girl called Georgia, memorializing the occasion with a verse inscribed on the flyleaf:

> May you enjoy to read, "oh boy,"
> The pranks of the Central High:
> And profit by the lessons taught
> In your habits, by and by.[1]

Despite their poetic limitations, these lines manage to describe the two main benefits that adults hope children will gain from such books: enjoyment and improvement. When speaking of the "lessons taught," the Walkers no doubt had in mind the fairly obvious messages about respectable behavior and socially acceptable virtues that the authors of series such as "The Girls of Central High" built into their texts. But American girls' school series of the early twentieth century reflected other lessons as well, lessons that addressed contemporary cultural concerns about gender, ethnicity, and democracy. Directed primarily to a white middle-class audience, girls' secondary school fiction offered a print culture that modeled for readers the qualities they would need and the roles they would assume as middle-class proponents and protectors of a democratic American society. At the same time, however, the stories undermined their own democratic ideals through plots and discourses that emphasized the same class and ethnic divisions that their more overt rhetoric questioned.

Of course, the cultural messages of these series were shaped by historical and generic context. Although school stories appeared in American literature as early as the eighteenth century, it is no coincidence that they were most popular in the Progressive Era, a period in which education was a topic of abiding public interest and in which educational theory and practice underwent significant changes. In constructing their new visions, educational reformers responded to shifting demographic patterns (especially in terms of urbanization and immigration), to new child labor laws, to changing vocational needs, to an increased sense of the school as a source of social reform, and to a general growth in the public's interest in education. One lasting change was that secondary schooling, a relative rarity for youth in the nineteenth century, became an essential element of their education in the twentieth century. As the century progressed, attendance at secondary schools increased, not just in numbers, but in proportion to the overall population. About half a million young people between the ages of fourteen and seventeen attended public high schools in 1900; over a million attended by 1912; and by 1920, the figure was 2,200,000.[2] Added to these numbers were those students who attended parochial and other private high schools and academies. Though secondary education was by no means a given for all young people during the Progressive Era, the growing prominence of high school in the contemporary culture meant that there was nonetheless a substantial audience for books about girls at both public and private secondary institutions. The limited evidence that exists concerning girls' actual reading patterns suggests that this audience was receptive to school stories. Surviving branch circulation reports from the New York Public Library in 1910, for example, indicate that such stories were popular with readers.[3]

Through their thematic and structural conventions, school series both reflected and helped construct some of the prevailing cultural narratives about the purposes and effects of American secondary education. Primary among these narratives were those dealing with the formation and continuance of democracy and democratic ideals. Many people believed that education, particularly public education, represented the country's best hope for assimilating immigrants, promoting social mobility, and diffusing the tensions between labor and capital. Reformers saw the school as an essential tool for implementing necessary social changes and for shaping the lifelong attitudes of future adult citizens. Such ideas were basic to Progressive Era educational philosophy. Few seriously questioned the notion that effective schooling could form the habits and beliefs that would take the chaotic America of large immigrant populations, swift technological change, and urban-industrial displacement, and mold it into a functioning democracy.

For some writers, democratic and patriotic rhetoric was merely a facade for xenophobia. Educator Ellwood P. Cubberley insisted that the country needed "a national campaign to eliminate some of our national weaknesses and dangers," one of which, he implied, was the threat posed by "the foreign-born in our midst."[4] Other writers, however, clung to a higher philosophical ground, genuinely seeing public education as one of democracy's strongest examples and hopes. In his study *Our Public Schools,* Oscar Corson wrote,

> The free public school system of the United States represents the nation's most serious attempt to make valid the fundamental statement in the Declaration of Independence that all men are created equal and are endowed by their Creator with certain inalienable rights ... for the public school is the one place in all the world where there is guaranteed absolute equality of educational opportunity to all, where wealth and ancestry, in and of themselves, count for nothing, and where brains and character and industry are certain to win the recognition they merit.[5]

Though stated more hyperbolically than most, Corson's idealistic description of the connection between education and democracy reflects a view typical of the time. Not all educators were as sanguine as Corson about the existing level of "democratization" in the public schools, but most contemporary writers did not question the importance of such a goal, not only for the benefit of individuals, but also for the very continuation of the democratic process. Public schools, wrote Charles Robbins in 1918, must develop "that unity of spirit upon which the highest success of a democracy depends.... The great work of the school is to give all increased breadth of vision, greater tolerance of spirit, [and a] stronger desire for the welfare of all."[6]

For many reformers and educators, then, secondary education ceased to represent an option only for the rich, and became instead a necessity for all, a requirement for true American citizenship. Although history has shown that secondary schooling never completely fulfilled its proponents' idealistic dreams, neither educators, politicians, nor school story writers in the Progressive Era relinquished their belief in the egalitarian potential of secondary education, nor their vision of a resulting society that mitigated class distinctions. As William Reese writes in *The Origins of the American High School,* "the idea that American high schools could expand their mission and their clientele, fulfilling democratic ends, became an article of faith among educators" in the twentieth century.[7]

The high school series of the time demonstrate this faith, presenting characters who champion the political structures of democracy as well as its social responsibilities, particularly egalitarianism and tolerance of diversity. But existing along with these noble messages are subtexts that support the views of revisionist historians such as Michael Katz, who contends that, rather than creating self-reliant, socially mobile, democratic citizens, American secondary education instead trained a docile, punctual working class and a self-satisfied middle class, neither of which was prepared to challenge the inequities of a capitalist, class-based system, and whose school-learned values could easily be conscripted to benefit corporate interests.[8] Girls' school series of the Progressive Era illustrate both the worthy and the oppressive potentials of secondary education.

Nine girls' series published between 1900 and 1920 qualify as "high school series"—that is, they feature secondary school as a significant setting for more than one volume and often for the entire series.[9] Four of these nine are set at single-sex public high schools. Of these four, two were written by Josephine Chase, a prolific author of juvenile fiction who wrote her first series, the "Grace Harlowe High School" books, after working as a secretary for the Henry Altemus Company of Philadelphia, a firm that published many of the popular children's series of the early twentieth century. The earliest of the girls' public school series, the Harlowe High books were published between 1910 and 1911 under the pen name "Jessie Graham Flower, A. M." Chase's second public school series, written under the pseudonym of "Pauline Lester," was the four-volume "Marjorie Dean High School" series.[10] The other two single-sex public school series are the "Friendly Terrace" books (1912–1916) by Harriet Lummis Smith; and the seven-volume "Girls of Central High" series (1914–1921) produced by the Stratemeyer Syndicate under the pen name "Gertrude Morrison."[11]

Four other series are set at private girls' boarding schools or academies: the first three volumes of the "Helen Grant" series (1903–1905), written by Amanda M. Douglas; the four-volume "Fairmount Girls" series, by Etta Anthony Baker, (1909–1911); the four-volume "Hadley Hall" series, by Louise Breitenbach, (1912–1915); and Edith Kellogg Dunton's "Nancy Lee" series (1912–1917), written in four volumes under her pseudonym "Margaret Warde." The ninth series, Margaret Ashmun's five "Isabel Carleton" books, takes place in part at a coeducational day school in Madison, Wisconsin. This school appears to be public, though it is not specifically identified as such. Isabel herself graduates from high school after the first volume, but subsequent titles include some of the school adventures of her younger sister, Fanny.[12]

Virtually all these series establish "democracy" as a central ideological value, defining the term both politically and socially. In general, the girls in these stories accept without question political structures such as majority rule and free elections, although none of the books pays more than passing attention to the issue of women's suffrage. In social terms, the series equate "democracy" with a belief in the fundamental legal and moral equality of all people, whatever their class. Students earned respect and admiration by virtue of their scholarship and behavior, not their social background. In this regard, the books continue what William Reese has identified as a major tenet of democratic educational philosophy in the nineteenth century: the belief that the ideal secondary school should function as a meritocracy in which advanced education is available to any bright student regardless of her or his financial status or social connections.[13] The books also inextricably link democracy with constructions of what it means to be an American. Significantly, however, school stories focus little attention on issues of race and ethnicity, despite the public prominence of these topics during the Progressive Era. As a result, the books define "American" as only that which conforms to the paradigm established by white, English / Northern European culture.

The public school stories provide the most direct discourse of democracy, since the tolerance described in the private school stories often leans more toward *noblesse oblige* than true egalitarianism. This distinction between public and private is often made explicit. *Peggy Raymond's School Days,* a public school story in the Friendly Terrace series, couches its rhetoric of democracy in terms of this dichotomy, making clear that attending public schools offers a girl her best chance to develop American democratic ideals. In the story, rich and snobbish Genevieve Alden has recently transferred to Girls' High School from a "select" private boarding school because her father has declared that "as long as his daughter was an American he was going to have her brought up like one, and that's why Genevieve is continuing her education in the public schools." At the "select" private school, the narrator says, "scholarship had been matter of minor importance," while "wealth and family were ... of paramount importance." At Girls' High School, however, Genevieve finds that "her world was upside down.... Her algebra teacher did not care in the least whether she was the daughter of Charles Alden, wealthy manufacturer, or

[of] John Sznwalski, teamster." The hypothetical teamster's obviously ethnic name is no accident: when the notions of immigration and ethnicity do surface in these books, they are often linked with the issue of democratic tolerance.[14] This same connection occurs in *The Girls of Central High*'s example of meritocracy in action. One of the most popular girls at the school is Irish Mary O'Rourke, whose father "was *merely* a day laborer" but who attains a position of class leadership based solely on her own abilities and friendliness (emphasis mine).[15]

Even private Fairmount Academy, the most exclusively upper-class institution represented in the nine secondary school series, makes its nod towards social equality and merit. As a school, Fairmount has few academic pretensions beyond those required for a girl's self-respect and her ability to converse intelligently in society. As the author explains in the introduction to *Frolics at Fairmount,* "Fairmount is a finishing school, pure and simple." Yet one of the students at Fairmount is Abby Anderson, a poor girl who plans to be a teacher and who is "so altogether conscientious and painstaking in her work, and such an excellent scholar" that the principal allows her to tutor some of the "younger pupils in return for her tuition."[16]

The democratic foundations of both public and private education in these series are directly connected to the formation of each character's personal integrity and to her status as a representative of socially and morally acceptable American girlhood. In the plot-driven series, heroines such as Marjorie Dean and Grace Harlowe are already nearly paragons when their stories begin. In the more complex, character-driven series, girls such as Nancy Lee and Alma Peabody of Hadley Hall must struggle and grow in order to realize their noble potential. But in all cases, the series strongly suggest that if readers are to assume similar places as model girls, they should begin by reforming the self so as to measure up to the stories' idealized definitions of proper gender roles and proper middle-class attitudes. School is presented not only as the space in which this self-formation can occur, but also as its driving force. The series make clear that the social influences and opportunities of school will help shape the heroines and their schoolmates into noble, "womanly" adults. As illustrations of this premise, the heroines are presented as fun-loving and energetic, willing to be leaders if social good will result, but unwilling to seek prominence for its own sake. The best girls are loyal to principles, to friends and family, and to the school itself. They also are (or learn to be) nurturing, charitable, and kind.

These gender-related virtues quickly become political, again within the framework of school. Through clubs, sororities, student government, and charitable endeavors, the schoolgirls are presented as participants in their own social destinies and in their larger communities. The public school stories in particular show girls organizing shows, bazaars, and other fund-raisers that involve and affect the entire community. Thus, these Progressive Era series were building on a notion that had been present in America since the earliest days of the Republic, namely that women, as mothers and nurturers, had an important role to play in the success of the nation. The school stories helped widen this idea to include some limited political impact and opportunity outside the home, even if still as preparation for future motherhood. To this extent, then, the books offered positive messages: the "new" girls of the twentieth century were not to be passive recipients of society's largesse, but could be active agents in society's improvement. In *The New Girl*, her study of British girls' culture from 1880 to 1915, Sally Mitchell notes that "[f]iction helps [girls] to shape acceptable images, determine what can be imagined, and envisage concrete situations that express formless emotions or unconscious desires."[17] Both implicitly and explicitly, American girls' school series contributed to that active imagining in terms of the private and public duties of womanhood and citizenship.

For the most part, Progressive Era school series "shape acceptable images" very clearly for their readers, without moral ambiguity. In each series, for instance, the way a given character responds to poor girls is an infallible barometer of moral worth. The heroines judge people based on individual merit, not wealth. Marjorie Dean risks being ostracized by the entire freshman class in order to befriend a shabby girl who lives in the poorest section of town. In *Grace Harlowe's Plebe Year at High School*, Grace initially speaks to her future best chum Anne simply because a few snobbish girls have snubbed Anne. When a jealous friend of Isabel Carleton lies to two poor German girls, telling them that Isabel said she was "too good to associate with them," Isabel cannot rest until she has cleared herself of the charge of elitism.[18] Conversely, any snobbish tendencies identify a girl as a villain or potential villain. Characters are at once stamped as unworthy if they prefer social position over personal merit, as is the case with one of Marjorie Dean's enemies, Rowena Farnham, who says to wealthy Constance Stevens, "You ought to associate with girls of your own class ... That Geraldine Macy is the only rich girl you ever go with. All the others are just middle class."[19]

Villain though she is, Rowena is right in one respect: it is primarily middle-class sensibility that informs the ideology and rhetoric of these books. In keeping with the spirit of reform that characterized the Progressive Era, however, all the series celebrate the joint middle- and upper-class value of charity, emphasizing that a true girl and a true American takes seriously her responsibilities to the less fortunate. In keeping with ideals exemplified by the then-popular settlement house movement and other active reforms, this charity is not merely something to be satisfied through ritual visits to the bedsides of the ailing or by a simple donation of food or money. Instead, the most effective charity is more robust, requiring the characters' active involvement. The books present a variety of charitable enterprises, most of them anchored squarely in established notions of females as nurturers. In both the Marjorie Dean and the Fairmount Girls series, the girls establish and support "day nurseries" for the children of factory workers. Though the upper-class Fairmount Girls' contributions are primarily financial and administrative, Marjorie Dean and her friends actually work in their nursery themselves. In *Nancy Lee's Spring Term,* charity is explicitly presented as a form of practical education. The entire school undertakes the care of an abandoned baby, with the students' eager participation marshaled into a "new elective course on baby-tending."[20] Most series also make clear that charity will be an essential element of each character's later life as a middle- or upper-class woman. Marjorie Dean's mother, for instance, spends most of her time engaged in charity among the town's poor. She and other like-minded mothers are so successful in their social work that their daughters, who would like to form a charitable club, can find no major good works in their city that remain to be done.[21]

Unsurprisingly, these narratives of charity bring class distinctions to the fore. In the pages of the high school series, middle-class readers can learn about the existence and the problems of the working class without running any physical or ideological risks. Physically, readers face no actual encounters with such dangers of poverty as infection, which many members of the middle and upper classes feared would result from forays into workers' tenements and neighborhoods. Miss Horton, the principal of Fairmount Academy, in fact refuses to allow the girls to visit "poor people" because one such family had previously "kept quiet" about having scarlet fever.[22] Ideologically, readers are encouraged to see themselves as working within the current class system, their attention turned to individuals' needs, not to larger questions of social justice. And since the characters' charitable activities are mostly confined to the domestic sphere of mothering and nurturing, readers' definitions of proper gender roles are not radically changed. The traditional roles are merely extended beyond the boundaries of one's own home into certain carefully circumscribed and socially acceptable public arenas.

Still, despite these emphases on the status quo, the books' narratives of charity help demonstrate one of the series' most dynamic messages: that girls have the power to mold their individual lives and their school and social communities. In many respects, the heroines of these school series can be seen as part of the tradition of "heroic femininity" that Shirley Foster and Judy Simons explore in their book, *What Katy Read.*[23] Readers see examples of girls organizing clubs, planning and carrying out fund-raisers, and administering important social services such as day care centers. Within these narratives, readers can learn political lessons about how to become effective community activists and even shapers of social policy.

Charitable activities are not the only narratives that offer girls access to power and that to some extent challenge prevailing gender stereotypes. Athletics, one of the most common tropes in girls' school stories, provides another such pattern. The Fairmount Girls series stresses the girls' expertise in riding, ice skating, and golf, using plots that often poke fun at male surprise or discomfort in the face of such prowess. Basketball, however, is the predominant sport used to redefine gender roles and to reemphasize the rhetoric of democracy. In her study of women's college fiction, Sherrie Inness demonstrates that basketball in such stories is almost always portrayed positively, as a way of validating athletic, physical women and undermining contemporary views that team competition made women more masculine or unsuited for motherhood. Inness writes, "Readers were encouraged to view athletic activities as not primarily preparation for domestic duties but as potential training for leadership roles outside the home."[24] The basketball narratives in secondary school books deliver much the same message.

One example occurs in the aptly titled *The Girls of Central High at Basketball.* Dr. Agnew, one of the characters' fathers, addresses his daughter on the subjects of athletics, gender, and loyalty: "Loyalty," he says. "That's the kernel—loyalty. If your athletics and games don't teach you that, you might as well give 'em up." He continues: "The feminine sex is not naturally loyal. Among boys it is different ... long generations of working and fighting together has made the normal male loyal to his kind. It is an instinct—and even our friends who call themselves suffragettes have still to acquire it."[25] Sexist though this passage is, its subtext actually proposes an important part for athletics in redefining gender roles. The implication of this speech is that girls' athletic programs, with their inter-school and inter-class rivalries, their emphasis on teamwork, and their development of girls' abilities to think quickly and coolly under pressure, replicate in miniature some of what were seen as the conditions of the male-dominated "public sphere." Underneath the praise of war and men's work and the condescension toward suffragettes is the suggestion that girls and women can and should learn how to function in this public world as they pursue such rights of democracy as voting.

The Marjorie Dean books provide a further example of the democracy of sport. Basketball in this series is almost wholly administered by students. Senior girls serve as team managers and coaches. Teams are selected through a democratic model based on merit and majority rule. When a rather snobbish teacher allows herself to be manipulated by Marjorie's enemies into calling for Marjorie's resignation from the team, the entire team as well as the student managers face down the teacher by refusing to recognize her authority, either as an adult or as a faculty member. Not only do they handle themselves with dignity and aplomb, but they also have the satisfaction of seeing the school principal, in the teacher's presence, agree with them. Within the requirements of literary realism (the mode of all the school series), this scene is certainly implausible. Within these series' cultural discourses of gender and democracy, however, the moment has tremendous resonance for readers. In addition to the dynamic of youth triumphing over adult authority, the episode offers a concrete example of the role that personal activism can play in an effective democracy.

The student-run basketball teams are but one example of student governance in these series. A major feature of the Hadley Hall books, for instance, is the female principal's plan, similar to those at colleges such as Wellesley, Bryn Mawr, and elsewhere, to make pupils responsible for their academic integrity and for establishing and upholding school rules. "I should like Hadley Hall to be self-governing," the principal tells the girls at Assembly. "To bring this about, you must make your own laws, and obey them."[26] The girls of Fairmount Academy undertake a degree of self-governance even without adult urging, deciding on their own to assess themselves a penalty of five cents whenever they use slang.

Up to this point, the cultural narratives in these Progressive Era girls' school series are quite healthy, encouraging as they do expanded gender roles, community activism, and increased tolerance of difference. But these messages have a price. As presented in these school stories, greater female agency for the white middle class often comes only at the expense of similar agency for poor, working-class, ethnic, and nonwhite females. Based as it is on the unequal relationships inherent in charity and on class markers such as distinctive language, dress, and attitude, the success of schoolgirl democracy requires the corresponding existence and perpetuation of the very inequalities that the characters' and narrators' direct commentaries ostensibly deplore.

Subtle but prevalent alternative discourses compete with the rhetoric of social mobility and tolerance. For instance, Isabel Carleton's younger sister Fanny has such strong "democratic" feelings that she insists on treating the maids as members of the family, but her view is offset by the fact that wiser characters such as Mrs. Carleton and Isabel laugh gently at Fanny's intensity, viewing it as an example of adolescent passion that will moderate in time. Plots are also often structured to support class distinctions. When one of the Carleton family's longtime maids gets married, only teenaged Fanny and eight-year-old sister Celia attend the nearby ceremony. In another example, Alice Long, a character in the Girls of Central High series, has to leave school to work in a factory. When she meets her former classmates on the street, she gives them the title of "Miss." The spirit of democratic tolerance supposedly inspired by secondary education apparently does not extend beyond the school building.

These tensions come in part because education itself, hailed by so many as the solution to ethnic, class, and economic inequities, is in fact a large part of the problem. Education level is not only one of the markers that defines social class, but it also creates the sort of speech and behavioral differences that identify a person's class status. The Fairmount Girls' five-cent slang penalty illustrates this point well. Mary, one of the girls, explains to the school's local adult benefactor why they chose to levy this fine. "You see, the girls, especially we older ones, realize that we use too much slang," Mary notes. "We passed a group of mill girls in town one day not long ago, and heard one say, 'Dollars to doughnuts it is!' and another answered: 'Betcher life it ain't!' It sounded dreadful! Then we began to understand how much worse it must sound from us, because we are having training which those poor girls never had."[27]

This passage is no doubt meant to demonstrate Mary's understanding and tolerance, albeit a condescending tolerance based on pity for lower-class ignorance. But an equally powerful subtext of difference and alienation reinforces the gulf between the working-class factory girls and the upper-class Fairmount girls, a gulf that yawns wide every time a member of one group or the other opens her mouth. Initially, this situation seems to support Progressive thinkers' belief in the necessity of universal secondary education: how better to bridge this gulf than to offer every young person the schooling that would erase such obvious class differences? But such a solution requires that education be used to homogenize the classes to a privileged middle-class standard, rather than to create a genuine demo-cratic tolerance of diversity and an appreciation of individual merit.

Thus the school stories employ a rhetoric of democratic tolerance and social equality at the same time that they suggest that class divisions either cannot be mitigated or can be overcome only by assimilating the working classes into the middle classes. This paradox exists in part because, like society at large, the authors of the series separated class from wealth. Since financial standing alone does not determine class, writers could con-fine the discourse of tolerance and equality solely to money while relocat-ing their discourse of class separation to indicators such as behavior, background, values, commodities, and speech. Based on these signifiers, almost all of the "poor" girls who are befriended by the heroines of school series are more properly seen as members of the middle and upper classes who have come to economic hard times. Their poverty is consistently jux-taposed with descriptions of their good family, their "well-bred" manners, their inexpensive yet "tasteful" gowns, their "refined" voices. With the exception of the very minor figure of Mary O'Rourke in the Girls of Cen-tral High series, there is not a single character attending any of these fic-tional high schools, public or private, whose background could be defined as working class using any class indicator other than income level. The inescapable message is that "universal" secondary education is in actual-ity restricted to those whose attitudes, background, and values are already at least middle class.

These messages about class also extend to race and ethnicity. School series may indeed present secondary education as available to the genteel poor, but as constructed in the stories, the genteel poor are virtually always white and native born. In all the series, as was typical of the time, ethnic and racial stereotypes abound. For every occasional positive presentation, such as that of Nora O'Malley, Grace Harlowe's wealthy Irish-Catholic chum, there are many broken-down Irish cleaning women, brogue-spouting old retainers, and servants such as Mary the recently-immigrated "hired girl" in *The Girls of Central High on Lake Luna,* who says, "Sure, and I was bogtrotter when I landed, and we did kape the pig in the kitchen, I admit it."[28] However, the few ethnic characters who do attend high school mostly escape caricature. Their behavior is indistinguishable from that of the privileged girls, suggesting the authors' faith in the Progressive Era view of the public school as a major instrument for assimilating immi-grants, a place where, as Charles Robbins wrote in 1918, "the little for-eigners [can] rapidly acquire a great deal of the American spirit."[29]

African Americans are even further removed from the ideal of universal education. Though black students sometimes exist in elementary school stories, they are completely absent from secondary school series. The very few black characters who do appear are usually minor menials who sometimes also serve as object lessons in charity and in the inescapable "otherness" of nonwhites, as the Fairmount Girls learn when they provide a birthday surprise of ten dollars to Minerva, an old black woman who sells fruit from a cart. The girls tell Minerva to buy something "sensible," assuming that she will understand the term as they do and will purchase a useful item such as a warm shawl. Dismayed when she instead buys a huge, ornate sideboard, the girls finally accept the views of Belle, the Southerner in their midst, who had tried to convince them that blacks did not think like whites and would never use money "sensibly." Though they eventually decide that Minerva's pleasure justifies her purchase, the Fairmount Girls come to construct racial difference in terms of hierarchy, with themselves at the top. The "other" thus remains inexplicable and subtly wrong.[30]

As one way of explaining and justifying the absence of working-class and racial or ethnic groups from secondary education, several of the high school series imply that these groups have in some way chosen their own exclusion. Class-related ignorance and stubbornness are sometimes cited: "Isn't it a pity," says Grace Harlowe's friend Anne, "that people like her [a woman who takes her ward out of school] can't understand that if a girl were allowed to finish her education, she could earn so much more in the long run than she could by working year after year in a mill?"[31] Implicit in most of these explanations is the idea that class attitudes and behavior are inherent, or at least learned at so early an age as to be unchangeable. This point is most forcefully made in the earliest of the nine series, Amanda Douglas' Helen Grant books (1903–1911). Mostly untouched by Progressive Era attitudes about the socially transforming power of universal education, this series hearkens back to an earlier notion: the idea that secondary schools are meant only for the most intellectually capable members of the population, a group that for Douglas seems to exclude most members of the working class. She counters any suggestion of economic or social injustice in this view by implying that most working-class people do not want or need secondary education in the first place.

This justification is illustrated by the contrast between Helen Grant and her cousin Jenny Mumford. The series opens with fourteen-year-old Helen about to graduate from grammar school. The daughter of a deceased mother and a scholarly, neglectful father, Helen lives with her farmer uncle, Jason

Mumford, and his wife Jane. The Mumfords' daughter Jenny had gone happily to work in a shoe factory at age fourteen, and Aunt Jane expects Helen to do likewise, despite Helen's clear intellectual abilities and her love of learning and culture. Since she disdains education, the shrill, Dickensian Aunt Jane argues that attending secondary school will serve only to give Helen airs above the family. But as Douglas presents the character, Helen is already "above" the Mumfords, due to her innate emotional, intellectual, and moral superiority. To Douglas, class status is merely an external emblem of such inherent traits. Progressive Era ideas that secondary education could promote not only economic and social mobility but could also shape mind and character would no doubt have seemed backward to her. In the Helen Grant series, people do not become what they are because of education; they come to education because of what they are.

This idea of innate class-related traits is strongest in the Helen Grant series, but it is present in subtler ways in other series as well. In *Marjorie Dean, High School Senior,* for instance, wealthy Veronica Browning pretends to be working her way through school as a maid, so that she can determine which girls will like her for herself and not her money. In what author Josephine Chase presents as a strong example of democratic tolerance, Marjorie and her coterie accept Veronica into their circle at once. Yet the power of the example is undercut in several ways. First, Veronica's identity as a maid is essentially erased. Unwilling to "embarrass" Ronnie by acknowledging her work, the other girls ignore her supposed occupation, eventually refusing to allow her even to mention it. Second, Chase suggests that being a maid cannot be simply an occupation; the label "maid" reflects one's fundamental character. Veronica, for instance, is unable to maintain her pose completely. Through her behavior and demeanor, the mask of the maid keeps slipping, showing the "real" girl beneath, to the confusion of her friends, who expect only certain predictable actions and ideas from a servant.

Finally, the language with which Chase describes both this slippage and Marjorie's reaction to it further deconstructs the egalitarianism of the story. The narrator notes, "For a girl who had been brought up in such humble circumstances, [Veronica] was astonishingly authoritative in her manner of speaking. Yet Marjorie could not help but admire her dauntless spirit of independence."[32] In Marjorie, the author has constructed a character meant to represent the ideal product of an education based on the principles of democratic equality and social mobility.

But the wording of this passage suggests that Chase does not believe that education should be able to erase all class markers. Girls raised in "humble circumstances" apparently should not be "authoritative," whatever their experience of the supposedly transforming effects of public high school. Personal agency, the passage implies, belongs to those either born to it or exposed to it early in life; one cannot be trained to it later. And the structure of the final sentence deconstructs its content of tolerance and admiration. The first word, "[y]et," is a transition expressing contrast, as in the sense "despite this." This diction suggests that Marjorie is being extremely broad-minded and even unusual in her willingness to admire Veronica "despite" the fact that Ronnie behaves in ways unexpected for a servant. The phrase "Marjorie could not help but admire" casts Marjorie's admiration as something drawn against her will. Finally, the reservations implied in the words "not" and "but" remove any remaining declarative assertion from the content of the statement.

In addition to their implications of inherent class differences, several of the series also suggest that poverty itself is as much a mental state as an economic one. In this way, the books avoid serious challenges to capitalist inequities. The authors had first mitigated the idea that capitalism itself could result in injustice to the working and lower classes by constructing narratives in which class status could be perceived to be innate, and in some cases, accepted even by those who might be expected to suffer from their position. In this narrative pattern, the responsibility for poverty belongs to the lower-class people themselves, rather than to the prevailing economic system. But this paradigm does not explain another pattern common to these series: the presence of innately middle- or upper-class characters whose reduced circumstances do not result from inherent personal traits, but from unfortunate external circumstances. On first consideration, this pattern might seem to offer a space in which to question the overall economic system, since it suggests that poverty is not necessarily the fault of the person who experiences it.

But the school narratives do not support such a questioning. While series heroines might occasionally muse about the arbitrary nature of economic success, the books more often either do not raise this question at all, or suggest that if only the poor-but-genteel girls would cultivate the proper attitude, their poverty would not be a burden. The Hadley Hall series, for instance, features impoverished-but-beloved Cordelia Everitt, the senior class president. Her unfailing cheerfulness in the face of deprivation and her focus on her many blessings make her one of the most popular girls in the school. Abby Anderson, however, the token "poor" girl at Fairmount Academy, has been soured by her reduced state. The narrator says, "Many of the girls had tried to be kind to Abby, but ... the marked differences between their circumstances and hers had made the poor girl over-sensitive ... her quick resentment was making her bitter."[33] The Marjorie Dean series offers a similar character in the person of Lucy Warner, who, as one of her classmates notes, "has always had a fixed idea that because she's poor, everyone looks down on her."[34]

In both cases, the wealthier girls redeem their angry classmates from the destructive effects of their bitterness by modeling alternative attitudes. The Fairmount Girls persuade Abby to spend the summer with them in Maine, where they all live and work together simply and harmoniously. As a result of Abby's exposure to this communal example, she "brought back to Fairmount ... a belief in the goodness of others instead of her former mistrust."[35] In keeping with the somewhat messianic tone of the Marjorie Dean series, Marjorie's conversion of Lucy Warner is more dramatic and even less credible, at least to modern readers. Despite suffering from fever and tonsillitis, Marjorie walks through the snow to visit an ailing Lucy. She wins Lucy's allegiance by forgiving her for writing nasty anonymous letters and by offering a little speech in which she asserts that "being poor doesn't count. It's the real you that makes the difference."[36]

Thus both authors adroitly shift the source of the problem of poverty from lack of money to lack of proper attitude, from the economic system to the individual. In the process, they often replace the working girls' burden of poverty with the burden of gratitude, meaning that truly egalitarian social relationships between the wealthy and the poor remain out of reach. One could argue, perhaps, that what such narratives offer poor or working girls is not guilt, but a form of agency: they learn that their happiness is in their own hands. While this interpretation should not be discounted, it is undercut by the powerful discourses of the wealthier girls' privilege. Even adolescent readers might have felt the disjunction as they read of Marjorie Dean, the possessor of a luxurious home, dainty frocks, and economic security, standing in Lucy Warner's "dismal," "bare," and "cheerless" house telling Lucy, with no context of authorial irony, that "being poor doesn't count."

Clearly, Progressive Era girls' school stories offered conflicting messages to readers. On the one hand, these books sincerely championed democratic tolerance and presented new constructions of girlhood that expanded previous gender roles with exciting opportunities for personal independence and control. On the other hand, these revised views were still based on class hierarchies and on cultural definitions of gender that limited women to fairly traditional roles within a mostly private sphere. As a result, the heroines in the school stories could further democracy and gain personal agency only if they could rely on the continuance of a lower level in the social hierarchy on which they could practice tolerance, nurturance, and charity. This lower level most often consisted of a steady array of poor, laboring, or nonprivileged characters. The books did demonstrate the expanded and dynamic part that white middle-class girls and women could play in supporting an effective democracy. Unfortunately, the price of this expansion was often the further inscription of the very class and ethnic divisions that the series' rhetoric of democracy tried so hard to erase.

NOTES

1. Handwritten note on flyleaf, Gertrude Morrison, *The Girls of Central High Aiding the Red Cross* (New York: Grosset & Dunlap, 1921).

2. Joel Spring, *The American School, 1642–1985* (New York: Longman, 1986), 94.

3. For instance, Etta Anthony Baker's "Fairmount Girls Boarding School" books were cited by three different branches as "popular with girls," "asked for," and "never in." At least six other school stories were similarly identified. I would like to thank Robert Sink, archivist of the Rare Books and Manuscripts Division of the New York Public Library, for providing me with this information.

4. Ellwood P. Cubberley, *Public Education in the United States* (Boston: Houghton-Mifflin, 1919), 481.

5. Oscar Corson, *Our Public Schools: Their Teachers, Pupils, and Patrons* (New York: American Book Company, 1918), 9.

6. Charles Robbins, *The School as a Social Institution* (Boston: Allyn and Bacon, 1918), 118.

7. William J. Reese, *The Origins of the American High School* (New Haven, CT: Yale University Press, 1995), 260.

8. Michael Katz, *Class, Bureaucracy, and Schools: The Illusion of Education Change in America* (New York: Praeger, 1971).

9. Full titles and dates of the series analyzed for this essay are as follows:

Series set in single-sex public high schools: (1) "The Friendly Terrace Series" by Harriet Lummis Smith (published initially by L.C. Page; reprinted by A.L. Burt); *The Girls of Friendly Terrace* (1912); *Peggy Raymond's Vacation* (1913); *Peggy Raymond's Schooldays* (1916); *Peggy Raymond at "The Poplars"* (1920); *Peggy Raymond's Way* (1922); (2) "The Girls of Central High Series" by Gertrude Morrison (published by Grosset & Dunlap; reprinted by World [Stratemeyer Syndicate]): *The Girls of Central High* (1914); *The Girls of Central High on Lake Luna* (1914); *The Girls of Central High at Basketball* (1914); *The Girls of Central High on the Stage* (1914); *The Girls of Central High on Track and Field* (1914); *The Girls of Central High in Camp* (1915); *The Girls of Central High Aiding the Red Cross* (1921); (3) "The Grace Harlowe High School Series" by "Jessie Graham Flower, A. M." [Josephine Chase] (published by Henry Alte-mus Co.): *Grace Harlowe's Plebe Year at High School* (1910); *Grace Harlowe's Sophomore Year at High School* (1911); *Grace Harlowe's Junior Year at High School* (1911); *Grace Harlowe's Senior Year at High School* (1911); (4) "The Marjorie Dean High School Series" by "Pauline Lester" [Josephine Chase] (pub-lished by A.L. Burt): *Marjorie Dean, High School Freshman* (1917); *Marjorie Dean, High School Sophomore* (1917); *Marjorie Dean, High School Junior* (1917); *Marjorie Dean, High School Senior* (1917).

Series set in private girls' secondary schools: (1) "The Alma of Hadley Hall Series" by Louise M. Breitenbach (published by L.C. Page): *Alma of Hadley Hall* (1912); *Alma's Sophomore Year* (1913); *Alma's Junior Year* (1914); *Alma's Senior Year* (1915); (2) "The Fairmount Girls Series" by Etta Anthony Baker (published by Little, Brown): *The Girls of Fairmount* (1909); *Frolics at Fair-mount* (1910); *Fairmount Girls at School and Camp* (1911); *Fairmount's Quar-tette* (1914); (3) "The Helen Grant Series" by Amanda M. Douglas (published by [Lothrop], Lee, and Shepard): *Helen Grant's Schooldays* (1903); *Helen Grant's Friends* (1904); *Helen Grant at Aldred House* (1905); [six additional titles focus on Helen's college years and her teaching career]; (4) "The Nancy Lee Series" by "Margaret Warde" [Edith Kellogg Dunton] (published by Penn): *Nancy Lee* (1912); *Nancy Lee's Spring Term* (1913); *Nancy Lee's Lookout* (1915); *Nancy Lee's Namesake* (1917).

Series set in a coeducational high school: "The Isabel Carleton Series" by Margaret Ashmun (published by Macmillan): *Isabel Carleton's Year* (1916); *The Heart of Isabel Carleton* (1917); *Isabel Carleton's Friends* (1918); *Isabel Carle-ton in the West* (1919); *Isabel Carleton at Home* (1920).

10. See Pauline Lester, *Marjorie Dean, High School Junior* (New York: A. L. Burt, 1917); and *Marjorie Dean, High School Senior* (New York: A. L. Burt, 1917).

11. According to the Stratemeyer Syndicate Archives at the New York Public Library, the ghostwriter for "The Girls of Central High" series was W. Bert Fos-ter, a prolific author of books for both boys and girls.

12. This example reflects another important aspect of Progressive Era edu-cation for women, namely the professionalization of housework and mothering through courses in what was variously identified as "domestic science," "domes-tic arts," or "home economics." The Peggy Raymond and Isabel Carleton series, in particular, stress the value of such courses to the creation of "modern" women.

13. Reese, *American High School,* 45–47.

14. Smith, *Peggy Raymond's School Days,* 20, 76.

15. Morrison, *Girls of Central High,* 59.

16. Baker, *Frolics at Fairmount,* xi; *Girls of Fairmount,* 74–75.

17. Sally Mitchell, *The New Girl: Girls' Culture in England, 1880–1915* (New York: Columbia University Press, 1995), 141.

18. Ashmun, *Isabel Carleton's Year,* 63.

19. Lester, *Marjorie Dean, High School Junior,* 201.

20. Warde, *Nancy Lee's Spring Term,* 212.

21. Lester, *Marjorie Dean, High School Junior,* 176.

22. Baker, *Girls of Fairmount,* 82.

23. Shirley Foster and Judy Simons, *What Katy Read: Feminist Re-readings of "Classic" Stories for Girls* (Iowa City, IA: University of Iowa Press, 1995).

24. Sherrie Inness, *Intimate Communities: Representation and Social Transformation in Women's College Fiction, 1895–1910* (Bowling Green, OH: Bowling Green State University Popular Press, 1995), 82–94. Quotation on 85.

25. Morrison, *The Girls of Central High at Basketball,* 19.

26. Breitenbach, *Alma at Hadley Hall,* 37–38.

27. Baker, *Girls of Fairmount,* 56–57.

28. Morrison, *The Girls of Central High on Lake Luna,* 62.

29. Robbins, *The School as a Social Institution,* 122.

30. Baker, *Girls of Fairmount,* 252–262.

31. Morrison, *The Girls of Central High on Lake Luna,* 58.

32. Lester, *Marjorie Dean, High School Senior,* 53.

33. Baker, *Girls of Fairmount,* 75.

34. Lester, *Marjorie Dean, High School Junior,* 155.

35. Baker, *Girls of Fairmount,* 107.

36. Lester, *Marjorie Dean, High School Junior,* 232.

7

TURNING CHILD READERS INTO CONSUMERS:

CHILDREN'S MAGAZINES AND ADVERTISING, 1900–1920

Catherine Van Horn

A *Children's Magazine* column writer who pleaded with her youthful readers in 1908 to pay more attention to the periodical's advertising pages showed signs of the stress that the new mass-marketing age could place on children's publications. Advertising had been a part of publishing in the United States since the colonial era, but only in the latter part of the nineteenth century—with an increase in industrial production and the rise of branded, mass-marketed goods, among other developments—did it become a key form of press financing. Newspapers and magazines that traditionally had made money through political party subsidies or through subscriptions and single-copy sales instead increasingly sought revenue from advertising.[1] When a publication's growing dependence on advertising met with advertiser ambivalence about the publication's worth, disaster loomed: "(T)hey say I don't bring enough letters to our advertisers, yet," the column writer told *Children's Magazine* readers, "Suppose they discharge me! Oh dear! Who will help me?"[2]

That the columnist discussed advertising with the magazine's readers emphasizes the importance both advertisers and audiences held for turn-of-the-century publications. As mass-magazine publishers and national advertisers developed closer ties in the late nineteenth century, the traditional relationship between a periodical and its readers became a three-way affair. Magazine publishers relying on subscriptions for profit had to please readers. But an increasing reliance on advertising dollars meant publishers had to satisfy both readers and advertisers. Some magazines

dropped their prices, diversified their content, or targeted specific advertising "classes" to build up their circulation base, striving to draw in more
of the middle-class men and women that advertisers wanted to reach.[3]

Older elite magazines such as *Century* and *Harper's* and newer middle-
class magazines such as *Munsey's, The Saturday Evening Post,* and *Ladies
Home Journal* proved successful at the new turn-of-the-century formula,
growing fat on the advertising pages carried in each issue.[4] However, publishers of children's magazines faced a more difficult time, suffering as
they did at the time from serving a readership not yet defined as a significant advertising market.[5] While some early national advertisers such as the
Charles E. Hires (root beer) Company had occasionally targeted children
with novelties, trading cards, and other advertising matter in the nineteenth century, what scant advertising there was in children's magazines
addressed mothers and families more than it did children.[6]

This was standard practice, according to advertising expert Nathaniel
Fowler in 1897. Although he pointed out in his *Fowler's Publicity* that
"the young of to-day are the buyers of tomorrow," he still recommended
that advertisers target parents more than children, "for comparatively few
children read advertisements." Even in children's publications, he advised,
advertisers should direct their messages to mothers, although it would be
"good policy" to occasionally appeal directly to children.[7]

Yet advertisers did not need children's magazines to reach the middle-
class women who already flocked to popular general circulation and gendered magazines. To bank their share of the growing pool of national
advertising dollars, publishers of children's magazines needed the advertising industry to consistently perceive children themselves as a valuable
advertising market. For that, they had to persuade children to pay attention
to advertising messages and gather proof for advertisers that children did
so. As they worked to make their advertising pages pay, publishers of children's magazines became pioneers in casting children in the role of an
advertising class.

Central to their efforts, this article asserts, was the personal relationship
that publishers and editors of children's magazines fostered with their
young readers, and with the children's parents by proxy. Christopher P.
Wilson had noted that the genteel editors of elite publications during the
Gilded Age had adopted an anonymous editorial voice, selecting articles
for their readers but otherwise remaining aloof from them. The new wave
of editors who began marketing their more commercial magazines to the
masses in the late nineteenth century rejected aloofness in favor of per-
sonification and a more intimate relationship with their audiences, carried

on through such devices as signed editorials, advice columns, and letters pages.[8] Perhaps because of their audience, editors of quality children's magazines during the genteel era already had worked to personalize their voices. The trend continued at the turn of the century, as magazines drew children into personal relationships with the publications produced both to entertain and educate them.[9]

General interest children's magazines after the Civil War largely eschewed the moralistic approach used in their antebellum counterparts in favor of publications that entertained in a wholesome fashion. Still, children's magazines deemed to be of quality often retained a sense of the didactic—a predilection for using their articles and other editorial matter to guide their young readers down the path of honesty, virtue, and social responsibility. Some of that direction came through columns that developed a personal voice for the publications, places where editors connected with readers through the exchange of advice, letters, or creative work.[10]

The development of this personal relationship would prove useful as children's magazines cajoled readers to pay attention to advertising and asked for help in their commercial enterprise. Not all editors would be as overtly manipulative as was the *Children's Magazine* columnist who threatened both her dismissal and the appearance of a spanking machine on her readers' doorsteps if they failed to help draw advertising to the magazine. Nonetheless, quality children's magazines worked closely with advertisers in the early twentieth century to use the personal relationship between magazine and youthful reader as a way to construct advertising and its needs as a natural part of children's periodical reading.

Three quality children's magazines that worked to create a relationship with upper-middle-class readers in 1900 and after carried titles that emphasized just for whom the editors wrote. The New York–based *St. Nicholas,* often lauded as the most popular quality children's publication of its era,[11] assumed the subtitle *An Illustrated Magazine for Young Folks* for most of its long run (1873–1940). *Little Folks: An Illustrated Monthly for Youngest Readers,* publishing first in Boston and then in Salem from 1897 to 1926, left no doubt in its title as to which readers should find its pages attractive. The same held true for *John Martin's Book: The Child's Magazine,* published in the New York area from 1912 to 1933.

Publishers and editors moved well beyond titles, however, to create a community of readers within their pages who looked to each other and to the magazine for friendship. Early in its history, for example, *St. Nicholas* provided social space in its magazine for readers and editors to meet. Mary Mapes Dodge acted as editor for the upper-middle-class magazine from its inception in 1873 as a child of Scribner & Co. in New York, through its transfer to The Century Co. in 1881, and until her death in 1905. The magazine was intended both to please and to instruct, instilling a traditional sense of morality and character in children while also preparing them to keep pace with the changing world. Dodge quickly established an editorial and instructional voice for the magazine in early columns and provided space for letters and reader contributions, but it was the St. Nicholas League's debut in November 1899 that created a long lasting and powerful personal relationship between the magazine and its readers.[12]

The St. Nicholas League was a children's club whose motto was "Live to Learn and Learn to Live" and whose aim was to stand "for intellectual advancement and for higher ideals of life." Subscribers and non-subscribers alike could join the league by sending for a free membership badge that entitled them to participate in assorted writing, photography, and other creative monthly competitions fronted each month by personal comments from the league's editors. Winners' work, which was to be verified as original by parents or teachers, earned prize badges and publication within the handful of pages devoted to the league each month. Children also could write into the league's "Letter Box." The league became wildly successful, eliciting substantial response from children and praise for the quality of the competitors' work by Albert Bigelow Paine, the league's editor until 1910. As historians have noted, the league served as an early proving ground for many writers, including Edna St. Vincent Millay, F. Scott Fitzgerald, William Faulkner, and E. B. White.[13]

Little Folks offered nothing as elaborate as the St. Nicholas League, but its editors nonetheless provided several opportunities for young readers to interact with the magazine beyond the story pages. The S. E. Cassino Co. published *Little Folks* under the editorial guidance first of the husband-and-wife team of Charles Stuart Pratt and Ella Forman Pratt, experienced editors of children's magazines, and then of M. O. Osborne.[14] Like *St. Nicholas,* the magazine intended both to entertain and teach, to be a "playfellow" that nonetheless stimulated readers "to be fearless, cheerful, unselfish, and above all true and honorable." Throughout its history, the magazine invited readers to see their names in print either by writing to the *Little Folks* "letter bag" or by being one of the many winners of the assorted puzzle or drawing competitions in the publication's "play department" directed by the editors. On occasion, the editors wrote in first person as they praised children's artwork from the last competition and established the rules for the next one.[15]

In contrast, Morgan Shepard, the owner and editor of *John Martin's Book* who published under the name of John Martin, built a personal relationship with his readers not through competitions but through letters and columns that used first-person remarks to address children or their parents. Prior to becoming a magazine editor, Shepard claimed various careers as a miner, Central American revolutionary, cow puncher, street car driver, and bank clerk. He then established a business of writing and mailing first-person story letters from John Martin to young children, sending through the mail perhaps as many as 2,000 letters per month. In 1911, Shepard's letters began appearing in *St. Nicholas* as editorial material "for very little folk." In November 1912, Shepard began housing his whimsical letters inside his own upper-middle-class magazine saturated with the sentimental personality of John Martin. The magazine aimed "to teach without preachment and guide without coercion" and to be a "perfectly natural friend" to children. While the magazine omitted a reader's letter page, and Shepard generally declined to run children's names in his magazine, Shepard often directly answered mail from children and their parents in a column using his John Martin persona. He also occasionally invited children to visit him at his publication house.[16]

Although they went about the task in different ways, the editors at each of these three magazines worked to establish more personal relationships with their youthful readers than the story pages alone would have allowed. A clue that readers may have viewed the magazines on the personal level promoted by editors is contained in the language used in their published letters. Children often addressed a magazine as "you" in their letter texts, emphasized how they waited eagerly each month to welcome their friend into their homes, and shared news about themselves as a friend might do. "Mama told me a long time ago that if I would pull one of my teeth that was loose I might write you a letter," wrote Josephine H. King from Augusta, New York, to *Little Folks* in 1900. "Of course you know I did it, for here is the letter."[17]

Once a personal relationship had been established between children and their magazines, publishers and editors could capitalize on the bond to ask readers for assistance in soliciting subscribers and advertisers. Subscribers came first. Magazines after the Civil War turned heavily to offering premiums as a way to induce subscribers to renew and to bring others into the fold with them, and children's magazines were no different.[18] *The Youth's Companion,* for example, a nineteenth-century weekly paper directed toward children but inclusive of the whole family, excelled at mobilizing readers for subscription purposes, offering a storehouse of goods from which children could choose in return for bringing new readers to the publication.[19]

St. Nicholas, John Martin's Book, and *Little Folks* all offered premiums to different degrees and, in varying levels of intensity, pursued children's recruitment efforts. Of the three magazines, *Little Folks* was the most active in asking children to recruit on its behalf, sometimes moving well beyond its regular premium catalog of dolls, sleds, toy guns, and bicycles. One year, *Little Folks* publishers considered offering a premium contest that would bestow a pony upon the winner who recruited the most subscribers.[20]

As they appealed to children and their parents for subscription help, the magazines often noted that the efforts of loyal subscribers on behalf of the magazine actually produced a better magazine for all:

> We believe that there is no magazine published today that has a more loyal family of subscribers than *Little Folks Magazine*. We have yet to find a subscriber who is not always ready and willing, yes anxious, to say a good word for the magazine. Even the mothers and fathers of our subscribers tell their friends about it, and many have in this way secured new subscribers.
>
> All seem to realize that the larger the number of subscribers the better it will be possible for us to make the magazine.[21]

Children's magazines used similar language to justify their requests for readers to pay attention to advertisers, although reader benevolence was now to extend to include support of advertiser goals. *St. Nicholas* had directed children to pay attention to advertising as early as 1900, but when a new advertising manager debuted at the magazine in 1911—and was personally introduced to *St. Nicholas* readers in the advertising pages—the magazine began explicitly asking readers for help for itself and for its advertisers.[22] The personal relationship the magazine had built between itself and its juvenile readers now included advertisers, and *St. Nicholas* readers were told they had a responsibility to maintain the relationship.

That responsibility extended beyond simply paying attention to advertising. It also included writing letters to advertisers who "want to get acquainted" and purchasing advertised goods.[23] When companies complained in 1912, for example, that *St. Nicholas* advertisements drew attention but not sales from readers, the advertising editor discussed the matter with readers:

> You know we must all stand by the advertisers who patronize *St. Nicholas* because they are your friends as well as ours. They believe it is well worth their while to get you as much interested in what they have to sell as it is for them to interest your father and mother; so whenever you get a chance to say a good word for the St. Nicholas advertisers or buy what they advertise in our magazine, just do it, because you will know you are getting the best goods that can be bought and that you are securing the personal service of the manufacturer himself.[24]

Such requests for children to help the magazine by helping advertisers appeared from the start in *John Martin's Book*. Because the magazine was aimed at children younger than the 8- to 16-year-old readers targeted by *St. Nicholas,* Shepard often directed his discussions about advertising both to children and to parents. Sometimes he talked directly to parents, as he did in a message in his debut issue of November 1912. "In the twentieth century we must face the idea of commercialism," he wrote mothers in a full-page message in which he asked them to show their appreciation for the magazine by using advertised products.[25] In the same issue, he used poetic form to explain to children what the magazine's advertising pages were all about:

Come, Children, take a careful look through the last pages of YOUR BOOK. Each page is like a Ship that brings big cargoes of a host of things. Each page has lots of news to tell of things to buy and things to sell.

Each page is like a Merchant too, who wants to be the best for you. He sells the best with might and vim, so you will come and buy again. Of course, he hopes that MOTHER sees how very hard he tries to please. And as for FATHER he will see how very good we try to be.

As for the Man who writes these lines, he makes a bow and then declines to praise the things that will not do to buy for Mother or for you. In other words: He'll not endorse what is not good for you, of course. He really thinks it always pays to gain his gold in other ways. It wouldn't be quite fair and square. That's what I mean, my DEARS—so there.[26]

During its first year of publication, *John Martin's Book* received a letter from a teacher who complained that his magazine contained too much advertising. His advertising manager explained in a full-page response that the magazine accepted only truthful advertisements about products that better the home, losing money on those advertisements rejected for the good of the children. The "representation of the market-place" in the magazine in no way meant "a bowing down before Mammon." Rather, advertising support helped a wholesome magazine for children. "Come now!" the advertising manager wrote. "It isn't so bad after all. Help us live up to our ideals."[27]

Little Folks aspired to similar ideals—and to a similar age group—as did *John Martin's Book*. Its publisher also tried to interest the magazine's readers and their families in supporting advertisers as a way to support the publication, but his efforts focused mostly on the parents assumed to be reading the magazine to their children. As early as 1898, the publisher invited parents to help affirm that they did indeed pay attention to its advertisers as a means to help the magazine:

You can help LITTLE FOLKS a great deal by reading the advertisements from time to time, and if of interest to you by writing our advertisers. Nothing of a questionable nature is allowed in our columns. It is not an easy matter to induce advertisers to use space in children's periodicals for they claim that children are not buyers, and this sounds so plausible that they really believe it. The publisher claims that many LITTLE FOLKS subscribers have their parents read the magazine to them not once but many times, and that their parents are very careful in their selections of whatever their children read or have read to them. This should make an advertisement in LITTLE FOLKS very profitable. The publisher would like to have a great many mothers and fathers write him their ideas about this matter. That would help to get more advertisements perhaps. Some day when there are more subscribers and more advertisers, LITTLE FOLKS may be enlarged.[28]

Unlike *John Martin's Book* and *St. Nicholas*, *Little Folks* was not above running reading notices or editorial plugs for advertisers, adding more bang for the advertising buck. Yet, despite years of such service and of soliciting reader support for advertisers, the difficulty in drawing advertisers appears to have forced *Little Folks* ultimately to focus heavily on subscription revenue as the foundation for the magazine. In 1920, the publisher directed a message to readers to explain that high costs and a "policy" calling for reliance on subscriptions over advertising to avoid crowding stories had kept the magazine small. Perhaps a more honest reason, though, for insubstantial amounts of advertising might have been the fact that *Little Folks,* unlike *John Martin's Book* and *St. Nicholas,* made little sustained effort to turn its young readers into consumers. While *Little Folks* mostly capitalized on its relationship with parents to solicit advertising attention, the other magazines worked to construct child readers themselves as consumers of advertising and influences on parental purchasing.

St. Nicholas, for example, worked both to naturalize advertising for its readers and to construct them as a target market for the advertising industry by drawing upon the strength of its popular St. Nicholas League. The success of the League in stimulating children's creative attention during the first year of its existence apparently spurred *St. Nicholas* publishers to replicate the club in the magazine's advertising pages. *St. Nicholas* had been the brainchild of Roswell Smith, one of the founders of the elite *Scribner's Monthly* and an early advocate of magazine advertising. When a reorganization of Scribner & Co. in 1881 left Smith with ownership of both *St. Nicholas* and the adult monthly—now renamed *The Century*—he began to actively solicit advertising for the publications, one of the earliest members of the elite magazine publishing club to do so.[29] The adventurous advertising nature of the renamed Century Company continued into the 1900s when *St. Nicholas* became one of the first quality children's magazines to actively introduce advertisers to children. An announcement in the October 1900 St. Nicholas League pages advised members that a new branch of the league would be forthcoming:

> The work of the successful competitors in the St. Nicholas League, as shown from month to month in this department, has appealed to readers of all ages, and the suggestion has been made by the publishers that to enlist boys and girls in the work of making the advertising pages more attractive would be entertaining and profitable to the young folks themselves, irrespective of the value to our advertisers.[30]

Throughout the history of the St. Nicholas Advertising League, from 1900 to 1917, its editors directly addressed participants as a group, in effect coalescing them into a club in the same manner as did the league's sibling in the editorial pages. At its inception, the advertising league "invited" readers into the new environment, offering them the opportunity to participate in a contest to create advertisements for the magazine's advertisers using the same rules as established by the regular league.[31] As part of the contests, readers received substantial instruction on what worked as an advertisement and what did not. Advertising league editors frequently reminded contestants that learning about advertising was educational for them and important for the future.

In the first years of the advertising contests, the focus was largely on participants creating actual advertisements that would help companies "in making direct sales or gain publicity," and, as did the regular league, the advertising league sometimes published the winning work. Winners won cash prizes ranging from $1 to $5, and their names and those of the competitors worthy of an honorable mention appeared in monthly reports on previous contests.[32] Advertiser response was occasionally noted in the magazine, and some advertisers purchased outstanding material created through the early contests for $3.

Assigning *St. Nicholas* readers to create advertisements helped the children to learn about advertising and might also have helped companies learn what kinds of pitches would sell to the children who had been paid little attention by the advertising industry. Yet, within a few years, such contests began to disappear, in part because the children had been trained. "All the advertising competitions printed in St. Nicholas have practically been planned to teach the St. Nicholas readers how to advertise," an advertising editor reported in 1904. "This object has been accomplished. The recent contests show that the young workers have learned what advertising means."[33]

As well, the advertisers may have been less interested in reader-produced advertising now that the industry had begun to professionalize the process of copy creation and copy testing. Around the turn of the century, advertising agencies such as N. W. Ayer & Son had begun taking the burden of copy writing away from companies, and advertising research was on the rise.[34] "Modern advertising has ceased to be a matter of mere guesswork," the advertising league editor told readers in 1905.[35] Contests in subsequent years required readers to use existing advertisements to complete puzzles or games in various ways, to show how products were or could be used in their homes, or to reason why companies not advertising in the magazine should do so. On occasion, competitors also had to include letters about such topics as their pets or brothers and sisters that served as market research for the magazine and its advertisers.[36]

As Ellen Gruber Garvey has pointed out, the *St. Nicholas* advertising contest served as a bridge for young readers between the familiar editorial pages and the more foreign advertising pages. Garvey noted that the advertising contests were infused with the familiar editorial elements of play and fiction. Additionally, the editorial tendency to personalize the relationship between the magazine and its readers could be found in the contests—in the educational lessons provided by the advertising editors, in the praise and reproach offered on competitors' efforts, and especially in the personalizing of the advertising judges, and sometimes of the advertising editors, which allowed readers to imagine a relationship with them.

Participants were told in 1909, for example, that the contest judges had reviewed the work for the "Vacation Competition" while on a vacation of their own at the New Jersey seashore home of one of the judges. They sailed the judge's boat into the bay and then repaired to a table to evaluate the entries that were being rustled by wind blowing through portholes, working despite the lure of the sun and the breeze.[37] In 1913, the advertising editor created a fictional partner in Alexander the Little, who was given the responsibility for organizing the advertising contests. Alexander was a sometimes mischievous little boy who interacted with the editor in the contest's pages to introduce and explain the contests in entertaining ways.[38] Alexander's appearance in the advertising contests showcased how effectively *St. Nicholas* could bridge the gap between editorial and advertising pages in its effort to naturalize advertising in the magazine.

Having already established a personal presence in the contests, the advertising editor created a fictional character closer to the children's age who provided an outlet for dialogue between the two and storytelling within the ad contest framework. This bridge between the editorial stories and the advertising section then extended further with Alexander's appearance in actual advertising. A full-page ad from "The Man Who Writes the United States Tire Company Advertisements" ran in June 1913 under the headline "Alexander gave me a peek into his letter file." The ad reprinted children's responses about Nobby Tread bicycles gleaned from an advertising competition, noting that Alexander had called the advertiser to *St. Nicholas* offices "to show me something that would please me."[39]

St. Nicholas was not the only site for advertising contests in the early twentieth century. Contests were popular devices both for companies themselves to use in their advertising and for adult magazines such as *Ladies Home Journal.*[40] *The American Boy,* a popular boys' magazine publishing since the turn of the century in Detroit, used at least one contest to solicit comment from its readers about what products should be advertised in its pages.[41] The *Children's Magazine,* whose advertising columnist had a penchant for spanking machines, ran mindless contests in 1908 that sometimes required competitors to get three adults to send away for advertising circulars or booklets.[42] *John Martin's Book* ran at least one advertising contest,[43] but Shepard chose another route to naturalize advertising for his very young magazine readers: advertisements that mimicked the storytelling children loved.

Advertisements in children's magazines after the turn of the century slowly began to address children themselves, especially in those publications whose publishers and editors worked to construct their readers as a target market. While child-oriented advertising gradually appeared in *St. Nicholas* after 1900, it constituted nearly the entire advertising section right from the start in *St. John's Book.* Shepard served as a copywriter for the companies who chose to advertise in his magazines, creating advertisements for children that resembled the editorial pages in content and appearance. One writer who grew up reading the magazine recalled that the advertisements were written "in a way that made them seem like pages that were not advertising."[44]

Shepard often wrote the poems or stories that appeared in the advertisements, and his efforts so pleased some advertisers that his work for Ivory soap and other products occasionally appeared in other children's magazines by "special permission" of *St. John's Book.* Shepard was not averse to taking material he had written for another venue and making it commercial. The poem used in an ad for Colgate & Co., for example, began life in a book and became transformed into an illustrated advertisement with the addition of the last four lines:

I like to watch my Daddy shave;
It's wonderful to see
How big and fine a shaving place
My daddy's face can be.

The shaving suds make mountains and
His big cheek makes a plain;
His razor slides into the suds,
And leaves a shaving lane.

Each side the lane the suds are high,
Like foamy ocean waves.
It must be fun to be as old
As Daddy, when he shaves.

I wish that I were big and old;
I'd shave with might and main,
And slide my razor through the suds,
And make a shaving lane.

When I'm a man I'm going to make
The soap suds high and thick.
My Daddy makes his shaving lane
With Colgate's Shaving Stick.[45]

Shepard asserted that letters came from children and their families who enjoyed reading the ads as much as they did the editorial stories. He would use such letters in *John Martin's Book* trade advertisements designed to convince the industry that his ads appealed to "little people, who never outlive early impression, whether these impressions be of a literary character or commercial."[46] To reinforce his assertion, Shepard borrowed from *St. Nicholas* in creating for his readers simple advertising puzzles whose solutions required the perusal of the advertising pages.

Readers were then invited to send back the puzzles, which had coupons stamped with advertiser names and addresses on their flip side, proof for advertising companies that the children and their parents had read the magazine's advertising. In return, young readers would receive poster stamps, bookplates, or other small tokens of appreciation for proving to advertisers that marketing in children's magazines paid. "It has always been said by Wise Acres that a magazine made for you Children is a poor place in which to put advertising," Shepard wrote in 1914. "... See if you can't prove to the Wise Acres that you are much more important than they have the old-fashioned habit of thinking you are."[47]

Not all of the "wise acres" in the advertising industry converted to the children's magazine viewpoint that advertising in children's periodicals paid during the early twentieth century. *St. Nicholas* and *John Martin's Book,* and to a much lesser extent *Little Folks,* carried pages of advertisements from prominent national advertisers such as Borden's, Knox, Kellogg's, Steinway, Sapolio, Procter & Gamble Co., and Colgate & Co. Yet their advertising page counts paled next to those of the popular adult magazines of the era, and the advertising industry scarcely noticed children as a target market in its trade literature prior to World War I, despite the persistent advertising in the trade journals by *St. Nicholas, The American Boy, The Youth's Companion,* and other children's magazines.[48]

"Advertisers do not, as a rule, look favorably upon young people's periodicals as advertising media, the impression probably being that the youngsters have no money to spend, which is true enough in the majority of cases," a *Printer's Ink* writer reported in 1899.[49] That may have been true, but children's magazines after the turn of the century exerted much effort within their pages to accustom children to paying attention to advertising, and much effort outside their pages to convince advertisers that their young readers had impressionable minds and constituted a large influence upon their parents' buying habits. "Talk to the Dictators of 180,000 Homes!" *The American Boy* exclaimed in 1910 in *Judicious Advertising.* Boys were buyers, the advertisement claimed, but, even more, they wielded "a mighty power over father and mother." And besides, advertisers could imbed in a boy's brain "impressions that you will continue to cash in on through that boy's youth and manhood."[50]

The advertising industry began discovering the youth market after World War I, the revelation coming perhaps not coincidentally after George Creel, the Committee on Public Information, and other wartime propaganda agencies showed how effectively children could be mobilized into action for a cause. The *St. Nicholas* advertising managers who had nurtured the magazine's advertising league for years would have cringed at the closing remarks of one 1920 article that noted that the "child market" was now just beginning to get the attention it deserved. "Perhaps," the author wrote, "some bright fourteen-year-old boy or girl will even show us a new and more effective line of advertising copy."[51]

Of course, some publishers and editors of children's magazines had been working for nearly two decades to prepare children to do just that. Capitalizing on their personal relationships with readers, the magazines had extended their editorial friendships into the advertising arena, using progressive-style pleas for cooperative help along the familiar editorial elements such as fiction, play, and instruction to help bridge the gap that had once separated children's magazines from what Morgan Shepard called "commercialism."

Ellen Garvey has argued that to conceive of a split between editorial and advertising sections is to falsely define the experience of magazine readers who consumed a publication whole.[52] If young readers indeed interacted with turn-of-the-century magazines in totality—as their letters to the magazines seem to assert—then efforts by publishers, editors, and, by extension, advertisers in the early twentieth century to place the new child-targeted advertising endeavors into familiar editorial frameworks became key in preserving an integrated experience. Their efforts promoted the construction of advertising as a "natural" part of children's reading well before the general advertising industry worked to do the same.

NOTES

1. For the rise of mass marketing, see Susan Strasser, *Satisfaction Guaranteed: The Making of the American Mass Market* (New York: Pantheon Books, 1989), and Richard S. Tedlow, *New and Improved: The Story of Mass Marketing in America* (New York: Basic Books, 1990). For an insightful overview of the relationship between advertising and magazines at the turn of the century, see Richard Ohmann, *Selling Culture: Magazines, Markets, and Class at the Turn of the Century* (London: Verso, 1996). For additional sources on the transformation of magazine financing, see, for example, James D. Norris, *Advertising and the Transformation of American Society, 1865–1920* (New York: Greenwood Press, 1990), 27–45; Stephen Fox, *The Mirror Makers: A History of American Advertising and Its Creators* (New York: William Morrow and Company, Inc., 1984); William Leach, *Land of Desire: Merchants, Power, and the Rise of a New American Culture* (New York: Pantheon Books, 1993), 42. Some of these studies draw on the magazine advertising history in Frank Presbrey's *The History and Development of Advertising* (Garden City, NY; Doubleday, Doran & Company, Inc., 1929) and in several volumes of Frank Luther Mott's *A History of American Magazines, 1865–1885* (Cambridge, MA: Harvard University Press, 1938). For a similar account of the transformation of newspaper financing, see Gerald J. Baldasty, *The Commercialization of News in the Nineteenth Century* (Madison, WI.: The University of Wisconsin Press, 1992). For a look at the culture of advertising during this period, see T. Jackson Lears, *Fables of Abundance: A Cultural History of Advertising in America* (New York: Basic Books, 1994).

2. "The Jolly Joker's Puzzled Pages," *Children's Magazine* (September 1908): 111.

3. Norris, 27–45.

4. Sidney A. Sherman, "Advertising in the United States," *Publications of the American Statistical Association* 52 (December 1900): 3–5; Norris, 27–45.

5. Frank Munsey, the well-known publisher of the famous *Munsey's* and an early advocate of magazine advertising, gave up on the children's magazine

Golden Argosy from 1883 to 1888 in part because of its inability to attract advertisers who wanted "money-spenders" and not dependent children. Frank A. Munsey, *The Founding of the Munsey Publishing House* (New York: De Vinne Press, 1907), 21–22. That the advertising industry and its trade publications largely ignored children as a target market during this period may be a factor in the absence of substantive discussions in standard advertising histories about advertising to children before the broadcast age. See, for example, Roland Marchand, *Advertising the American Dream: Making Way for Modernity, 1920–1940* (Berkeley, CA: University of California Press, 1985); Daniel Pope, *The Making of Modern Advertising* (New York: Basic Books, 1983); Michael Schudson, *Advertising, the Uneasy Persuasion; Its Dubious Impact on American Society* (New York: Basic Books, 1984). Strasser makes brief reference to historical advertising to children in her *Satisfaction Guaranteed.* In several of his many works on children's advertising and marketing, James McNeal overlooks early efforts when he asserts that children did not constitute a target market until World War II. See James U. McNeal, *A Bibliography of Research and Writings on Marketing and Advertising to Children* (New York: Lexington Books, 1991), and James U. McNeal, *Kids as Customers: A Handbook of Marketing to Children* (New York: Lexington Books, 1992). Stanley C. Hollander and Richard Germain assert that some advertisers did target children earlier in the twentieth century in their focus on the development of target marketing. See Stanley C. Hollander and Richard Germain, *Was There a Pepsi Generation Before Pepsi Discovered It? Youth-Based Segmentation in Marketing* (Lincolnwood, IL: NTC Business Books, 1992).

6. Charles E. Hires, "Some Advertising Reminiscences 1869–1913," *Printers' Ink* 94 (July 24, 1913): 17–24; Ellen Gruber Garvey, *The Adman in the Parlor: Magazines and the Gendering of Consumer Culture, 1880s–1910s* (New York: Oxford University Press, 1996).

7. Nathaniel C. Fowler, *Fowler's Publicity* (Boston: Publicity Publishing Company, 1990), 581–582.

8. Christopher P. Wilson, "The Rhetoric of Consumption: Mass-Market Magazines and the Demise of the Gentle Reader, 1880–1920," in *The Culture of Consumption: Critical Essays in American History, 1880–1980*, ed. Richard Wrightman Fox and T. J. Jackson Lears (New York: Pantheon Books, 1983), 39–64; Ohmann, 227–230.

9. R. Gordon Kelly, *Mother Was a Lady: Self and Society in Selected American Children's Periodicals, 1865–1890* (Westport, CT: Greenwood Press, 1974), 30–31.

10. Kelly, 3–4, 30–31.

11. Anne Scott MacLeod, *American Childhood: Essays on Children's Literature of the Nineteenth and Twentieth Centuries* (Athens, GA: The University of Georgia Press, 1994), 119; Martin Gardner, "John Martin's Book: An Almost Forgotten Children's Magazine," *Children's Literature* 18 (1990): 145–159.

12. Fred Erisman, "St. Nicholas," in *Children's Periodicals of the United States*, ed. R. Gordon Kelly (Westport, CT: Greenwood Press, 1984), 377–388;

Susan R. Gannon and Ruth Anne Thompson, *Mary Mapes Dodge* (New York: Twayne Publishers, 1992), 106–107.

13. "Announcement," *St. Nicholas* 27 (November 1899): 80–82; "The Closing Year," *St. Nicholas* 29 (November 1901): 82–83; Greta Little, "The Care and Nurture of Aspiring Writers: Young Contributors to Our Young Folks and St. Nicholas," *Children's Literature Association Quarterly* 17 (Winter 1992–93): 19–23; Gannon and Thompson, *Mary Mapes Dodge,* 124–126.

14. Beverly W. Talladay, "Little Folks: An Illustrated Monthly for Youngest Readers," in Kelly, 282–285; "Little Folks advertisement, *Little Folks* (September 1898): Little Folks Advertiser pages, not numbered.

15. See, for example, "Round-Rabbit Round-Ups," *Little Folks* (March 1907): 170a.

16. Anne Menzies, "John Martin's Book: The Child's Magazine," in Kelly, 234–239; Martin Gardner, "John Martin's Book: An Almost Forgotten Children's Magazine," *Children's Literature* 18 (1990): 145–159; Allan Harding, "John Martin Leaders Morgan Shepard A Strange Life," *The American Magazine* (August 1925): 24–26, 132–134; "Dear John Martin: An Interview," *The Playground* (November 1923): 454–455; "For Very Little Folk," *St. Nicholas* 38 (January 1911): 267; John Martin, "John Martin's Letter to You," *John Martin's Book* 1 (November 1912): pages not numbered; "John Martin: His Book and His Dream," business prospectus held in the Mark M. Jones Papers collection, Box 7, Folder 53, Rockefeller Archive Center.

17. Letter from Josephine H. King, *Little Folks* (October 1900): Little Folks Advertiser, page ii.

18. See Mott, vol. 2.

19. See Mott, vol. 2. See also L. Felix Ranlett, "The Youth's Companion as Recalled by a Staff Member," in *The Hewins Lectures 1947–1962* (The Horn Book, Incorporated, 1963): 85–104.

20. "With the Publisher," *Little Folks* (1912–1913), full-page column bound in the back of volume 16 with the advertising pages.

21. "With the Publisher," *Little Folks* (1912–1913), full-page column bound in the back of volume 16 with the advertising pages.

22. "St. Nicholas League Advertising Competition No. 112," *St. Nicholas* 38 (April 1911): 562–569.

23. See, for example, "Report on Advertising Competition No. 136," *St. Nicholas* 40 (June 1913): 20; "Report on Advertising Competition No. 137," *St. Nicholas* 40 (July 1913): 18; "Report on Advertising Competition No. 143," *St. Nicholas* 41 (January 1914): 22.

24. "Report on Advertising Competition No. 125," *St. Nicholas* 40 (June 1913): 20; "Report on Advertising Competition No. 137," *St. Nicholas* 39 (July 1912): 14.

25. "Merely Money," *John Martin's Book* 1 (November 1912): unnumbered page fronting advertising section.

26. "The Merchant Ship," *John Martin's Book* 1 (November 1912): unnumbered page at the start of the advertising section.

27. John A. Offord, "Merely Money," *John Martin's Book* 2 (September 1913): unnumbered page.

28. "To Mothers and Fathers," *Little Folks* (November 1898): vi.

29. James Playsted Wood, *Magazines in the United States* (New York: The Ronald Press Company, 1956), 272; Ohmann, 26.

30. "A New Competition for League Members," *St. Nicholas* 27 (October 1900): 1142.

31. See, for example, "The St. Nicholas League," *St. Nicholas* 27 (October 1900): advertising page 13.

32. See, for example, "Supplementary to announcement on page 285 of this issue of St. Nicholas." *St. Nicholas* 28 (January 1901): advertising page 13.

33. "St. Nicholas Advertising Competition No. 42," *St. Nicholas* 32 (December 1904): advertising page 22.

34. Lears, 94.

35. "Report on Advertising Competition No. 41," *St. Nicholas* 32 (January 1905): advertising page 16.

36. See, for example, "Advertising Competition No. 161," *St. Nicholas* 42 (May 1915): advertising page 28.

37. "Report on Advertising Competition No. 93," *St. Nicholas* 37 (November 1909): advertising pages 20, 22.

38. "St. Nicholas League Advertising Competition No. 137," *St. Nicholas* 40 (May 1913): advertising pages 18, 20.

39. United States Tire Company advertisement, *St. Nicholas* 40 (June 1913): advertising page 30.

40. Helen Damon-Moore, *Magazines for the Millions: Gender and Commerce in the Ladies Home Journal and the Saturday Evening Post 1880–1910* (New York: State University of New York Press, 1994); Untitled, *Printers' Ink* (February 8, 1905): 16.

41. See, for example, "Deciding the Advertising Contest," *The American Boy* (December 1913): 24.

42. "The Jolly Joker's Puzzle Page," *Children's Magazine* (February 1908): xii.

43. "One Thousand Dollars," *John Martin's Book* 2 (February 1913): unnumbered page.

44. Gardner, 151.

45. "The Shaving Lane" advertisement, *John Martin's Book* 5 (July 1915): back cover.

46. See, for example, "John Martin's House, Inc." advertisement, *Judicious Advertising* (May 1914): 106.

47. Untitled column, *John Martin's Book* 3 (March 1914): unnumbered page.

48. For exceptions, see "The St. Nicholas Competition," *Profitable Advertising* (March 1903): 873; Walden Fawcett, "Influence of Children Upon Sales,"

Printers' Ink (January 23, 1913): 33–38; "Boy Scouts as a Market," *Printers' Ink* (June 4, 1914): 74–77.

49. Untitled, *Printers' Ink* (November 8, 1899): 28.

50. "Talk to the Dictators of 180,000 Homes," *Judicious Advertising* (December 1910): 16.

51. Ray Giles, "New Methods of Merchandising to Children," *Printers' Ink Monthly* 1 (November 1920): 17–18. See also Wesley E. Farmiloe, "The Boy and Girl as Advertising Prospects," *Judicious Advertising* (May 1918): 85–88; Helen A. Ballard, "The Child Appeal as a Factor in Merchandising a Product," *Printers' Ink* (June 19, 1919): 93–96; Leonard Peake, "Advertising to the Grown-Up of Tomorrow," *Printers' Ink Monthly* 2 (January 1921): 80–87; Paul C. Hunter, "The Modern Pied Piper," *Judicious Advertising* (September 1921): 61–65; Don Gridley, "Ideas That Are Making Sales to and through Children," *Printers' Ink Monthly* 7 (November 1923): 31–32; Charles G. Muller, "Don't Overlook the Sons and Daughters of Mr. and Mrs. Consumer," *Printer's Ink* (May 21, 1931): 57–62; E. Evelyn Grumbine, "This Juvenile Market," *Printers' Ink* (July 19, 1934): 12, 16–18, 20.

52. Garvey, 3–5, 51–79.

8

LEARNING TO BE A WOMAN:
LESSONS FROM GIRL SCOUTING AND
HOME ECONOMICS, 1920–1970

Rima D. Apple and Joanne Passet

Increasingly, historians have been studying the importance of such popular culture as film, radio, and music in the lives of adolescents. Crucial but neglected in this creative research has been attention to the role of less dramatic but perhaps more pervasive print messages provided by the American school system and girls' social organizations. Girl Scouting and home economics classes represent typical experiences for girls in twentieth-century America. Between 1920 and 1970, millions joined Girl Scout troops—some stayed only a year or two, but many others maintained their memberships into adulthood.[1] At the same time, American girls often were required to attend home economics classes as a part of their primary and secondary school education. Common as these two parallel experiences were, we know little about them and the messages they conveyed to American girls about domesticity and citizenship.[2]

Textbooks served as the basic tools for students in home economics classes; in many instances their grades depended on a careful reading of these texts. Similarly, Girl Scout manuals explained the various aspects of Scouting and, most importantly, outlined the specific requirements for acquiring merit badges, the focus of most Girl Scout activities. Scouts would have read them very closely.[3] Hence, Girl Scout manuals and home economics textbooks reached millions of impressionable girls. Given the vast numbers who participated in home economics training and the Girl Scouts, analyses of their manuals and textbooks are critical to understanding of the development of twentieth-century American youth culture.

On the surface, Girl Scouts and home economics appear quite different. Home economics was a mandatory course of instruction in many school districts across the country; Scouting was voluntary. Home economics classes met in school rooms; Scouting activities occurred in a variety of venues, from church basements to Girl Scout "Little Houses" to campgrounds. Yet, despite these differences, home economics and Girl Scouting share significant commonalities. Both were obviously gendered. Girl Scouts enrolled only girls; merely a minuscule number of boys attended home economics courses before the 1970s when federal legislation mandated coeducation. Both also were undeniably moralistic and nationalistic, each overtly designed as a means of character and citizenship training. And, not surprisingly, Scouting and home economics emphasized domesticity for the girl and the future woman, a domesticity shaped, as we shall see, by the "needs of the nation" and often based on self-sacrifice. Most critically, then, both Girl Scouting and home economics consciously sought to prepare girls for their future as the women of America.

Singly and together, Girl Scouting and home economics sanctioned, sanctified, and reinforced a domestic image of the American woman. In the narrowest sense, she was responsible for the health and well-being of her family. But, as Scouting and home economics underscored, the definition of family and home included one's civic duty to promote the health and well-being of one's community and nation. Yet, Girl Scout manuals and home economics textbooks did not promote a static image of domesticity: three significant changes occurred between 1920 and 1970. First, the locus of domesticity fluctuated. At times there was a greater stress on the domestic role in the private family, while at other times there was greater emphasis on roles outside the home and within the larger community. Second, throughout the period of study, experts—typically medical experts—played an expanded role in defining and limiting the extent of girls' and women's domestic roles. Finally, a loss of autonomy occurred as girls' activities in both Scouting and the home economics curriculum called for less and less self-reliance. In its place, impressionable adolescents were taught to follow the directions of experts.

By the interwar period, both Scouting and home economics had become solidly entrenched in American culture. Home economics had grown out of the domestic science and cooking school movements of the nineteenth century. The Lake Placid (NY) Conferences in the early 1900s promoted home economics as a general science curriculum for girls. "Domestic science" or "household arts" textbooks of the period dealt almost exclusively with foods and cooking, suggesting that well-fed families would result in a productive citizenry. By the end of the 1910s, federal funding under the Smith-Hughes Act of 1917 had firmly established home economics in the public schools of this nation.[4] Many championed this course of study as the educational solution to critical social problems plaguing the United States in the early decades of the twentieth century. In a common justification of home economics education in 1919, Alma Binzel noted: "Much of what is unwise in the rearing of children is due to the indifference, the inertia, and the lack of insight that rise from unpreparedness for the responsibility. Each generation of graduates from the eighth grade and high school courses in home economics," she continued, "should increase the number of homes in which babies and children will have better chances of survival and health."[5] Such rationales helped generate support for home economics among politicians and school administrators, but at the same time changed the tone and content of this education for girls. They moved home economics from a general-education, science-based program to one more focused on the development of domestic skills, albeit domestic skills in the service of the community and the nation.

Other factors in the immediate aftermath of the war also fostered the development of a domestic-based, community-oriented home economics curriculum. For one thing, texts continued to emphasize patriotism and one's patriotic duty to strengthen the nation. Then too, the achievement of women's suffrage encouraged a broader outlook and reinforced the notion of civic maternalism. Passage of the Shepard-Towner Maternity and Infant Protection Act of 1921 distributed federal matching grants to the states for prenatal and child health clinics, information on nutrition and hygiene, and visiting nurses for pregnant women and new mothers. Spurring many women to action, it led them to become directly involved with state- and community-level social service agencies, dramatically demonstrating the powerful potential of maternalistic ideology.[6] Though patriotism, suffrage, and the Shepard-Towner Act more directly affected adult women, reverberations echoed in the calls for home economics education for girls. One of the earliest textbooks for the teaching of home economics made this connection quite explicit:

> With the declaration of peace, [home economics studies] assume a new significance and appear as an indispensable part of [a girl's] education. This is true because every girl needs instruction regarding better and more healthful living, and training in those practices which will enable her to live her daily life more intelligently, to rear her children more thoughtfully, and to serve her community and country more efficiently.[7]

The Girl Scouting movement was similarly affected. Juliette Low founded the Girl Scouts of America in 1915, patterning it on the overtly patriotic and nationalistic Girl Guides of England. These traits intensified after the war as the trends affecting home economics also influenced the Girl Scouts. During Scouting's early years, in which the organization grew slowly, Scouts consulted a manual entitled *How Girls Can Help Their Country* (1913), adapted from the Girl Guides' handbook, *How Girls Can Help the Empire.*[8] This handbook, which like home economics texts assumed that girls would grow up to become mothers, included a short section on the "Care of children" and listed "child nurse" as one of the badges girls could earn. This skill-oriented domestic badge, like many other badges of the era, required the Scout to take care of a child or infant, to make poultices, to do patching and darning, and to know how to test bath heat, use a thermometer, and test the pulse.[9] The 1914 badge requirements naturalized motherhood, encouraged girls to *do*, but not to *think through* the problems and questions of child care.

Following the war, the manual changed significantly as Girl Scouting became more popular (the number of Scouts increased by a factor of 10, from little more than 8,000 in 1917 to over 83,000 in 1921). Many of the same influences stimulating the development of home economics are reflected in the philosophy of the Scouts during this period. Low herself stressed the importance of patriotism in shaping Scout activities. In 1919 she proudly pointed to the Scouts' "Americanization" work with the foreign-born. "Girl Scouts found a very special patriotic service in teaching through Girl Scout troop work the ideals of American citizenship to the children of foreign parents," she said. "Older scouts took great pride in starting troops in foreign settlements, training the tenderfoot scouts and teaching them about American citizenship."[10] Clearly, Girls Scouts were expected to take their learning and activities beyond their homes and immediate neighborhood. As Louise Stevens Bryant, education secretary of the Girl Scouts, explained in 1921, "The object of the Girl Scouts is to bring to all girls the opportunity for group experience, outdoor life, and to learn through work, but more by play, to serve their community."[11]

Another important element shaping Scouting and home economics in the interwar period was the contemporary image of womanhood, an image shaped by strands of Progressivism and maternalism, an image in which woman had the power, and even more importantly the calling, to reshape and reform American society. Her greatest power resided in the home, where by applying her domestic skills, she would maintain a healthy, happy family. Success in the home, though, also commanded wider recognition because the nation's strength depended on healthy, happy citizens. Thus, by using her skills in the home, woman could improve individual as well as collective health and happiness.

Though a woman had the potential and the responsibility to create the conditions necessary for a strong citizenry, she did not always possess the necessary knowledge. A woman's success in the domestic sphere and beyond often derived from her ability to learn from scientific and medical experts. The tremendous explosion of advice literature emanating from commercial publishers and governmental agencies, as well as the growth of parenting education and child study clubs, shows that society believed this to be true.[12]

In the interwar period, Girl Scout leaders and home economists reveled in the possibilities of this powerful and educated womanhood, and enthusiastically promoted this theme in their publications. They stressed the importance of the domestic role, and recommended activities that encouraged girls to educate themselves with the most modern scientific information. Such themes were not new in the interwar period; nonetheless, they did receive increased emphasis—so much so that by the Twenty-fifth National Girl Scout Convention in 1939, the organization's slogan was "Half a million future homemakers." Lillian Gilbreth, a keynote speaker at that convention, most cogently illuminated the link between citizenship and domesticity when she described homemaking as "the biggest and finest job in the world because an adequate and happy family life laid the foundations for all happiness and adequacy elsewhere."[13]

The 1920 edition of the Girl Scout manual, *Scouting for Girls,* epitomizes the new model of womanhood, combining duty and self-sacrifice with domesticity, and insisting that in Scouting, girls and young women "are learning in the happiest way to combine patriotism, outdoor activities of every kind, skill in every branch of domestic science and high standards of community service."[14] Even such mundane household tasks as sewing, darning, and cooking, this manual emphasized, are important and should be done responsibly and cheerfully. To make this point most definitively, the manual reminds Scouts that the famous author Louisa Alcott was accomplished in "all the homely, helpful things that neighbors and families did for each other in New England towns." Alcott, it suggests, was an altruistic paragon to be emulated. "And let every Scout who finds housework dull, and feels that she is capable to bigger things, remember this," the manual read. "The woman whose books for girls are more widely known than any such books ever written in America, had to drop the pen, often and often, for the needle, the dishcloth and the broom."[15]

The themes of domesticity and female self-sacrifice are traditional enough to hearken back to a nineteenth-century example, yet the methods recommended are modern. Household chores will take less time when the girl learns the "scientific, business-like way" to accomplish them "with the quickest, most efficient methods, just as any clever business man manages his business."[16] Thus, by marrying traditional roles with modern methods, the 1920 Scout manual simultaneously and subtly denigrates women's ways and elevates those associated with men.

The manual continues to reinforce the idea of female as traditional and male as modern in its discussion of badge requirements, which often involve modern, scientifically informed domestic tasks. Household Economics, for example, will be "the great general business and profession of women, if it is raised to the level or [sic] the other great businesses and professions, and managed quickly, efficiently and economically, [and] will cease to be regarded as drudgery and take its real place among the arts and sciences."[17]

Similarly, the discussion on child care values contemporary medically sanctioned practices over women's traditional experiences. Consequently, there is an emphasis on the careful scheduling of the child and on early toilet training. In order to earn the Child Nurse badge in 1920, a Scout has to care for a child under two for at least two hours a day for four weeks (a minimum of fifty-six hours). During this time, she has to handle all the necessary work for routine care, including feeding, bathing, and dressing. Other required activities for the badge are more "academic": the Scout is expected to answer questions such as "How can a baby be encouraged to move itself and take exercise?" Several reference books are listed, but answers to all these questions are included in the manual's discussion of child care. Of greater consequence to this study, however, is the clear expectation that by 1920 the Scout should *think* about why she does certain things with an infant. Thus, these badge requirements are in stark contrast to the earliest requirements for a child care badge. A Girl Scout earning a child care badge after the war is expected to have hands-on experience with a child *and* to demonstrate her ability in problem solving.

An examination of the 1920 manual reveals several reasons for this greater emphasis on cognitive training. As in the earlier manual, there is the traditional, gendered assumption that some day each Scout would have a home and family of her own to tend. Her education and activities as a Scout will make her a better wife and mother. But earning such domestically oriented badges also promises her influence beyond the narrow confines of her individual home. All Scouts should consider working towards a merit badge in homemaking, the manual advises, because "Every Girl Scout knows that good homes make a country great and good; so every woman wants to understand home-making."[18] Moreover, such practical knowledge "will add to the efficiency and happiness of the nation ... the women of today have a better chance to control these things than ever before."[19] The nation needed successful homes. Over and over again, the 1920 manual insists that women play a pivotal role in the health of the nation; it clearly draws the connection between a girl's Scouting activities and her future role of homemaker and mother.

The emphasis on learning by doing, especially in relation to child care, persists in the 1929 edition of the Girl Scout manual, as does the connection between family and nation. Thus, Scouts are reminded that "There always are and always will be children to be taken care of. There is no way in which a girl can help her country better than by fitting herself to understand the care of children."[20] To earn the Child Nurse badge, a Scout still needs to demonstrate that she can independently and responsibly care for a child, but by 1929 the child can be older (any age up to five) and the period of care is reduced from fifty-six hours during one month to twenty-four hours spread over three months. Still, the Scout is expected to "perform all the necessary work covering daily care of a child, including feeding, bathing, dressing, preparing for bed, arranging bed and windows, amusing, giving fresh air and exercise, and so forth." She again has to exhibit her knowledge of the rationale for these tasks. One of the activities, for example, requires her to "bring a chart or a poster, which you have drawn or made of pictures you have cut out, showing the foods suitable for a child up to five years of age." While this version of the child care badge demands less in the way of "academic" knowledge, the Scout learns by doing and by being responsible. Other badge requirements are more creative and active, requiring the Scout to plan and give a party with games and refreshments for a group of children.

In many respects, the widely read home economics textbooks of the period mirror Girl Scout manuals. Not surprisingly, they emphasize a woman's domestic responsibilities, including child care. And they make the assumption, sometimes tacit, sometimes expressed, that girls will manage homes in the future. Home economics courses provided the most explicit preparation for this vision of domestic womanhood, and these texts, like Girl Scout manuals, connect the health of the home and family to the health of the nation. In other words, they stress that the well-being of the United States rests on the shoulders of American womanhood. As *Problems in Home Living,* a textbook published in 1929 for junior high students, explains: "To the extent home standards are high, the standards of the nation are raised."[21]

These textbooks, however, differ from Girl Scout manuals in one very significant respect. Home economists were at the forefront of the movement to bring modern science into the American household. Accordingly, home economics texts elevate with greater vigor than Girl Scout manuals the need for scientific knowledge and training based on science. They embrace women's traditional domestic responsibilities but assert that "to meet these responsibilities requires knowledge of nutrition, health, social relations, and the allied sciences as well as devotion and a spirit of sacrifice."[22] Many of the details of child care are similar in the two genres, but home economics textbooks provide more frequent scientific or medical rationale for their instructions. In their 1929 textbook, *Care and Training of Children,* Goodspeed and Johnson articulate girls' and women's need for this modern information. For them, the proof of appropriate child care is the creation of a "good citizen." In order to do this, the mother must be "guided by the latest knowledge and most approved skill that those who have spent their lives studying methods of infant care are able to suggest to us."[23] Breast-feeding, for example, is usually touted in textbooks, manuals, and many other forums of American society at this time. But home economics texts are more likely to justify maternal nursing with the expert-based rationale: "all doctors agree that the most satisfactory way to feed the baby is by nature's method."[24] Though rarely impugned directly, women's experiential knowledge slowly is being replaced by scientific and medical expertise.

Home economics textbooks and Girl Scout manuals also differ in the area of projects required. Both underscore the importance of hands-on learning, but to earn a child care badge, a Scout has to care for a child by herself for a specific period of time. In contrast, home economics textbooks employ demonstrations, removing the student from a position of responsibility and making the educational process more didactic and less experiential. Goodspeed and Johnson encourage the home economics teacher to find a child who can visit with the class an hour or two a week for "supervised play," a far cry from the critical role the Scout was expected to assume in order to earn a child care badge. Similarly, by the late 1920s and early 1930s, the discussion of bathing in home economics texts takes on a very different tone. Students are instructed about the best ways to prepare the materials needed for the baby's bath, but a mother or school nurse does the actual bathing while girls are restricted to practicing on baby dolls in the classroom.

By the late 1920s and early 1930s, both home economics textbooks and Girl Scout manuals began promoting a more narrowly defined image of womanhood. Girls still read about domesticity and self-sacrifice, but those texts instruct them "to like dishwashing and carrot cleaning because they are details of a whole which is interesting and charming."[25] Texts and manuals urge young women to learn all they can about modern homemaking and child care so they can assist their beleaguered mothers. As the 1936 text, *A Girl's Problems in Home Economics,* describes the modern mother:

> She gets up before the rest of the family, prepares breakfast, sends the child off to school and father off to work, takes care of the baby, cleans up the breakfast dishes, does a little necessary laundry, does the day's marketing, gets lunch, clears up the luncheon dishes, prepares the baby's lunch, does a little ironing while the baby sleeps, does some necessary sewing, takes the baby out of doors, prepares dinner, feeds the baby and puts him to bed, serves dinner, and sits down after this meal with her mending basket too tired to talk.[26]

What is a girl to take from this bleak description? Authors of this and other texts of the period recommend that she study her mother's life and learn where she can assist her best, for instance, by helping prepare breakfast or dinner, or by doing some of the shopping. One student assignment takes little note of the Depression and instead cultivates the consumerist side of modern homemaking. "Talk over with mother the problem of equipping the kitchen with labor-saving devices," the text advised. "List the ones you both think would add leisure and save physical work. Gather information as to kinds, costs, and expected results of various kinds. Call a family council and see if you can not contrive a plan whereby you will be enabled to purchase the desired machine."[27] The rhetoric and pedagogical activities in home-economic texts of the 1930s have narrowed significantly from those promoted in earlier books. Increasingly, domesticity is confined to the home.

In other aspects as well, these texts describe a changed world with altered expectations for girls. With greater insistence, they teach the importance of cooperation in the home. When this theme appeared in earlier publications it represented one arena among several; now it often is presented to the exclusion of other venues. In the same manner, the sphere of child care is more restrictive. Chapters on child care describe the part students can play in helping with younger siblings. Again, focus is restricted almost exclusively to the family. Moreover, the shift from experiential to didactic learning is accelerated. In the home economics textbooks, few if any exercises involve actually caring for a child. Instead they may recommend that the student visit baby shops and examine the ready-to-wear garments on sale there. Whereas earlier home economics textbooks, and particularly Girl Scout manuals, exalted a girl's childcare responsibilities and required girls to care for infants and children independently, texts published a decade later imply that girls are incapable of that responsibility. This change is vividly illustrated when one contrasts the badge requirements in 1920, when a girl had to care for a child for two hours a day for four weeks, with an admonition appearing in a 1933 home economics textbook:

> ... the schoolgirl should not try to assume much responsibility for [young infants]. She can help most probably by finding out what is the baby's schedule and doing all she can to prevent this schedule from being broken. She may help in such things as selecting the clothing for the baby, wheeling it out in the air and sunshine, avoiding disturbing the baby while asleep, and making its bed. The actual handling of the baby should be done by her mother or the nurse.[28]

No longer is a girl expected to demonstrate her abilities. In fact, she is blocked from providing direct physical care.

At the same time, the value of experiential learning is devalued and the role of scientific and medical experts is enhanced. One author in 1942 went so far as to insinuate that students who learn modern scientific methods should correct ignorant mothers. "A mother singing a lullaby while rocking her child to sleep is a picture of mother love often described in poetry and song," she advised. "But modern science teaches that rocking and singing a baby to sleep makes much work for the mother, so for her sake and for the child's sake as well [it] should be left out of the baby's routine."[29] Such texts tell students consistently that the physician knows best as they direct students to authoritative literature.

The Girl Scout manuals of the early 1930s depict girls as capable of becoming modern, scientific homemakers. As in home economics texts, Scouts are expected to learn appropriate child care methods from doctors and nurses and to become conscientious mothers. But Scouts also are expected to be actively involved in child care. The 1929 child care badge requirements stipulate that the Scout care for a child under five years for a minimum of twenty-four hours over a three-month period. Moreover, she must assume responsibility for all the necessary work of daily care, such as feeding, bathing, dressing, and so forth.

For many more years, direct child care remained an important activity for girls interested in this badge. Nonetheless, the growing influence of medical practitioners in baby and child care is evident in both home economics textbooks and Girl Scout manuals by the end of the 1930s. The 1940 requirements again specify a minimum of twenty-four hours of care over a three-month period. Now, however, Scouts should only "be responsible for the care that the baby's doctor feels you can safely assume."[30] Just as the information about child care should come from physicians—undercutting female experiential learning, so too should permission to care for children come from a medical practitioner—not the mother. By the end of the decade, the requirement that a Scout be responsible for the daily care of a child had been dropped. In order to earn the child care badge, she needs a doll to demonstrate how to bathe, dress, and feed a baby. A similar elevation of the physician's role as advice giver is seen in home economics texts of the period.

The growing expectation that women and girls should accept professional direction is only one aspect of the changing idealization of womanhood and girlhood presented in this literature by mid-century. While a girl's knowledge of homemaking and child care continues to be touted for its benefits to family and the larger community, it is applauded also as an avenue for self-discovery. Now, the motives for studying child care are very different. As one home economics text argues in 1941, a girl can gain "considerable understanding of herself" through the study of children.[31] In addition, learning about children would enable her to care more responsibly for her younger siblings, a traditional argument for instructing girls in child care. "Then, too, in many localities caring for children is one of the chief sources of income for girls," explain Laitem and Miller in *Experiences for Homemaking*.[32] By the 1940s, one reaches outside the home for financial benefits, to babysit. Initially, girls were expected to learn how to care for children for the sake of the larger community, out of self-sacrifice; in the literature of the 1940s, the motivation becomes self-enhancement and monetary rewards.[33]

By the 1950s and 1960s, these trends are firmly established in home economics and Girl Scout publications. The 1953 *Girl Scout Handbook* sums it up best. "Homemaking is an art, a profession, and a business for every girl and woman," the manual reports. "Art and science have given us certain tools, skills, and devices which will prepare you to run your home happily and well."[34] It is important to learn these skills from experts. This change in emphasis is clearly seen in the new requirements for a child care badge. The Scout is no longer a responsible caretaker of a young child, rather she is expected to "help an adult care for a child for a whole day."[35] Moreover, the child care section now provides detailed information on babysitting and being a responsible sitter. Home economics textbooks of the late 1950s and 1960s exhibit a similar focus; often the chapters on child care in home economics textbooks deal exclusively with the issue of babysitting.

This examination of home economics textbooks and Girl Scout manuals makes clear how the role envisioned for American girls and women changed in the middle decades of this century. During the years under consideration, American girlhood and womanhood were inexorably intertwined with domesticity; yet, their authority in that sphere was severely compromised. Though the passage of years did not dim the importance of domesticity in their lives, the scope of their influence shrunk. The early decades applauded woman's power and encouraged girls to consider their wider domestic responsibilities in the public sphere; by mid-century, the focus had shifted to the private sphere and became virtually restricted to the middle-class nuclear family. Females remained responsible for the domestic arena, but increasingly they were dependent on direction from others. Over the century, the importance of medical and scientific experts grew as girls, and women, were increasingly directed to follow the instructions of physicians and other professionals.

Some may readily accept this analysis of home economics textbooks, but object that Girl Scouting did more than stress the importance of domesticity. After all, when most people think of Scouting activities they conjure up camping, backpacking, and water sports. Yet, despite that image, the overwhelming proportion of badges awarded in Girl Scouting from its earliest years have been in the domestic arena. As a matter of fact, the first badge ever awarded was for "child nurse."[36] Subsequently, household arts and health and safety accounted for over half of the badges awarded each year.

Clearly, Girl Scout manuals and home economics textbooks mirrored each other's image of womanhood and girlhood; these and other aspects of the movements suggest a close relationship between the two.[37] For example, Lillian Gilbreth, a leader of the home economics movement, also was a pivotal leader of the Girl Scouts throughout much of this period. The required child care projects in Girl Scouts and home economics both have elements that echo popular psychological theories, such as behaviorism. Passion about women's responsibilities reflect the rhetoric of the Progressivism and calls to patriotism that permeated much of American culture in the early twentieth century. Domestic tasks are taught in language similar to that of the efficiency movement and Taylorism. At the same time, the average family size is shrinking and the U.S. population is increasingly mobile. Historians need to address the relationship between these movements and developments in Girl Scouting and home economics in order better to understand the factors influencing the lives of American girls and women.

Moreover, this study of the rhetoric and ideology of home economics textbooks and Girl Scout manuals begs the crucial question of how effective this literature was in promoting its image of American womanhood. Definitive answers are beyond the scope of this essay, but preliminary data suggest a relatively good fit between rhetoric and practice. As noted above, badges in areas of domestic interest remained popular through the 1970s. Anecdotal evidence, such as reports about Scouts working at well-baby clinics, Low's praise of Scouts in the Americanization campaign, and articles about Scout troops sewing clothes for wartime orphans, hint that Scouts took seriously the guidance of the manuals.[38] Questions about activities of individual troops and Scouts, and the factors influencing their selection of badges and other projects, are yet to be explored.[39] Anecdotal evidence published in textbooks for home economics teachers and annual school reports suggests that students were imbued with the images promoted in home economics texts. Commented one high school student quoted in a 1930 home economics teacher's manual: "My observation and study during this [child study class] project will enable me to bring up other children in a way that they will be better physically, morally, and mentally, and will make them better citizens of their state, ready to serve their country."[40]

While both Girl Scout manuals and home economics textbooks naturalized the domestic role of women and girls, the meaning of domestic responsibility was not fixed. Moreover, it functioned on several levels simultaneously. One level was social and relational; the other, individualistic. Over time, the relative importance of the familial home and the wider social sphere for women's domestic work fluctuated. The interwar years saw an expansion of woman's domestic sphere from private home to world-at-large, but by the Cold War era much of the focus was on the isolated family unit. Projects promoted in Scouting manuals and home economics textbooks underwent significant transformation on yet another level. Initially, Scouts and students of home economics were expected to learn by doing, a hands-on approach that encouraged individual responsibility and independent action; in later decades, class assignments and Scouting activities centered more and more on observation, removing girls from positions of responsibility.

Girl Scouting and home economics education were parallel character-training movements in the middle decades of the twentieth century, linked by a mutual focus on the need to learn how to become effective home-makers. The pressure to learn appears consistently in Scouting and home economics literature from the interwar period through the Cold War. Learning, however, means different things in different periods: the education championed in manuals and textbooks shifts from developing skills through "learning by doing" to more didactic instruction and observation, from a focus on critical thinking to an emphasis on identifying and following authoritative sources. By the Cold War era, texts taught girls how to be successful babysitters by heeding the advice of experts.[41] Thus, these changes in the rhetoric surrounding the image of educated girlhood provide us with an important window for studying the transformation of the idealization of American womanhood in the rapidly changing middle decades of the twentieth century.

NOTES

1. Juliette Low formed the first girl guide units in America in 1912, in 1913 she worked for the establishment of a national organization, and in 1915 it became known as the Girl Scouts of America.

2. Several historians have explored the gendered messages Scouting conveyed to American girls, comparing early Girl Scout and Boy Scout manuals, and deconstructing the content of Scouting novels for girls. See Laureen Tedesco, "Making a Girl into a Scout: Americanizing Scouting for Girls," in *Delinquents and Debutantes: Twentieth-Century American Girls' Cultures*, ed. Sherrie A. Inness (New York: New York University Press, 1998), 19–39; Rebekah E. Revzin, "American Girlhood in the Early Twentieth Century: The Ideology of Girl Scout Literature, 1913–1930," *Library Quarterly* 68 (July 1998): 261–275; and Sherrie Inness, "Girl Scouts, Camp Fire Girls, and Woodcraft Girls: The Ideology of Girls' Scouting Novels, 1910–1935," in *Nancy Drew and Company: Culture, Gender, and Girls' Series*, ed. Sherrie A. Inness (Bowling Green, OH: Bowling Green State University Popular Press, 1997).

3. The Girl Scouts also produced another publication, a journal entitled *The American Girl*. We have not included it in this study for several reasons. First, the publication was not required reading for Girl Scouts, and in its early years it reached only a relatively small number of Scouts. Second, by the mid-1920s, though the magazine continued under the auspices of the Girl Scout organization, it was conducted as a separate *commercial* publication, its subscription was voluntary, and it was not tied as closely to Girl Scout activities. Because of our focus on required reading, we have not included Scouting novels in this essay.

4. Rima Apple, "Liberal Arts or Vocational Training? Home Economics for Girls," in *Re-thinking Home Economics*, ed. Sarah Stage and Virginia B. Vincenti (Ithaca, NY: Cornell University Press, 1997), 79–95.

5. Alma L. Binzel, "For the Homemaker: Making Children Worth While," *Journal of Home Economics* 11 (January 1919): 28.

6. Molly Ladd-Taylor, *Mother-Work: Women, Child Welfare, and the State, 1890–1930* (Urbana, IL: University of Illinois Press, 1994); and Seth Koven and Sonya Michel (eds.), *Mothers of a New World: Maternalist Politics and the Origins of Welfare States* (New York: Routledge, 1993).

7. Anna M. Cooley (et al.), *Teaching Home Economics* (New York: Macmillan, 1919), vii.

8. *75 Years of Girl Scouting* (New York: Girl Scouts of the United States of America, 1986), 10.

9. W.J. Hoxie, *How Girls Can Help Their Country* (New York: Knickerbocker Press, 1913), 86–89, 130.

10. Juliette Low, "Girl Scouts as an Education Force," Bulletin, 1919, No. 33, Department of the Interior, Bureau of Education (Washington, D.C.: Government Printing Office, 1919), 7–8.

11. Louise Stevens Bryant, "Education Work of the Girl Scouts," Bulletin, 1921, No. 46, Department of the Interior, Bureau of Education (Washington, D.C.: Government Printing Office, 1921), 3.

12. For more on the push for educating mothers, see Rima Apple, "Constructing Mothers: Scientific Motherhood in the Nineteenth and Twentieth Centuries," *Social History of Medicine* 8, no. 2 (1995): 161–178.

13. "It Happened at the Convention: A Résumé of the Twenty-fifth National Girl Scout Convention, Philadelphia, October 23–27, 1939" (New York: Girl Scouts, Inc., n.d.) [copy located in the archival collection of the Girl Scouts of the USA, Inc., New York, New York], 3.

14. *Scouting for Girls: Official Handbook for the Girl Scouts,* 3rd ed. (New York: Girl Scouts, Inc., 1920), 1.

15. *Scouting for Girls,* 3rd ed., 24.

16. *Scouting for Girls,* 3rd ed., 25.

17. *Scouting for Girls,* 3rd ed., 105.

18. *Scouting for Girls,* 3rd ed., 106.

19. *Scouting for Girls,* 3rd ed., 105.

20. *Girl Scout Handbook,* rev. ed. (New York: Girl Scouts, Inc., 1929), 294.

21. Margaret M. Justin and Lucile Osborn Rust, *Problems in Home Living* (Philadelphia: J.B. Lippincott, 1929), ix.

22. Justin and Rust, 360.

23. Helen C. Goodspeed and Emma Johnson, *Care and Training of Children* (Philadelphia: J.B. Lippincott, 1929), 3.

24. Goodspeed and Johnson, 39.

25. Alice Mary Kimball, "Girl Scouts Play at Homemaking," *Journal of Home Economics* 25 (March, 1933): 196.

26. Mabel B. Trilling, Florence Williams, and Grace G. Reeves, *A Girl's Problems in Home Economics: Clothing, Home, Food, Family* (Chicago: J.B. Lippincott, 1931), 631.

27. Trilling, Williams, and Reeves, 627.

28. Mata Roman Friend and Hazel Shultz, *Living in Our Homes* (New York: D. Appleton, 1933), 21–22.

29. Carlotta C. Greer, *Your Home and You: Unit Course in Home Economics* (Boston: Allyn and Bacon, 1942), 267.

30. *Girl Scout Programs and Activities* (New York: Girl Scouts, Inc., 1938), 247.

31. Helen H. Laitem and Frances S. Miller, *Experiences in Homemaking* (Boston: Ginn, 1941), iii.

32. *Girl Scout Programs and Activities,* iii.

33. For an examination of the origins of babysitting after World War II, see Miriam Formanek-Brunell, "Truculent and Tractable": The Gendering of Babysitting in Postwar America," in *Delinquents and Debutantes*, 61–82.

34. *Girl Scout Handbook: Intermediate Program* (New York: Girl Scouts of the U.S.A., 1953), 349.

35. *Girl Scout Handbook* (1953), 476.

36. "In Memoriam: Elizabeth Purse Ellis," *Girl Scout Leader* (June 1967): 27.

37. Some contemporary articles that discuss similarities and links between Girl Scouting and home economics education include: Alice Mary Kimball, "Girl Scouts Play at Homemaking," *Journal of Home Economics* 25 (March 1933): 195–197; and Grace T. Hallock, "The Girl Scout Takes to Homemaking," *Journal of Home Economics* 22 (December 1930): 969–972.

38. Particularly useful would be a careful, insightful study of *The American Girl,* which was published monthly and thus would reflect more immediate environmental and situational developments, such as the Depression and World War II.

39. Historians have not yet examined the lessons troops learned when they met in "Little Houses" (houses and apartments designed as Girl Scout centers where Scouts could practice their homemaking and housekeeping skills).

40. Quoted in Treva E. Kauffman, *Teaching Problems in Home Economics* (Philadelphia: J.B. Lippincott, 1930), 65.

41. Our focus on the shift from the interwar admonition to help change the world to the Cold War concern with babysitting is not meant to deny that other aspects of Girl Scouting and home economics continued to encourage girls to reach out beyond their immediate environment. However, the fact that the sphere of child care narrowed from the world to the individual home points to a less integrative perspective on women's roles.

9

KATE CHOPIN AND
THE BIRTH OF
YOUNG ADULT FICTION

Bonnie James Shaker

Kate Chopin *and* the Birth of Young Adult Fiction.[1] I am reminded of the
need to clarify my employment of this common coordinating conjunction
by another scholar who acknowledges the many potential meanings of
"and" in titles.[2] Neither a compounding agent for singular nouns nor a sig-
nifier that necessarily communicates a coexistence between two separate
entities, the "and" in my title is intended to suggest an intersection between a writer and an historical occurrence in fiction, an intersection that
has been little discussed critically, and an intersection that, because of its
undertreatment, may be met with some skepticism.

Admittedly, young adult fiction is difficult to define as a genre, let alone
locate in origin. Caroline Hunt's nearly exhaustive literature review on the
topic is a lament "that virtually no theoretical criticism attaches to young
adult literature *as such.* Theorists in the wider field of children's literature
often discuss young adult titles without distinguishing them as a separate
group and without, therefore, indicating how theoretical issues in young
adult literature might differ from those in literature for younger children."
What Hunt foregrounds as a vacancy of independent criticism indeed
points to the problem of defining young adult fiction as a genre in and of
itself. Yet Hunt admits that such a genre exists, if by no other means than
through the institutionalized consent of those who study the problem, and
she reproduces their consensual knowledge when she hands it down to us
as received wisdom: "no one, as far as I know, seriously suggests that
young adult literature as a separate category begins before World War II
(Seventeenth Summer) or, alternatively, the late 1960s *(The Outsiders).*"[3]

Yet for all of her meticulous research, Hunt does not consider Barbara A. White, who argues persuasively that young adult literature became a stable, recognizable, replicated form some twenty years earlier. In defining young adult fiction as a genre, White quotes James Johnson as saying, "The psychological climate of adolescence itself [must be] treated extensively," in order for a text to be considered young adult fiction. Additionally, White refers to W. Tasker Witham, who claims: "It was not until about 1920 that there began a general trend among American novelists to consider seriously and sympathetically the wide range of problems that may be considered primarily pertinent to adolescents."

Thus, White herself concludes that "The novel of adolescence followed closely upon two developments: the emergence in the late nineteenth and early twentieth centuries of a new stage of life, a period in which people in their teens are institutionally segregated from children and adults, and the creation of the concept of "adolescence" to explain and justify this period."

Focusing her study exclusively on "novels about female adolescence written for adults by American women," White concludes that novels of female adolescence, long ignored by early researchers of the genre, are distinguished by their heroines' "conflict over gender identity," or the struggles they encounter when faced with some rite of passage that moves them from a more gender-neutral girlhood to a female-gendered adulthood.[4]

Until we add the criteria of adolescent interiority (which required an authorial drawing of character not developed until the twentieth century) and the cultural understanding of adolescence as a distinctive life phase (generally attributed to psychologist G. Stanley Hall's *Adolescence*, 1904), novels featuring female protagonists from the eighteenth century onward, even those written by men, might qualify as young adult fiction. White, in fact, examines literary antecedents to heroines of "bonafide" adolescent novels for common patterns that help to explain the development of the young adult female novel, and finds them in Hannah Foster's *The Coquette* (1797), E.D.E.N. Southworth's *The Hidden Hand* (1849), and Louisa May Alcott's *Little Women* (1848), along with the short stories of regionalist authors Kate Chopin, Sarah Orne Jewett, and Mary E. Wilkins-Freeman.

Like White, I am interested in the literary antecedents to protagonists of accepted adolescent novels and what they have to tell us about the genesis of young adult fiction. Beyond her study, however, I am fascinated by the question of how such important literary "precedents"—fictional representations of older children on the brink of adulthood—came into being in the first place, prior to the construction, deployment, and accepted linguistic currency of a distinct life phase called "adolescence."

Consequently, I ask why young adult literature emerges within the culture of print as a full-blown genre on the heels of such late nineteenth century short fiction writers as Chopin, Jewett, and Freeman, and not such novelists as Foster, Southworth, or Alcott. This paper will address those questions in regard to one of the aforementioned authors, Kate Chopin. It will assert that ideological and market forces impacted the production and marketing of Chopin's fiction. It will further argue that, although a single case study, this kind of research has implications for the examination of other women writers at the turn of the twentieth century who engaged in constructing prototypes of young adult fiction, and thus deserves more attention by print culture historians.

To link Kate Chopin with the *birth* of young adult fiction, then, is a bold move, for clearly Chopin's writing is simply a step in the long process of development of English-language young adult literature representing white culture that began with Samuel Richardson's *Pamela* (1740). However, in choosing the metaphor of birth, I fully intend to invoke concepts of conception and delivery. Young adult fiction may have been conceived in the eighteenth century with the birth of its ancestor, the novel, but its gestation took much longer, and the form was not delivered until into the twentieth century. I will begin by confronting this seemingly unlikely connection between Chopin and young adult fiction's delivery.

Kate Chopin (1850–1904) is best known to us today as the daring author of *The Awakening,* that scandalous novel of 1899 that openly represented a white bourgeois woman's desires for autonomy and sexual fulfillment outside of the sanctified bonds of Victorian marriage. The importance of *The Awakening* as a subversive feminist text has come to define Chopin's place within the American literary canon, and the many narrative accounts of her novel's far-reaching effects—the furor it caused within polite society and among genteel editors, its banning from St. Louis' Public and Mercantile Libraries, Chopin's expulsion from St. Louis' Artist's Guild and the Wednesday Club, and her resultant despair that curtailed any further literary production—all have justified her inclusion in the canon on the strength of this single, ignominious novel.

However, such narrative accounts of Chopin's life and career have since been revised. More recent scholarship reveals that Chopin was just as often exculpated as she was excoriated by contemporaneous reviewers for *The Awakening*'s bold themes. Emily Toth convincingly demonstrates that *The Awakening* was never a banned book, nor was Chopin ever ostracized from her hometown's Artist's Guild or Wednesday Club; and Heather Kirk Thomas has cogently argued that when Chopin's literary production began to decline, she was suffering from ill physical health, not mental depression.[5]

Thus, while the myths surrounding *The Awakening* have served Chopin well in the effort to afford her recognition and respect within the academy, what has been lost in these early narrative accounts of her literary importance is the fact that, in her own day, Chopin was primarily known to and valued by her reading audience as an author of short fiction. Marketing her work first through periodicals, and then as collected volumes of short fiction in *Bayou Folk* (1894) and *A Night in Acadie* (1897), Chopin gained her national reputation as a short story writer, and was remembered in critical histories for some thirty years after her death for her accomplishments in the genre.[6]

Chopin was a short story writer by both necessity and choice. She wrote in a day when, as her predecessor Margaret Fuller observed, periodicals were the "only efficient instrument," not only from which readers could receive material, but also through which authors could disseminate it.[7] As a medium, the periodical was particularly hospitable to women. The attitudes Susan Koppelman expresses about the short story today—that it suffers from "a loss of status, currently being viewed by many in the literary world as an apprenticeship genre, preparation for fiction writers on their way to tackling the greater task of writing novels"—were under construction at the very moment Chopin was writing. This was precisely because Chopin's contemporary, William Dean Howells, one of the period's most influential magazine editors and main proponents of realism, was actively feminizing short story writing as he worked concomitantly to masculinize novel writing.

This construction of the short story as a gendered genre coincided with "the growth of the magazine industry['s] ... inexhaustible market for stories oriented toward specific audiences," so that opportunities for women's writing increased as venues for gendered writing—ladies' fashion magazines, family papers, and juvenile periodicals—emerged. Such market conditions lead Koppelman to conclude that "the fact that so many [women writers] settled on the short story as the literary form in which to develop their greatest skills had as much to do with the popularity of the genre and their consequent greater financial opportunities as it did with creative inclination."[8]

In the 1890s, when Chopin was writing and marketing her fiction, the term "woman writer" was close to an oxymoron. Susan Coultrap-McQuin, Anne Goodwyn Jones, Amy Kaplan, Mary Kelley, and Mary Ryan are just some of the scholars whose pioneering efforts have detailed how mid- to late-nineteenth-century ideals of white bourgeois femininity, such as privacy, domesticity, reproductivity, docility, dependence, and self-effacement, conflicted necessarily with the public, commercial, productive, active, independent, and self-promotive demands of writing and publishing fiction.[9]

However, periodical writing provided female authors with a facade behind which to camouflage any concerns that their writing might compromise their womanhood. Because writing periodical fiction allowed women to perform their work within the confines of their domestic domicile, it appeared that such work did not conflict with a woman's primary duties as wife and mother. Since such traditional roles were assumed to be a woman's first priority, periodical writing could be parlayed as a hobby along the lines of cross-stitch, which was effortlessly performed during leisured hours amidst much activity and interruption by family members. And such a "leisured activity" further allowed women to deny that any personal ambition motivated their doing it; some women even argued that they wrote in the name of some higher, public good.

"In an era when going 'out' to work represented a loss of status for women," Jane Benardete and Phyllis Moe observe, "writing was an acceptable occupation that allowed women to work in the home, while putting their education to use and turning their largely domestic experience to profit. In the post–Civil War decades," they continue, "the burgeoning list of periodicals for women and young folk offered such women a suitable market and the more talented among them found that writing was more rewarding in every way than telling stories to children, which, either as wives or spinsters, might have been their fate."[10]

One standard strategy women used to break into periodical writing was to begin with juvenile periodicals, the least-threatening and least-questioned venue of publishing for women because child care was a white Victorian woman's quintessential concern. Particularly new and unknown women writers published initially in highly acclaimed and widely circulating children's periodicals in order to garner a national audience, catch the attention of prominent adult magazine editors, and eventually break into other fiction markets.[11] As Jane Benardete and Phyllis Moe explain, these women "capitalized upon woman's traditional relation to children and the home. They were, in fact, ingenious entrepreneurs."

Kate Chopin was one such woman writer. In the thirteen years that Chopin was marketing her manuscripts (1889–1902), sixteen of the seventy-seven short stories she published were first printed in juvenile periodicals. Between 1891 and 1902, Chopin successfully placed one story in *Wide Awake,* four in *Harper's Young People,* and eleven, including her last, in the *Youth's Companion.*[12] She earned $787 from these magazines, a sum that made up over one third of her lifetime's $2,300 literary income.[13]

Thus, whether Chopin was doing so consciously, or whether she was simply following an established career path for women, juvenile periodicals served as her stepping-stone to broader literary acclaim. An incident in Chopin's career bears out the efficacy of such a strategy. When William Dean Howells, then an editor at *Harper's,* read Chopin's short story "Boulôt and Boulotte" in the magazine's companion juvenile *Harper's Young People,* he wrote her a personal note encouraging her to produce more pieces like it.[14]

Understandably, Chopin's juvenile periodical stories have been designated by some of the most respected Chopin scholars as children's stories. But there is evidence that the line between children and adult texts was less distinct for Chopin than it was in either the centuries before or after she was writing. Eleven of her stories originally published in juvenile periodicals were later included in the two collected volumes of short fiction published in her lifetime, *Bayou Folk* and *A Night in Acadie.* Significantly, neither of the volumes contains any notice by author or publisher that some of the stories therein were not marketed exclusively to adults.

Furthermore, Chopin's contemporary book reviewers seemed unaffected by the possibility that some of her short pieces were read by (or even intended for) juveniles. In his favorable article on Chopin dated August 1894, William Schuyler acknowledges without any reservations or annotations that among "the collection of twenty-three tales known as 'Bayou Folk,'" some stories originally appeared in the *Youth's Companion, Harper's Young People,* and *Wide Awake.* Schuyler describes the entirety of Chopin's work as sophisticated and cultured, claiming that it displays a "delicate and sensuous touch and the love of art for art's sake," terms that modern-day critics would be disposed to reserve for adult literature.[15]

In her highly regarded biography on Chopin, the third since Daniel Rankin's in 1932 and Per Seyersted's in 1969, Emily Toth, like the Chopin biographers before her, draws distinctions between Chopin's children's and adult texts. While Toth is one of the very few scholars to acknowledge that Chopin gained her national reputation by publishing in juvenile periodicals, she also writes that "Chopin—obviously chafing against the virtuous formula of children's stories—switched to writing adult stories in which she could portray the conflicts that most interested her: the problems of romance, independence, passion, and divided loyalties."[16]

Such a comment suggests a distinct demarcation between the time when Chopin stopped writing children's fiction and started producing adult literature. The problem with such an assessment is that it does not account for the fact that Chopin continued to publish in juvenile periodicals until the very end of her career, or that such conflicts described by Toth also appeared in Chopin's so-called children's literature.

Like the novels of female adolescence in Barbara White's study, five of Chopin's *Youth's Companion* tales make use of the theme of a young adult character's entry into gendered adulthood. "Aunt Lympy's Interference," "The Wood-Choppers," and "Polly's Opportunity" all center on dramas of young and single white females who must either face a downgraded social status by working for a living or lose their independence by opting for marriage. Similarly, "For Marse Chouchoute" and "A Wizard from Gettysburg" are each about teenage white boys growing up in the post-Reconstruction, Jim Crow South, who must learn to adopt the New Paternalism as a method of white male mastery over the variously colored underclass in order to maintain their social power and economic privilege.[17]

Thus, though Chopin clearly was restricted from portraying erotic desire in periodical fiction available to young readers, her juvenile periodical stories are indistinguishable from her other work in their tone, style, reading level, dialectic diversity, and artistic sophistication. As a result, it is difficult to establish criteria by which to distinguish Chopin's juvenile from her adult literature. For instance, although another Chopin story, "With the Violin," is a tale in the didactic, eighteenth-century children's literary tradition about a man who turns suicidal despair into worldly success after he has had a divine visitation on Christmas Eve, the story appeared in an adult publication, the St. Louis *Spectator.*

Similarly, although Chopin's "After the Winter" was originally purchased by the *Youth's Companion,* the *Companion* never printed it, and it eventually appeared in the *New Orleans Times-Democrat,* another paper with an adult audience.[18] The implications that this interchangeability of potential readerships holds for a reading of Chopin's fiction can be explored if we look at *Youth's Companion,* the periodical second only to *Vogue* in the number of Chopin stories it printed, and the periodical that was her single largest source of income throughout her career.[19]

Chopin's relationship with the *Companion* enabled her to have a national showcase for her work from the beginning of her career to the very end of her life. Chopin published her first *Companion* story, "For Marse Chouchoute," only eighteen months after she debuted "Wiser than a God" in the *Philadelphia Musical Journal* in December 1889; and her last two stories ever to find their way into print, "The Wood-Choppers" (May 29, 1902) and "Polly," published as "Polly's Opportunity" (July 3, 1902), did so in the *Companion,* just two years before she died.

Reasons why Chopin would want to see her work published in the *Companion* were many. Beyond the fact that, as a juvenile periodical, the *Companion* offered her the protection of a relatively safe and acceptable venue for public work and recognition, in the 1890s when Chopin was writing, the *Youth's Companion* was among the most widely circulating periodicals in the country, and possibly even the world.[20] Begun by Nathaniel Willis and Asa Rand in 1827 as a Sunday school weekly reader, the four-page weekly folio was a children's "companion" to one of the most important religious newspapers of the age, the Boston *Recorder.* But by the 1890s, the *Companion* had severed its somber Puritan roots; it averaged twelve pages per issue, was printed on high quality paper, and was beautifully illustrated.

After Daniel Sharp Ford and John W. Olmstead purchased the *Companion* from Willis and Rand in 1857, Ford took only ten years to buy out his partner. He then turned the periodical's initial 4,800 circulation into more than 500,000 by the mid-1890s. Ford accomplished this feat through the use of many methods. In terms of marketing, Ford was among the first editors to support his magazine's printing costs through the sale of advertisements in an effort to keep its subscription prices low. He further instituted a premiums system, whereby current subscribers received prizes for garnering additional subscriptions. But two other changes were just as important, if not critical avenues to the magazine's phenomenal success. First, he began to value a model of children's literature that more closely imitated contemporaneous adult fiction. By this move, Ford implicitly implemented his second change: he broadened the magazine's audience base to include the composite age groups and sexes of the entire Victorian family.[21]

Ford's endorsement of such fiction emerged along with a growing market of juvenile literature that was borrowing from and modeling itself after the most popular adult fiction of the day. From Martha Finley's *Elsie Dinsmore* (1867), a "girls' novel" imitation of the overwhelmingly popular adult domestic novel, *The Wide Wide World* (1850) by Susan Warner, to Louisa May Alcott's cross-genre novel, *Little Women* (1868), clear distinctions between children's and adults' texts were breaking down in the latter half of the century.[22] Following suit, then, the fiction Ford favored for the *Companion* appealed not exclusively to juvenile readers, but to a dual audience of young adult and adult readers. Child readers were accommodated with verse, riddles, and short, short stories on a separate "Children's Page."

Thus, regardless of its front-page profile as a *youth's* companion, the periodical was, in fact, marketed to a mixed audience of children, young adults, and adults, a deliberate strategy that gave it as much in common with the so-called genteel papers of the Gilded Age (*Century, Scribner's, Harper's,* and *Atlantic*), as with magazines more exclusively targeted at young readers (*Our Young Folk* and *St. Nicholas*).

The *Youth's Companion*'s marked success can be attributed in large part to this broad, mixed-audience appeal. Its fiction attempted to accommodate the interests of all members of the family, in part by including renowned authors and poets who were recognized by adults. Harriet Beecher Stowe, Elizabeth Stuart Phelps, Mary E. Wilkins Freeman, Sarah Orne Jewett, Alfred Lord Tennyson, Henry Wadsworth Longfellow, and Walt Whitman all wrote for the *Companion*.[23] Similarly, articles on such timely topics as science, health, the environment, education, politics, and current events, though tailored to a younger reader, were nonetheless authored by leaders in these fields, among them Theodore Roosevelt, Grover Cleveland, Booker T. Washington, Henry M. Stanley, Lillian Nordica, and P. T. Barnum.[24] In addition, advertisements for medicinal remedies, household and garden instruments, and male and female hygiene products clearly were directed at parents rather than at their children.

Furthermore, the *Companion's* self-identification began to reflect its unique marketing strategy more prominently as the years progressed. The words "a family paper" began appearing regularly on a back-page editorial statement in 1865. The phrase appeared again as a subtitle on page six of each issue in the mid-1890s, and then, finally, as part of the masthead in 1903. Thus, editor Ford continued to increase the *Companion's* circulation not only by attracting new generations of subscribers, but by retaining previous ones who, though having outgrown an exclusively juvenile market, nonetheless appreciated a paper "for all the family."

Chopin's fiction published in the *Companion* embodied this mixed-audience appeal. It belonged primarily to the genre of the family story, a short story version of the popular adult female domestic novel, which, like the novel, represented characters of various ages and both sexes in a domestic setting.[25] But her fiction occasionally featured the middle ground of that age span, what we recognize today as the young adult, by addressing the concerns specific to older girls and boys on the brink of adulthood. Because her fiction's sophisticated reading level required at least a teen-age, if not adult, reader, Chopin's *Youth's Companion* texts were never exclusively children's stories, but rather, cross-audience pieces that were suitable for older children and adults, alike.

It is this exclusion of the child character and child reader and focus on the intermediate-to-adult character and reader, or adolescent, that I believe positions Chopin as a writer on the cusp of young adult fiction. A reading, writing, and decision-making "subject," Chopin, was, herself, nonetheless subject to representation through contemporaneous discursive and cultural practices.[26] Her choice to author a particular type of fiction, then, is a measure of both her cultural circumscription as a woman writer and her ambition. In order to live within such contradiction, Chopin fashioned herself into a seasoned veteran of the periodical marketplace, honing her writing skills in such a way as to maximize the commercial opportunities available for her fiction.

Through scholarly recognition of this kind, we can begin to see how young adult fiction arises within the culture of print from considerations other than the literary. By representing her adult concerns in young adult bodies, Chopin blanketed the publication markets of both adult and juvenile magazines, creating better odds for placing her fiction. By targeting that period between childhood and adulthood as a moment of dramatic conflict, Chopin contributed to the narrative construction of adolescence by coding concerns specific to that age group as watershed moments. And by representing fictionally this period of development as a distinctive life phase, she articulates young adulthood as such, hailing the identity of the young adult into being and inadvertently constructing a readership who can identify with it. Thus, it is through more than purely aesthetic intent that Chopin de facto contributed to the birth of young adult literature and its entrance into print culture history.

NOTES

1. The author wishes to thank the University of Iowa Press for granting permission to reprint portions of this essay, which was originally published in "Kate Chopin and the Periodical: Revisiting the Re-Vision," in *The Only Efficient Instrument: American Women Writers and the Periodical, 1837–1916*, ed. Susan Alves and Aleta Cane (Iowa City, IA: University of Iowa Press, 2001), 78–91.

2. See a brief discussion of the "and" in Juliet Mitchell's "Psychoanalysis and Feminism" in *The Daughter's Seduction: Feminism and Psychoanalysis*, ed. Jane Gallop (Ithaca, NY: Cornell University Press), 1, 14.

3. Caroline Hunt, "Young Adult Literature Evades the Theorists," *Children's Literature Association Quarterly* 21 (Spring 1996): 4, 5.

4. Barbara A. White, *Growing up Female: Adolescent Girlhood in American Fiction* (Westport, CT: Greenwood Publishing, 1985), xii, 5, 12, 20.

5. See Emily Toth, *Kate Chopin* (Austin, TX: University of Texas Press, 1990), Appendix III, "The Alleged Banning *of The Awakening*," 422–425; and Heather Kirk Thomas, "'What Are the Prospects for the Book?'" in *Kate Chopin Reconsidered: Beyond the Bayou*, ed. Lynda S. Boren and Sara de Saussure Davis (Baton Rouge, LA: Louisiana State University Press, 1992), 36–60.

6. See Edwin Anderson Alderman and Joel Chandler Harris (eds.), *Library of Southern Literature,* vol. 2 (Atlanta: Martin & Hoyt, 1909), 863–866; Fred Lewis Pattee, *A History of American Literature Since 1870* (New York: Century, 1915); Fred Lewis Pattee, "Chopin, Kate O'Flaherty," in *Dictionary of American Biography* vol. 4, ed. Allen Johnson and Dumas Malone (New York: Scribner's, 1930), 90–91; and Arthur Hobson Quinn, *American Fiction: An Historical and Critical Survey* (New York: D. Appleton-Century, 1936), 354–357.

7. Fuller writes, "The most important part of our literature, while the work of diffusion is still going on, lies in the journals, which monthly, weekly, daily, send their message to every corner of this great land, and form, at present, the only efficient instrument for the general education of the people." Quotation taken from Kenneth M. Price and Susan Belasco Smith (eds.), *Periodical Literature in Nineteenth-Century America* (Charlottesville, VA: University Press of Virginia, 1995), 6.

8. See Susan Koppelman, "Short Story," in *The Oxford Companion to Women's Writing in the United States,* ed. Cathy N. Davidson and Linda Wanger-Martin (New York: Oxford University Press, 1995), 799, 802. See also Amy Kaplan, *The Social Construction of American Realism* (Chicago: University of Chicago Press, 1988).

9. Susan Coultrap-McQuin, *Doing Literary Business: American Women Writers in the Nineteenth Century* (Chapel Hill: University of North Carolina Press, 1990); Anne Goodwyn Jones, *Tomorrow Is Another Day: The Woman Writer in the South, 1859–1936* (Baton Rouge: Louisiana State University Press, 1981); Kaplan, 65–87; Mary Kelley, *Private Woman, Public Stage: Literary Domesticity in Nineteenth-Century America* (New York: Oxford University Press, 1984); and Mary P. Ryan, *Empire of the Mother: American Writing about Domesticity, 1830–1860* (New York: Institute for Research in History and Hawarth, 1982).

10. Jane Benardete and Phyllis Moe (eds.), *Companions of Our Youth: Stories by Women for Young People's Magazines, 1865–1900* (New York: Frederick Ungar, 1980), 9.

11. See Koppelman, 801.

12. *Wide Awake* published "The Lilies"; *Harper's Young People* published "A Very Fine Fiddle," "Boulôt & Boulotte," "The Bênitouis' Slave," and "A Turkey Hunt"; and the *Youth's Companion* published "For Marse Chouchoute," "A Wizard from Gettysburg," "A Rude Awakening," "Beyond the Bayou," "Loka," "Mamouche," "A Matter of Prejudice," "Polydore," "Aunt Lympy's Interference," "The Wood-Choppers," and "Polly." Publication data taken from Chopin's Account/Memo Books, 1888–1895 and 1888–1902, Kate Chopin Papers, Missouri Historical Society, St. Louis. See also Per Seyersted,

Appendix, *The Complete Works of Kate Chopin* (Baton Rouge, LA: Louisiana State University Press, 1969 [1993 Printing]), 1003–1032. *The Complete Works* is generally accepted as the standard edition of Chopin's fiction.

13. These figures include ten stories that the juvenile periodicals paid for, but did not print. *Harper's Young People* bought, but never published "Old Aunt Peggy," as did the *Companion* with "A Red Velvet Coat," "After the Winter," "Madame Martel's Christmas Eve," "Ti Frère," "A Little Country Girl," "Alexandre's Wonderful Experience," "A December Day in Dixie," "The Gentleman from New Orleans," and "Millie's First Party." Figures are calculated from Chopin's Account/Memo Books. Also, see Toth's account of such events, *Kate Chopin,* 372–373.

14. Toth writes that the Howells note no longer exists. Ironically, Howells never accepted one of Chopin's subsequent manuscripts. See Toth, *Kate Chopin,* 192; see also Per Seyersted (ed.), *Kate Chopin: A Critical Biography* (Baton Rouge, LA: Louisiana State University Press, 1969), 54.

15. Per Seyersted and Emily Toth (eds.), *A Kate Chopin Miscellany* (Natchitoches, LA: Northwestern State University Press, 1979), 118.

16. Along with Toth's *Kate Chopin,* 183, 198, and 207, see also Barbara C. Ewell, *Kate Chopin* (New York: Ungar, 1986), 51.

17. I address the ideological work such fiction performs in Bonnie James Shaker, *Coloring Locals: Racial Formation in Kate Chopin's Youth's Companion Stories, 1891–1902* (Iowa City, IA: University of Iowa Press, 2003). See also Daniel S. Rankin, *Kate Chopin and Her Creole Stories* (Philadelphia: University of Pennsylvania Press, 1932).

18. See Toth's biographical account of this piece in *Kate Chopin,* 201, and 204–205.

19. *Vogue* published nineteen of Chopin's stories, though it only paid her a little over $200 for them. *Companion,* by contrast, paid Chopin $750 for the twenty stories it accepted, though it only printed eleven. Figures calculated from Chopin's Account/Memo Books.

20. With the exception of mail-order papers, the *Companion* outpaced other American magazines in 1885 with a circulation of 385,000; it fell behind *Ladies' Home Journal* and *Comfort* in 1890 with a circulation of 500,000; and it was fourth in line in 1895 with 600,000 subscribers. Although Richard Cutts' claim that the *Companion* had "the largest audience of readers in the world" in the 1890s appears unreliable against Mott's figures, Cutts may be correct in his suggestion that American family magazines in general enjoyed greater circulation figures than their contemporaneous European counterparts. See Frank Luther Mott, *A History of American Magazines,* vol. 3 (Cambridge, MA: Harvard University Press, 1938), 6; and vol. 4 (1938), 16–17; and Richard Cutts, *Index to the Youth's Companion, 1871–1929* (Metuchen, NJ: The Scarecrow Press, 1972), xiv.

21. Information on the *Companion* is summarized from Cutts; R. Gordon Kelly (ed.), *Children's Periodicals of the United States* (Westport, CT: Green-

wood Press, 1984), R. Gordon Kelly, *Mother Was a Lady: Self and Society in Selected American Children's Periodicals, 1865–1890* (Westport, CT: Greenwood Press, 1974), and Mott, *History of American Magazines,* vol. 2 (1938), 262–274.

22. *The Adventures of Tom Sawyer,* too, fits into this cross-genre category. Others have already observed that Twain himself was equivocal on the point, writing to William Dean Howells, "It is *not* a boy's book, at all ... It is only written for adults," yet stating in the book's preface, "Although my book is intended mainly for the entertainment of boys and girls, I hope it will not be shunned by men and women on that account, for part of my plan has been to try to pleasantly remind adults of what they once were themselves." Quoted in Peter Hunt (ed.), *Children's Literature: An Illustrated History* (Oxford: Oxford University Press, 1995), 239. My account of the emergence of children's literature as a genre is taken from the following: Anne Scott MacLeod, "Children's Literature in America from the Puritan Beginnings to 1870," 102–129; Julia Briggs and Dennis Butts, "The Emergence of Form (1850–1890)," 130–165; and "Children's Literature in America (1870–1945)," 225–251, all in Hunt, *Children's Literature.*

23. The same strategy is used today to develop popular, long-running children's television programs. *Sesame Street* is a prime example.

24. Mott writes that "many an adult liked the simpler manner which these great adopted for the benefit of the *Companion* readers." See Mott, *History of American Magazines*, vol. 2, 270.

25. See MacLeod's essay in Hunt, *Children's Literature*, 126–128; and Mott, *History of American Magazines,* vol. 2, 268, for discussions of the family story genre.

26. I take the pun on subjectivity from chapter one ("Representing Subjects Subject to Representation") in Ann Marie Hebert, "Straight Talk: Theorizing Heterosexuality in Feminist Postmodern Fiction" (Ph.D. diss., Case Western Reserve University, 1995).

10

READING NANCY DREW IN URBAN INDIA:
GENDER, POSTCOLONIALISM, AND MEMORIES OF HOME

Radhika Parameswaran

In her introduction to this book, Anne Lundin charts the historical and theoretical contours of scholarship on print culture for youth. She writes about the contributions of reader-response theorists to what we know today about the reading cultures of children and young adults in the United States. Reader-response theorists argue for the importance of studying readers' engagement with popular literature within the social context of their everyday lives. Since the pioneering work of literary feminist and reader-response theorist Janice Radway on women's interpretations of romance novels,[1] cultural studies in the United States has witnessed a boom in studies of people's experiences with popular culture. Scholars from a variety of disciplines including history, journalism, English, sociology, anthropology, and education have examined the impact of everyday material culture such as soap operas, fiction, talk shows, tabloids, and shopping catalogs on consumer's social identities.

While the recent academic attention to popular culture is a welcome respite from the earlier focus on high culture, much of the research that exists concentrates on Europe, United States, Canada, and Australia. It is only recently, with the appearance of academic journals such as the *International Journal of Cultural Studies,* that we have seen a strong commitment in cultural studies to research about popular culture in non-Western settings. In the current context of widespread consumption of global popular culture, it is important to pay attention to people's engagement with popular media in geographic areas that are not part of the Euro-American world.

Furthermore, the history of books, reading practices, and contemporary print cultures in the Third World have received little attention until the last decade. Because urban, cosmopolitan cultural formations in the Third World have not been the focus of the social sciences, especially anthropology, we know little about the production and reception of print media, which in many Asian and African countries are more common in metropolitan spaces. With respect to South Asia, cultural studies scholars have begun making inroads into the study of popular culture such as global television and audience reception of television texts.[2] However, with the rise in film and television studies, popular literature has receded into the margins.

The lack of knowledge about children's and youth reading in the non-Western world is thus part of a more widespread neglect of a vibrant print culture in areas such as South Asia where reading, writing, and the politics of literacy have been major forces in their colonial history and in the postcolonial experiences of modernity. At the most basic level, scholars still need to gather information about adolescents' and children's reading around the world. Apart from an empirical concern with recording basic data on reading practices in the Third World, more urgent questions that address historical and theoretical issues are: How has European colonialism and its impact on contemporary language use affected children's leisure reading in Asian and African contexts? Does the social formation of girls' gender identities in the non-Western world influence them to read fiction just as girls do in the United States? In a global era when mobile, diasporic populations from the Third World are traveling to and living in the West, how do memories of reading, youth, and childhood recall and constitute a sense of home? Do non-Western readers perceive Nancy Drew to be a neocolonial, global symbol of the United States' economic and cultural power?

In this essay, I explore answers to these research questions by analyzing interviews I conducted with a group of Indian women about their experiences in reading Nancy Drew fiction. At the time of the interviews, all these women were living and studying in the United States at a large Midwestern university. My qualitative research involved three stages: seeking out women's responses to an e-mail questionnaire, conducting personal interviews with selected women who filled out my questionnaires, and moderating three focus group sessions (five, six, and six women in each group) which included all the women I interviewed in individual sessions. Out of the thirty women who received my questionnaires, twenty-two responded, and seventeen of these consented to personal and focus group interviews. A qualitative, methodological approach seemed ideal for my study on Indian women's childhood and adolescent reading, because I wanted to capture the nuances, details, and contextual moments that surrounded their childhood reading practices.

The women themselves were fairly homogenous in terms of age, class, education, residence, religious background, and family structure. All twenty-two who participated were between the ages of twenty-two and twenty-eight. With two exceptions, they all grew up in large Indian cities such as Mumbai, Chennai, Bangalore, Calcutta, Hyderabad, Bhubaneshwar, and New Delhi. All had attended schools and colleges in urban areas where the medium of instruction was the English language, although they had also learned to write and read in at least two vernacular Indian languages. Twelve had attended private Catholic schools for girls, six had attended coeducational central government schools, and four had attended exclusive private boarding schools for girls. All were Indian citizens by birth except two, who were born in Zimbabwe and Kenya but attended school and college in India. At the time I conducted the study, all had lived in the United States for two to four years and were attending graduate school in various disciplines including history, sociology, engineering, pharmacology, chemistry, computer science, and business. Except for two women who were Christian, the rest were Hindu, and all who participated in the study were middle and upper middle class with respect to their parents' incomes and education. Of the twenty-two, eighteen women's mothers worked or had worked at some point outside the home.

My analysis of adult Indian women's memories of reading Nancy Drew books shows that pleasure in reading popular culture texts is experienced and understood *within* historical and cultural contexts, and that reading Nancy Drews was a social experience that involved explicit and overt mediation by parents, relatives, peers, and schoolteachers. Additionally, talking about their childhood reading of Nancy Drew books, as I will argue in this essay, was an avenue for these young women to express and experience nostalgia about "home" and India. Indian women's nostalgic framing of their childhood Nancy Drew reading as a memory about the "good old" days back at home presents an interesting and paradoxical dimension of our lives in times of diasporic modernity. What does it mean when non-Western people recount nostalgia about their homelands through their experiences of reading Western popular literature such as Nancy Drew books? What are the implications of such cross-cultural reading experiences for theoretical discussions about authentic and inauthentic postcolonial identities?

My curiosity about Indian women's childhood reading, especially their memories about reading Nancy Drew books, was originally piqued at a social gathering for international students at a small, private university in the Dallas–Fort Worth area in Texas. Attending the gathering as an international student from India, I found myself in a group of people where there were students from several countries in Europe (Germany, Sweden, and Norway), Africa (Kenya and Cameroon), and Asia (China, Japan, and India). The conversation within the group suddenly turned to our childhood experiences and what we did for fun as children. For many of us, reading topped our list of favorite activities. In the course of our conversation, I found that along with me, two Indian women from Bombay, three women from Kenya, and one from Cameroon had all read similar kinds of children's fiction, and we had all read and enjoyed Nancy Drew books in the English language, much to the surprise of the other foreign students from Germany, Japan, and China. This essay is an extended exploration of my initial curiosity about Nancy Drew reading as a postcolonial experience that is shared among women who were born and raised in the former British colonies in South Asia and Africa.

Despite her popularity among readers around the world, research on Nancy Drew's impact on girls' and women's identity formation has only recently entered the academic arena. Pointing to the multiple reasons for the neglect of girls' series books in scholarly research, Sherrie Inness writes: "Girls' reading has long been considered unimportant when compared to adult reading. Girls' series books have been quadruple outcasts from critical circles because they are written for young readers, are targeted at girls, are popular reading, and, even worse, are series books, which often have been regarded with disdain by literary critics."[3] Gradually, however, with the tide of interdisciplinary attention to popular culture and the entry of feminist scholars in the academy, we have witnessed a surge of interest in the Nancy Drew phenomenon.[4] Popular passion for Nancy Drews and scholarly interest in the economic and cultural aspects of Nancy Drew reading came together during the Nancy Drew conference in Iowa City in 1993. The edited book *Rediscovering Nancy Drew,* which contains proceedings from the 1993 conference, provides valuable information and analysis of Nancy Drew's popularity, including the production and publishing of Nancy Drew books, readers' perceptions and responses to Nancy Drew, and collectors' roles in archiving and recording knowledge on Nancy Drew.

Fortunately, research on women's Nancy Drew reading has critically examined Nancy's privileged, white, upper-class heterosexual life in the

United States, a powerful First World nation. As with many mainstream popular culture texts, which reflect and perpetuate hegemonic values about the meanings of gender, race, class, and ethnic identities, Nancy Drew books relied on dominant representations of marginalized people to accentuate and define the normality and wholesomeness of Nancy Drew's life and her identity.[5] Among the scholars who critique Nancy Drew books for producing skewed representations of non-white people, Melinda de Jesús' essay takes us outside and inside the U.S. context to reflect on Nancy Drew as imperialist fiction. She argues in her essay that Nancy Drew reading, for herself, a Filipina American, and for her mother, a Filipina, was essentially an experience that reinforced cultural imperialism, American colonization, and hegemonic Western feminism. My essay provides additional insights regarding the complexities of cultural imperialism and cross-cultural reading experiences by showing how girls in India negotiate popular literature from British and American culture simultaneously. In analyzing the implications of Indian women's Nancy Drew reading for theoretical debates about cultural imperialism, this essay demonstrates that our leisure reading practices are dynamic, lived phenomena that include capitulation *and* resistance to dominant discourses.

For many young Indian women, reading Nancy Drews represented welcome relief from the pressure of studying and doing homework as children. Although all the women spoke about their Nancy Drew reading as pleasurable, I was struck by the even stronger feelings of frustration most expressed regarding access to these books and the scant leisure time they had as children to read fiction. In seeking out women's responses to how they gained access to Nancy Drew fiction in India, I found that there were essentially five regular sources that they relied on: school libraries, peer and family networks, bookstores, private clubs where their parents were members, and private lending libraries.

Buying Nancy Drew fiction at bookstores or getting series fiction and comics as gifts were reserved for special occasions because these books were fairly expensive—about twenty to thirty rupees (sixty to eighty cents approximately) in the 1970s—and many women wrote that their parents could not afford to buy them Nancy Drew books on a regular basis. Birthdays and festivals were some events when women said they could ask for and expect to get books as gifts. Relatives who visited would also take women out shopping and buy them books. Five women wrote that whenever their fathers went out of town on business trips, they would bring back books for them as a special treat. During personal interviews, ten women described Nancy Drew reading as a part of their experience of relaxed summer holidays when they took long train trips to visit relatives around the country. Sharmila, whose strongest memories of reading Nancy Drews were connected to her summer travels, contrasted her busy and stressful life as a student in the United States with the quieter and more restful pace of her life in India:

> Those two summer vacations when I went through my Nancy Drew obsession were wonderful. My aunt who lived in the United States brought back several Nancy Drews for me. Usually, my parents would have bought me one or two Nancy Drews to read on the trip but that summer I had something close to seven I think. Those train trips were great. I feel like I can never get that part of my life in India back. It's gone forever. I feel no one relaxes in this country and soon I will be part of this hectic life.

For Sharmila, a middle-class woman whose parents were teachers, getting Nancy Drew books and other fiction as gifts was thus part of a seasonal pattern of summer vacations and family travel. Apart from three upper-class women who described the well-stocked libraries in their parents' private clubs, most middle-class women said that as girls they were constantly "on the prowl" to find Nancy Drew books. Motivated by the constant need for fiction during summer vacations, four women spoke about becoming entrepreneurs in their early teens, that is, starting small collections of fiction contributed by the neighborhood children to start a commercial library. Describing the small library she and her two friends supervised, Sudha said, "We called it the Cheery Chums Library. We collected all our friends' books and then charged a daily fee for book rentals. The fee was nominal and we got all the money for running the library."

Given the lack of public libraries other than university libraries and the high prices of children's fiction, lending libraries for all the Indian women who participated in this study were one of the main sources for leisure reading materials. Private lending libraries in India are different from the public libraries in the United States. Lending libraries in urban India are small, privately owned one-room stores, where only popular fiction, popular magazines, and maybe a few video and audio tapes are stacked on shelves, and there is very little room to sit down and read. The purpose of these libraries is for library patrons or members to walk in, quickly browse, choose what they want, check items out for a daily fee, and leave. The books themselves are rented out by the library owner (a small business entrepreneur, rather than a trained librarian). People become library members for a fairly modest fee and a deposit amount to cover missing or damaged books.

Adult Indian women's comments about their ritual everyday visits to these libraries to obtain Nancy Drew books suggests the difficulties these library owners had in fulfilling their young customers' appetite for reading. In her written responses about finding Nancy Drews at the local lending library in her neighborhood, Seema wrote:

> I read all the Nancy Drews at Anwar library during one summer holiday when I was in the seventh class [grade]. I remember a friend urging me to read one, *The Ghost of Blackwood Hall,* and I enjoyed it so much that I read the rest of them—eight books—in two months. I'm not a slow reader. I was reading other books too of course. And then I ran out and would be so hopeful every time I visited the library. My older brother always got frustrated because I would insist on looking at the same eight books every time to make sure I did not miss any new ones.

For yet another woman, memories of visiting the lending library in her neighborhood in Bhubaneshwar to borrow Nancy Drews were tied up with similar hopes and dreams of seeing new books. After being disappointed for months, she reached a point where she decided to talk to the library owner:

> I was very surprised. I was a shy child you know, actually very shy. My mother was with me that day. I spoke to Prabhu Uncle who owned the library. I asked him why he was not getting any more Nancy Drews. He said he had been to Bombay and could not find any that were cheap. I begged him to go back and said I would take care of the library when he was gone! I went to the back of the book I had just finished, I think it was *The Mystery of the Tolling Bell,* and asked him to find all the earlier books.

Two other women reported feelings of anger when they arrived at the library only to find that the new Nancy Drew books they had reserved the day before had not yet arrived. One of these women wrote that she had begged the library owner to call the patron who still had the Nancy Drew books to come right away and return them. Apart from two upper-class women who reported that the lending libraries in their neighborhood had a fairly good stock of Nancy Drews, most women remembered that lending libraries could not satisfy their desire for reading about their favorite girl detective. Despite these frustrations, for many women, their visits to lending libraries and their relationships with the owners of these libraries were experiences that recalled the personal and intimate quality of community relationships they had in India.

For instance, one woman in a focus group session provoked several responses when she said, "I used to nag my library chaccha [uncle] everyday about getting more Nancy Drews, but he never got upset! He would just smile and tell me to read very, very slowly because Nancy was special and deserved careful attention. He was a part of my life. It's not the same here—going to the public library." Other women reacted immediately to this comment and soon there were several stories that recalled childhood relationships with lending library owners. Unnathi remembered that the owner of the library in her neighborhood would often stop by her house to give her a new book because he lived very close, "His son and my brother used to play cricket together so sometimes he would bring his son over with him, and I was such a pest about bugging him for new books." Chethana, who was the last one to comment before the group moved on to a new topic, said, "Guru uncle used to embarrass me in the beginning when I started reading Nancy Drews. He would refer to me as the Nancy girl."

While small lending libraries with limited funds could barely keep pace with adolescent Indian girls' demands for Nancy Drews, school libraries that stocked many more Nancy Drew titles were guilty of allotting little time for fiction reading. Sixteen of the twenty-two women bitterly complained about the brief one- or two-hour library classes they had each week to visit the school library. Some women who attended private Catholic convent schools for girls wrote that during the library period, they were all marched down to the library, ordered to get their books, and then had to sit down quietly to read these books, which they were not allowed to take home. The policy of reading fiction during only these library periods meant that these girls often had to read a book in fragmented fashion over three or four weeks.

Erica vividly remembered that she started the book *The Clue in the Old Stagecoach,* "I read chapter one and was just beginning to get lost in the book when Sister Maria interrupted me to collect the books. I looked at her hard and asked her why I could not take the book home just this once. I actually held on tightly to the book and believe me, I was brave because nobody misbehaved with Sister Maria." Other women talked about how difficult it was to stop and begin reading Nancy Drew books over an extended period of time because each chapter built up to such a suspenseful end and left you hanging. Poonam, who ranked Nancy Drew as the favorite author of her early teens, said, "Reading a Nancy Drew was not like reading *Little Women* or an abridged version of some Dickens book, you know. I would try to read only up to the middle of a chapter in a Nancy Drew book so I could bear to leave and not wonder what happened to Nancy."

Complaining about the limited time allotted for fiction reading at school, one woman compared her busy and stressful childhood in India to young teens' lives in the United States. Drawing on her interactions with children, adolescents, families, and relatives who lived in the United States, she wrote:

> Even children in India work so hard and we have so much pressure to perform well in schools. Our teachers probably were told to make us do well on state board exams. Our school had a reputation for the highest marks on the state board exams. It's not like here, you know, where these children are so pampered. When I baby-sit here, I am shocked. The two children I baby-sit this semester play all evening and the boy is twelve years old!

Paradoxically, some women's memories of stressful teen years studying, doing enormous amounts of homework, and attending lessons with tutors were also tied to special and pleasurable moments spent reading Nancy Drew books. Several women wrote that they experienced intense pressure from parents to perform well in school. However, only one woman thought that this was unfair. Instead, for many women, their Nancy Drew reading felt all the more relaxing and fun because they felt they deserved it as a reward for being good students. Five women said that the promise of reading Nancy Drews in the summer holidays after their final exams in April helped them get through the days and nights of studying during the weeks leading up to the exams.

These women's framing of their childhood and adolescence as stressful, but that the stress was unavoidable, and their rationalization of the pressure that middle-class Indian parents impose on young adults to perform well on exams, is partly influenced by their current location in the United States. These new immigrants, who had moved very far way from home for the first time in their lives, recount memories of living in India through the filter of a somewhat uncritical and romantic nostalgia. In coping with the changes of living in a new environment, these women cast their stressful adolescence as a necessary recipe for success. It is important to note here that young Indian women's reluctance to criticize their parents during interviews and focus groups could also arise from my own position as an insider and the public nature of focus group settings. Speaking negatively about one's parents and family members in a group situation where we were all new to each other (and thus violating social conventions) may have been too uncomfortable for some women.

Some parents actively encouraged Nancy Drew reading because they thought it would improve their children's English literacy. Because these books were expensive, parents who wanted their children to read fiction to improve English language skills became members of a lending library; others asked their children to share Nancy Drew books with friends. One woman recalled that her mother had, in fact, been responsible for her interest in Nancy Drew books:

> My mother spoke to my best friend who was my neighbor and she went to the same school as I did. My friend used to read Nancy Drews and she always did so well in her English classes. My mother spoke to her mother and found that reading Nancy Drew books was helping my friend learn to read and write in English. Suddenly I found my friend pestering me to read Nancy Drews and when I asked her why she told me my mother had asked her to get me started on Nancy Drews.

Two other women said that their parents complained a lot when they asked them to buy comics and candy at the train stations during summer trips, but were willing to buy them Nancy Drew books or other series books even though these books were more expensive. These women also spoke about receiving Nancy Drew books as gifts from relatives and adult family friends because their parents had explicitly requested relatives to choose books as gifts instead of dolls, toys, and comics.

Another aspect of parental involvement in Nancy Drew reading pertains to parents' anxieties about the influence of television on their children's English-language writing, reading, and speaking skills. While the primary battle for parents revolved around the impact of television on children's homework assignments, a secondary battle, according to eleven women, concerned children relinquishing reading fiction for watching films on television. Shobana and Ritika reported that their parents, who had always criticized them for not paying enough attention to their homework because they were reading Nancy Drew fiction, were now suddenly upset when they switched on the television after school. Shobana remembered the tactics her mother had employed to motivate her to continue reading:

> My mother was really proud of my vocabulary and speaking skills in English. She felt that my Nancy Drew reading had a lot to do with my English and then when I started watching television she got nervous. She would ask me to invite a couple of my friends over in the evenings. She would then bribe us with all kinds of tasty snacks like samosas, pakoras, and chapatti and jam to get us to read together.

Ritika's father, who had been similarly concerned about the increase in her television watching, also attempted to discourage this behavior:

> My father hated us to watch TV. When we started watching TV, we stopped going so frequently to the library to get Nancy Drews and other books to read. My father actually spoke to Mr. Salim Khan, the library owner and the next time we went to the library, Salim Uncle told us that if we came to the library every other day to get books we would get every sixth book free! I only found out that my father asked him to do this two years ago when I went to say goodbye to Salim Uncle. I was leaving for America when I went to see him.

Preethi said that once television arrived in her home, her parents started taking them out more often to bookstores to buy books and offered to accompany her during visits to lending libraries. "I was so shocked to get three Nancy Drews at one time because I usually had to beg and beg for one," Preethi wrote in answer to my question about the Nancy Drew books she owned. My own parents, who also possibly had similar concerns, did not buy a television for a long time. I remember being the only person in my neighborhood in ninth grade who did not have a television at home.

These urban middle-class parents' perceptions of Nancy Drews as facilitating and supplementing English-language education provided at schools is not surprising given the emphasis placed on English-language skills in postcolonial India. The English language was introduced in India in the early part of the nineteenth century by the official machinery of the British colonial system for a range of complex reasons: to train urban Indian elites in the English language so they could assist in administration, to deploy English literature as a way of introducing a higher form of civilization to colonial subjects, and to encourage the widespread use of English among the vast Indian population through the education of native elites. With the passage of an 1835 law, the English language became a part of Britain's official colonial machinery. Enamored of the advantages of English education, since it promised access to the corridors of power and intimacy with the powerful, Indian members of the upper castes and classes themselves began to seek an English education.[6]

The origins of the English language in India during British colonialism, its subsequent growth as the language of higher education and commerce, and its intimate links with the urban upper and middle classes in India's postcolonial phase have been noted and discussed by several scholars.[7] Connecting the proliferation of English in urban India with the "increasing concentration of the privileged English-speaking class with greater leisure in the metropolitan cities," Svati Joshi writes that knowledge of English promises "success in the job market, social mobility, and cultural superiority." English, despite government policies to promote regional languages, remains the language that ensures access to higher education and economic benefits.[8]

Although most women did not speak or write about fiction reading as a tool that was used by their English teachers, three of the twenty-two women discussed nontraditional teachers who incorporated fiction into their pedagogy. Malathi's teacher had students in her class read Nancy Drew books and summarize the plots in brief essays, which they then had to give their classmates to read and evaluate, and thus help improve each others' writing skills in English. In addition, Preethi reported that they had "Elocution" or public speaking classes in school where they had to read out aloud passages from Nancy Drew books. Priya said that her fifth-grade teacher used Nancy Drews to test their spelling: "We were broken up into groups in class and each group was assigned to read a chapter in a Nancy Drew book. When we came across difficult words we were supposed to spell them out to each other or write them down to learn the spelling. Our teacher would then give us a spelling test on the words we learned."

Echoing fiction reading practices that follow gender boundaries in the United States, the adult Indian women in my study also talked about brothers, fathers, and male friends and cousins reading different kinds of fiction. Several women recalled that when they were reading Nancy Drew books, their brothers mostly read Hardy Boys and the British Billy Bunter series books. However, ten of the twenty-two women reported that their brothers and male cousins were casual readers of Nancy Drews. Bhavani, whose entire family read voraciously for pleasure, wrote that her two brothers would ask her for Nancy Drews when they ran out of their own books. In discussing train trips she enjoyed as a child, Meera wrote about the "precious night and day train trips during winter and summer vacations when I could read uninterrupted." Meera also added that her brother would typically finish reading his books in a few hours and then would request to borrow her comics and Nancy Drew books.

Although they read different books, most women remembered that their male siblings read as much as they did until their late teens. These readers reported that adult men chose to pursue social activities outside of the home rather than reading, in contrast to young Indian women whose mobility becomes much more restricted as they enter adulthood. This study did not probe women's adult reading. However, in a related ethnographic study on adult Indian women's reading practices in India, I found that girls continued to pursue reading as a primary leisure activity into their adulthood for a complex range of reasons. Although women expressed enthusiasm for the pleasure that leisure reading provided them, they also suggested that parents' rules about curfew times, frustrations with sexual harassment on streets, and discomfort with the overwhelming male presence in public spaces influenced their choice to read in the private spheres of home and in the gender-segregated environment of college campuses.

Adult Indian women's feelings of admiration for Nancy Drew and their sense of identification with her character focused on her relationships and the sense of adventure and discovery that was built into each chapter and the entire narrative. Fourteen of twenty-two wrote that Nancy was brave because, despite not having a mother and being an only child without the companionship of siblings, she was able to manage and go on successfully in her life. One woman whose mother died when she was two described her emotional attachment to Nancy's character as a motherless child and said, "I used to think if Nancy Drew could find motivation and happiness in solving mysteries even though she was different from others—she had no mother you know—I could also behave similarly. I used to miss my mother very much when I was nine, ten, and actually until I was thirteen I think. Nancy Drew seemed very real to me then."

For many women, their pleasure in reading Nancy Drew books and their understanding of Nancy the girl detective were embedded in the "universal" quality of human relationships that transcended cultural and geographic boundaries. Sixteen of twenty-two emphasized their empathetic identification with the close father-daughter relationship in Nancy Drew books and talked about their own relationships with their fathers. During one focus group interview, discussions about Nancy's father, Carson Drew, became emotional moments because some women missed their own fathers who now lived far away in India. Drawing metaphorically on the supportive and warm character of Carson Drew, who encouraged his daughter in her adventurous pursuits, to describe how much she missed her own father, Keerthi said:

My father is very much like that ... just like Mr. Carson Drew ... he wanted to listen to everything I said even when I was a girl and probably told him stupid things. We are very close and many days I wish I could get his advice on everything like I used to in India. It's hard not being able to see him whenever I want to.

Yet others brought up similarities in Nancy's friendship with George and Bess and their own intimate friendships with girlfriends in school and college. However, in comparing the representation of fictional female relationships in Nancy Drew series books, seven women (a third of interviewees) said that they could recall discussions among friends on the quality of the friendship Nancy, Bess, and George shared. These women reported that they all rated their own friendships as much closer and more intimate because they shared and participated in many everyday rituals on a routine basis with their girlfriends, which they did not see reflected in Nancy Drew books. For instance, in a follow-up personal interview, Madhuri said, "We decided that we were much closer, after all, we did many more things together; walking to school, sharing our lunches, doing our homework, playing in the evenings ..."

Feminist scholars in the United States and Europe have expressed a sustained interest in the potential impact of strong heroines in fiction, heroines who defy Western culture's conventional standards of ideal femininity, and on girls' and women's identities.[9] In a qualitative study of adult women's memories about their childhood reading in the United States, Ana Garner found that many women discussed positively the role played by independent, bright, and enterprising heroines such as Nancy Drew in their choice of careers as lawyers, scientists, academics, and judges. These women wrote about the sense of identification they experienced with "sassy" childhood heroines in fiction because they were rarely exposed to strong female role models in the world around them and in their own families. The Indian women I interviewed also expressed their admiration for Nancy Drew. They were enthusiastic about Nancy's "unforgettable qualities" and used adjectives such as "persistent, brave, smart, loyal, clever" to underscore the affection they still had for their girlhood heroine. However, unlike the women in Garner's study located in the United States, none suggested that Nancy Drew might have been a role model or influenced them in their choice of careers or their decision to pursue higher education.[10]

Some reasons for the cross-cultural differences between Indian and American women in perceptions about Nancy Drew as a strong and positive role model may lie in the class, caste, age, and location of these particular informants. As upper-caste and middle- to upper-class women, these Indian readers represent a privileged group of Nancy Drew readers in the Third World. All but two women's mothers had attended college, and many came from families where education was valued for men *and* women. Fifteen of these twenty women reported that their mothers and other female relatives, including aunts and cousins, were doctors, bankers, entrepreneurs, teachers, school principals, professors, and scientists. While attending school and college in India, these women reported that they *and* their male siblings were equally expected by parents and other elders in the family to excel in school, to perform well in mathematics and science, and to secure professional jobs as adults.

Historically, these women represent a class of women who have benefited the most from reformist, anti-colonial nationalist movements in the nineteenth century that resulted in the entry of many urban middle- and upper-class women across Indian towns and cities into the public arenas of education and paid employment.[11] Middle-class Indian women in upper-caste families in the metropolitan areas in independent India received support and encouragement to get educated and succeed in male-dominated, upper-class professions such as law, medicine, accounting, and teaching. However, it is critical to understand here that these early historical efforts to promote women's entry into the public sphere were ultimately conceived within a patriarchal model because they did not advocate women's true autonomy from the roles of mothers, daughters, wives, or sisters, domestic roles that women, unlike men, were still expected to play. Additionally, in an effort to combat British colonizers' views about Indian culture as barbaric, elite male Indian anti-colonialists conceived of educated middle-class Indian as merely visible symbols of India's superior culture. Yet another more contemporary reason for the absence of talk or writing about Nancy Drew as a "role model" among the Indian women who participated in this study might be the absence of public discourse about role models and self-esteem in India, unlike the United States where such discussions on women's empowerment are a part of everyday media culture.[12]

At the time these women were young girls in India, the commodified, global forms of femininity imported to other cultures from the United States—thin, white, fashionable, and available to men—had not yet become pervasive through women's magazines or television. Additionally, these women who are now in the United States represent a relatively elite demographic group that has the economic and cultural capital to aspire to travel and study abroad in Western countries. Thus, language about the desirability of girls' cultivating rational (not emotional) intelligence, resisting patriarchal beauty ideals, or pursuing successful, professional male-dominated careers may not have constituted the social context within which these Indian women read Nancy Drew fiction.

These differences in experiences of gender and expectations of professional success do not imply that these women did not encounter patriarchal constructions of ideal womanhood. In fact, in focus group interviews, many women spoke about the different forms of surveillance and gendered expectations they experienced, such as pressures to dress modestly, learn domestic chores, and come home early before darkness set in. Women also recounted the many warnings they heard from mothers and other extended family members about becoming sexually active before marriage, dating, or engaging in public interactions with men who were not a part of their social circle. Reading about Nancy Drew for these Indian women was a part of the more idyllic world of girlhood when they had not yet confronted the more overt ideological construction of ideal femininity in Indian culture.

I found evidence of Nancy Drew functioning as a symbol of innocent girlhood in Indian women's lives in an ethnographic study of young women in India who read paperback Western romance novels.[13] These novels, which are imported to India from the United States and the United Kingdom, are commonly referred to as "Mills & Boons," after the publishing firm Harlequin Mills & Boon that produces these books. Some readers, who were defensive because parents and other authority figures disapproved of young women reading "trashy" literature that focused on sex and romance, legitimated their romance reading by explicitly referring to their childhood reading experiences. Twenty of the thirty women I interviewed in India legitimated their current romance reading as reading that "smart" women did by citing their enjoyment of Nancy Drew series books. Some readers argued that their fondness for Nancy Drew books when they were younger was an indication that they were not women who indulged in "stupid fantasies" now because they read romance fiction. Twenty-year-old Samhita, a Nancy Drew fan during her young teen years, argued:

> I read Nancy Drews until a few years ago. I really liked Nancy Drews because Nancy is so clever and she always was ahead of her boyfriend Ned. Then around the age of sixteen, I started reading Mills & Boons along with Nancy Drews. So what is the difference? The heroines in M&Bs are sometimes smart too just like Nancy but the stories are a different angle.

Echoing Samhita's defensive comments, other readers too presented the fact that they had read Nancy Drews earlier as evidence of their basically "sensible" nature. These informants implied that their admiration for Nancy Drew, who was independent and smart, during their early teen years was proof that their current reading of formula romance novels, which emphasized love, sex, and romance, was not deviant.

Some previous research and personal anecdotes about Nancy Drew reading have pointed to the alienating impact of the white, mostly upper-class world of Nancy Drew on women of color in the United States. In biographical essays about reading Nancy Drew, Njeri Fuller and Dinah Eng reflect on the emotional and psychological burden they had to confront in order to identify with Nancy's character. Fuller writes that she mentally transformed Nancy Drew into a black girl while Eng recollects that she "whited out" herself, that is, she denied her Chinese identity and imagined she was white so she could enjoy Nancy's adventures. Placing Nancy Drew within the historical context of the myth of white supremacy in the United States, Donnarae MacCann notes the representation of black people in Nancy Drew books that appeared in 1930 as comic, shifty, unreliable, and surly characters. MacCann writes that it was unfortunate that these stereotypical black characters were erased from later editions only to be replaced by white characters but not with more well-rounded or positive black characters.

Unlike Fuller, Eng, and MacCann, Melinda de Jesús takes her readers outside *and* inside the United States to analyze Nancy Drew reading as an integral part of internalized racism, cultural imperialism, and hegemonic white feminism. De Jesús examines the racial and cultural implications of Nancy Drew reading for herself, a second-generation Filipina American feminist, and for her mother, a first-generation immigrant Filipina. While acknowledging the feminist aspects of Nancy, especially her agency as a strong and independent girl, De Jesús writes that Nancy Drew books were overt symbols of American colonization and imperialism in her mother's life in the Philippines. In an American colony where the United States government had replaced military rule in the islands after the Philippine-American war, Nancy Drews arrived in her mother's life at the same time that American teachers began moving to the Philippines as a part of the mission to impart Western education and civilization.[14]

In the case of young women from India, the consumption of American fiction such as Nancy Drews in the phase of preadolescent girlhood is a leisure reading practice that follows and coexists with the early and late childhood reading of British fiction, comics, and fairy tales. Based on a triangulated analysis of Indian women's written and spoken responses in questionnaires, interviews, and focus groups, I found uniformity in their responses about the books and comics they had read as children. Among the reading materials listed were fairy tales from the Brothers Grimm and Hans Christian Andersen; paperbacks from Britain such as the Enid Blyton series books; comics from the United States such as *Archie, Wendy the*

Witch, Casper the Friendly Ghost, and *Dennis the Menace*; as well as the famous Asterix & Obelix and Tintin comic series that are translated into English from French. Prior to reading Nancy Drew books, twenty out of the twenty-two women recalled voraciously reading Enid Blyton series books, starting with the *Secret Seven* and moving on to *Famous Five, Five Find-Outers, Mallory Towers,* and the Carlotta series.

Although they had read Indian comics and tales, and some stories based on Indian history and mythology, most of the women's childhood reading consisted of imported books. An important reason for their childhood reading preferences for these books and comics can be located not in explanations about "colonial" reading tastes, but in the fact that English-language publishing in India, particularly in the area of children's books, is a relatively recent and postcolonial phenomenon. The British colonial history of English-language publishing in India, coupled with the lack of children's books in English written by Indians, means that for many young urban Indians, imported series books and comics from the United Kingdom and the United States were the staples of their childhood reading material. Scholars have expressed concerns about the implications of English-language publishing's early colonial history in India for the growth and autonomy of Indian publishing, and for the cultural identity of India's reading public.[15] Reflecting on the domination of English language publishing and reading among the urban elite, Urvashi Butalia writes: "The English book is ubiquitous. Publishing in English, from the time it was introduced in India, has come to occupy the largest segment of the market. Not only do books in English make up almost 50 percent of the numbers published in the country. India is one of the largest English publishing countries in the world, standing third after the US and UK in publishing."[16] Given the production costs and meager profit margins, most indigenous English-language publishing has been confined to textbooks because of the expanding market for educational materials and the growing numbers of schools and universities. It is only recently that private publishing firms such as India Book House, Orient Longman, and Jaico Publishers and quasi-government firms such as Children's Book Trust have begun producing leisure reading fiction for Indian children.[17]

When I asked the young Indian women I interviewed how they related to Nancy Drew, most reacted in a surprising and unexpected fashion. In focus group sessions and interviews, many women did not speak about the critical issue of reader identification, that is, their dilemma in connecting their own identity with Nancy Drew, a white American girl. Rather, they elaborated on the difficult transition they had to make from British fiction

READING NANCY DREW BOOKS IN URBAN INDIA

to American fiction. Tara, whose Enid Blyton collection was the envy of her friends, said, "I read my first Nancy Drew, *The Crooked Banister,* and remember having to read things twice and just missing the whole atmosphere of the British authors. I found Nancy Drews at first too abrupt, the people not well-defined, and nobody seemed to have enough personality or character." Another woman, Roopali, chimed in and said, "The sentences were short, there were few descriptions of scenes or characters, they did not eat as much good food or go on picnics like the British kids did." Summing up her difficulty with adjusting to the writing style in Nancy Drew books, Sudha remarked, "A little too gritty and a bit superficial after my Richmal Crompton and Enid Blyton books but by the third book I was into the writing style of Nancy Drew books." The reading of Nancy Drew books in India, which in part represents the economic power of American global publishing, and hence a form of neocolonialism, thus competes with the earlier cultural and economic imperialism of Britain.

In further discussions about the representation of Nancy Drew, none of these Indian women explicitly acknowledged the alienating effects on notions of selfhood and subjectivity that may be produced when children consistently immerse themselves in a fictional world that does not resemble their own. In fact, several women asked me to clarify the question: "When you were a girl, could you picture yourself or identify closely with anyone in Nancy Drew books?" Two clearly thought I was asking them a bad question and one of them said, "How can you ask us this? This was a story about an American girl. We don't live like that nor did we see things around us that looked like Nancy Drew's life."

Seven women suggested that they had thought of Nancy Drew as their American pen pal, somebody who lived far away but was a close friend with whom they regularly corresponded. Geeta, who cherished the ability she had as a girl to slip away into a fantasy world completely different from her own, said, "Nancy Drew would not be the same if she were anything but American. I loved visualizing and reading about her amazing life as a girl detective in America. I used to reproduce the images of Nancy Drew with pencil and watercolor paints." Anupama said she learned about how young girls in America lived, "Nancy Drew went swimming, dancing, skiing, dating, diving, and did all these things I could never do. She was my daring and interesting friend." Other women suggested that they could escape into Nancy's American life with ease as girls because there were no photos; instead, they said they loved the covers and pictures inside which were line drawings. Describing the time she used to spend gazing at the drawings, Priya wrote, "I loved those pictures. I could fill in whatever meanings I wanted. I knew Nancy was and looked different from me but those pictures let me imagine her as an American girlfriend, a girlfriend I could create."

Interestingly, during focus group discussions about the fantasy of escaping into Nancy Drew's life as an American girl, many women spoke about the ease with which they could forget reality when they were girls growing up in India. Several women emphasized their carefree lives at home where they had no responsibilities other than to work hard at school, and were continuously surrounded by friends and extended family members. For instance, during our interview, Sharon described her Nancy Drew reading one week when they had gone to visit her uncle's family in Calcutta:

> I loved reading about all the meals Nancy Drew ate. I imagined what the food would look like. I used to escape into Nancy's life completely ... I remember that vacation like it was yesterday. I read my favorite Nancy Drew, *The Clue of the Leaning Chimney,* and was completely gone. My mother called me several times and I did not respond. I then remember my uncle who was a doctor walked over and said that my mom had asked him to check my ears to see if I was deaf! I wish I could do that now.

Contrasting her inability to relax as a busy graduate student, Smita wrote that she was no longer capable of reading in the same way, "The only place I can relax now is at the movies where I cannot check e-mail or get a phone call or read. I remember being lost in Nancy Drew's life—imagining she was my American pal and we were doing things together you know."

Although they did not express criticism of Nancy Drew's specific ethnic or class background, a few women spoke about the aura of America that surrounded and permeated their Nancy Drew reading in India. Remembering the Nancy Drew books she shared with her friends at school, Payal said, "Nancy Drew was definitely 'cool' because she was American. If you were not reading Hardy Boys or Nancy Drews you did not belong in the 'cool' circle." Several women remarked that some of the most quintessential American elements of Nancy Drew's character that they remembered were her speedy roadster, her mansion, the city of River Heights, and her informal relationship with her attorney father, Carson Drew. Sarita said her cousins who lived in the United States were shocked and surprised when they visited India because just like them, she too was reading Nancy Drews. "I used to ask them all about America and we would play Nancy Drew games." Rather than emphasizing Nancy Drew's race or her upper-class status, these Indian readers focused on her nationality as an American girl.

Unlike Melinda de Jesús' Filipina mother, who imagined that she became Nancy Drew, these Indian readers claim that they had not identified with Nancy Drew in the sense of substituting themselves into her character. Instead they incorporated her into their world as an exotic friend. While women of color in the multiracial culture of the United States talk about transforming Nancy Drew into a black girl or of learning to suppress their own Asian ethnicity to become white, Indian readers who grew up in a fairly homogenous racial environment in India do not emphasize Nancy Drew's racial identity. Additionally, although these Indian women by no means live in the same American upper-class world of Nancy Drew, as elites in their own culture they may not have experienced a rupture between their own privileged world and that of Nancy Drew.

This essay's exploration of Indian women's Nancy Drew reading suggests interesting implications for the impact and influence of social contexts—history, location, and gender and class structures—on adult women's recollections and memories about their childhood reading. Contemporary cultural phenomena such as children's leisure reading practices in non-Western, postcolonial settings are linked in complex ways to the history of European colonialism. In this study of Nancy Drew reading in India, at the most visible level, the connections among class, cosmopolitan culture in urban spaces, and colonial history were manifested in the reading of imported English-language series fiction by middle- and upper-class Indian women readers. Discussing the influence of colonialism on urban Indian culture, Ashis Nandy writes: "In spite of the presence of a paramount power [colonialism] which acted as the central authority, the country was culturally fragmented and politically heterogeneous. It could, thus, confine the cultural impact of imperialism to its urban centers, to its Westernized and semi-Westernized upper and middle classes, and to some sections of its traditional elites."[18] Nandy's contention about the immersion of elites in India in Western culture could imply parallel developments and links among language, class, and colonial culture in other postcolonial locales in Africa and Asia. A less visible link to colonial history implicit in this study lies in the fact that Indian women readers' appetite for the fantasy world of English language series books is not a completely new artifact of our current global media culture.

In her insightful essay about the leisure reading practices of Indians in the mid- to late-nineteenth century, Priya Joshi shows us that, contrary to

British colonial imperatives, urban Indians did not seek out the "serious" high culture novels that the colonial administration advocated. "For one, the 'good' English novels that were part of the colonial curriculum and were entrusted with creating an Indian who was English in 'taste, in opinions, in morals, and in intellect' were in practice not the novels sought out by Indian readers for leisure reading," she writes. "The canon of popular literature and the books most avidly and spontaneously consumed by Indian readers were increasingly disjunct from those prescribed by the Department of Public Instruction."[19]

In her analysis of advertisements in the *Times of India* between 1861 and 1881, Joshi demonstrates that the demand among Indian readers for popular British literature such as the sensational, gothic, and melodramatic serial novels far exceeded their demand for more lofty novels by Dickens, Austen, Eliot, Thackeray, or Meredith. Joshi writes that these antirealist tales in which virtue always vanquished evil were reminiscent of pre-modern Indian tales and myths. Further, the forms of these popular novels also permitted adaptations with few cross-cultural restrictions. Joshi's persuasive argument that the success of British popular serial novels in India "had its roots in the failure of British high culture to penetrate fully the Indian marketplace of ideas" suggests that the consumption of certain kinds of British fiction among Indians was a form of resistance to colonial ideas about good literature.[20] The implications of Joshi's argument about Indians' resistance to reading only British high culture fiction and nonfiction in the nineteenth century casts a new light on Indian women's pleasure in reading Nancy Drew fiction. On the surface, given the greater economic power of American popular culture, and its inherently greater likelihood of becoming a pervasive force in the rest of the world, one could argue that Indian girls' voracious reading of Nancy Drew fiction is more evidence of American cultural imperialism in a Third World setting. However, Joshi's historical context of Indian readers' preferences for popular serial fiction as subversive resistance to British colonial pressures provides a different perspective on Nancy Drew reading, a perspective that cautions us against making hasty and sweeping judgements about contemporary cultural imperialism.

What does it mean when a group of non-Western women relive memories of "home" through their talk about reading popular American series fiction? Does this imply that their sense of self is engulfed by fictional characters from Western culture? Certainly, admiration for the material fantasy in Western popular literature—descriptions of food, houses, picnics—suggests that Nancy Drew reading is part of the predominantly one-way traffic in media culture from the developed world to the Third World. However, Nancy Drew books coexist with other lively and dynamic cultural forms and practices in many Third World readers' lives. Although the world of leisure reading was dominated by British and American popular fiction for these Indian women, their lives outside of their fiction reading were simultaneously and robustly immersed in their local cultures. Many women talked about celebrating Indian festivals, watching Indian films, eating Indian food regularly at home, speaking in vernacular languages with friends and family, and learning traditional Indian dance and music. So, rather than absorbing only Western culture through their leisure reading in a passive fashion, these Indian women may experience what Vinay Dharwadker defines as "cultural ambidexterity," that is, the ability to live and "act in two or more cultures without making unmixed, unilateral choices or commitments."[21] Dharwadker writes that culturally ambidextrous subjects avoid extreme resistance or complete collaboration and instead learn to function in two or more cultures in an ambivalent yet confident manner.

Adult Indian women's discussions about Nancy Drew as a filtered memory of their lives in India—relationships with lending library owners, friendships with other girls, relaxed summer vacations, and train trips— show us that the meaning of literature is embedded within our current experiences of modernity. Such modernity as this study shows is characterized by the increasing mobility of diasporic people who travel and live in the West but arrive here with a part of their imagination already rooted in Western culture. Furthermore, in my fieldwork, nostalgic discussions about childhood reading demonstrate that the setting and location of research is part of the "data" that we as scholars unearth and interpret. For instance, I found that focus group sessions about Nancy Drew reading functioned as significant cultural sites for women's shared memories about home.

With regard to gender, the study shows that reading series fiction did conform to gender boundaries, that is, Indian women reported that they read Nancy Drew as girls while their male siblings and friends preferred Hardy Boys. Although these women did read Hardy Boys books, they did not express the same enthusiasm or affection for these young male detectives as they did for Nancy Drew. So, at a certain level, Indian women's discussion of their childhood reading practices shows us that even across cultural boundaries, serial fiction such as Nancy Drew attracts and gives pleasure to girls from other parts of the world. As women who belonged to families in which education and professional success was valued for girls as well as boys, Nancy Drew did not serve as a strong symbol of "cleverness or intelligence" as she did for women in Ana Garner's study of women in the United States. Discourses of gender, class, and nationalism thus form the backdrop against which Nancy Drew is interpreted by these Indian women. Finally, the issue of gender and reader identification in this study also brings up interesting methodological problems. In interviewing adult women about childhood reading, one must be prepared for the critical lens of adulthood through which women now view their childhood. Identifying with a white girl may seem out of place to these adult women, who now live in the United States and could be just beginning to sense their racial and cultural difference from white Americans.

NOTES

The author would like to thank Daniel Crowley for his timely help in locating secondary sources for this essay.

1. Janice Radway, *Reading the Romance: Women, Patriarchy and Popular Literature* (Chapel Hill, NC: University of North Carolina Press, 1984).

2. See Purnima Mankekar, "Reconstructing 'Indian Womanhood': An Ethnography of Television Viewers in a North Indian City." (Ph.D. diss., University of Washington, 1993); Arvind Rajagopal, "Mediating Modernity: Theorizing Reception in a Non-Western Society," *Communication Review* 1, no. 4 (1996): 441–470; Steve Derne, "Film-Going Builds Self, Sexuality, and Power: An Ethnography of Men's Reception of Popular Films in India." (Unpublished manuscript, Department of Sociology, SUNY-Geneseo, Geneseo, NY); and Sara Dickey, "Consuming Utopia: Film Watching in Tamil Nadu," in *Consuming Modernity: Public Culture in a South Asian World,* ed. Arjun Appadurai and Carol Breckenridge (Minneapolis: University of Minnesota Press, 1995), 131–156.

3. Sherrie Inness (ed.), *Nancy Drew and Company: Culture, Gender, and Girls' Series* (Bowling Green, OH: Bowling Green State University Popular Press, 1997), 1.

4. See, for example, Melinda de Jesús, "Fictions of Assimilation: Nancy Drew, Cultural Imperialism, and the Filipina/American Experience," in *Delinquents and Debutantes: Twentieth-Century American Girls' Cultures*, ed. Sherrie Inness (New York: New York University Press, 1998), 227–243; Carolyn Dyer and Nancy Romalov, *Rediscovering Nancy Drew* (Iowa City, IA: University of Iowa Press, 1995); and Sally Parry, "The Secret of the Feminist Heroine: The Search for Values in Nancy Drew and Judy Bolton," in *Nancy Drew and Company*, ed. Sherrie Innes, 145–158; and Deborah Siegel, "Nancy Drew as New Girl Wonder," ibid., 159–182.

5. See Dinah Eng, "Befriending Nancy Drew across Cultural Boundaries," in Dyer and Romalov, 140–142; Njeri Fuller, "Fixing Nancy Drew: African-American Strategies for Reading," ibid., 136–139; Donnarae MacCann, "Nancy Drew and the Myth of White Supremacy," ibid., 129–135; and Melinda de Jesús, "Fictions of Assimilation" in *Delinquents and Debutantes*, ed. Sherrie Inness, 227–243. See also Inness, *Nancy Drew and Company.*

6. Hindu religious reformers Raja Rammohun Roy and Dwarka Nath Tagore in nineteenth-century India viewed English as the language that would help people to approach Western science and rationality, modern tools that would help to combat superstition. Kamal Sridhar points out that nationalist leaders like Jawaharlal Nehru, Subash Chandra Bose, Mahatma Gandhi, and Sardar Patel received education in India in English and then lived in England to pursue higher education. See Kamal Sridhar, "The Development of English as an Elite Language in the Multilingual Context of India" (Ph.D. diss., University of Illinois at Urbana-Champaign, 1977), 16, 18, and 110. Aijaz Ahmad writes that members of the English elite of India, who were active in the nationalist movement to overthrow British rule, arose from sites closest to the institutions of colonial power—administration, law commerce, English-language journalism, teaching staffs of colleges and universities." See Aijaz Ahmad, *In Theory: Classes, Nations, Literatures* (London: Verso, 1992), 76.

7. British efforts to strengthen and consolidate their rule in India can by no means be conceived of as diabolical and direct forms of domination over their colonial subjects. Gauri Viswanathan's detailed and theoretically sophisticated work on the colonial conditions that enabled the rise of English studies in India avoids precisely this simple model of domination as direct control and instead begins from the Gramscian notion of hegemony, which allows for ideology to be understood as a form of "masking" or illusion. The decision to fortify their position as colonial rulers—and to quell rebellion—through English emerged not only out of strong ethnocentric assumptions of superiority, but it also revealed an instrumental, administrative application of language, ultimately motivated by a sense of frailty in the colonial position. Viswanathan writes that, for the British who inhabited a colonial world of "imminent rebellion and resistance," English became a way to contain rebellion and inculcate awe and wonder of the Raj. See Gauri Viswanathan, *Masks of Conquest: Literary Study and British Rule in India* (New York: Columbia University Press, 1989), 11. See also Ahmad, *In Theory*; Svati Joshi (ed.), *Rethinking English: Essays in Literature, Language, History* (New Delhi: Trianka Publishers, 1991); Lachman Khubchandani, *Plural Languages, Plural Cultures: Communication, Identity, and Sociopolitical Change in Contemporary India* (Honolulu: University of Hawaii Press, 1983); Ashis Nandy, *The Intimate Enemy: Loss and Recovery of Self under Colonialism* (New Delhi: Oxford University Press, 1983); D. L. Sheth, "No English Please, We're Indian," *The Illustrated Weekly of India* 4 (August 19, 1990): 34–37; Sridhar, *Development*

of English; and Rajeswari Sunder Rajan, *The Lie of the Land: English Literary Studies in India* (New Delhi: Oxford University Press, 1992).

8. Joshi, 2, 21; Khubchandani, 67.

9. See Meredith Cherland, *Private Practices: Girls Reading Fiction and Constructing Identity* (Bristol, PA: Taylor & Francis, 1994); Ana Garner, "Negotiating Our Positions in Culture: Popular Adolescent Fiction and the Self-Constructions of Women," *Women's Studies in Communication* 22, no. 1 (1999): 85–111; Carolyn Heilbrun, "Nancy Drew: A Moment in Feminist History," in Dyer and Ramalov (eds.), 11–21; Nancy Romalov, "Mobile and Modern Heroines: Early Twentieth-Century Girls' Series" in *Nancy Drew & Company*, ed. Sherrie Inness (ed.), 89–100; and Bonnie Sunstein, "Reading the Stories of Reading: Nancy Drew Testimonials," in Dyer and Romalov (eds.), 95–112.

10. Garner, "Negotiating Our Positions in Culture."

11. See Partha Chatterjee, "Colonialism, Nationalism, and the Colonialized Women: The Contest in India," *American Ethnologist* 16, no. 1 (1989): 622–633; Kumari Jayawardena, *Feminism and Nationalism in the Third World* (London: Zed Books, 1986); Deniz Kandiyoti, "Identity and Its Discontents: Women and the Nation," *Millennium: Journal of International Studies* 20, no. 3 (1991): 429–443; and Ketu Katrak, "Decolonizing Culture: Toward a Theory for Postcolonial Women's Texts," *Modern Fiction Studies* 35, no. 1 (1989): 157–179.

12. Discourse on women's low self-esteem and the need for strong female role models for women is a part of prime-time news, sitcoms such as "Murphy Brown" and "Roseanne," cable channels such as Lifetime targeted to women, talk shows such as "The Oprah Winfrey Show," popular women's magazines such as *Cosmopolitan,* and self-help books. Such discourse on role models fits well into the therapeutic, individualist model of women's liberation that guides liberal feminism.

13. Radhika Parameswaran, "Western Romance Fiction as English-Language Media in Postcolonial India," *Journal of Communication* 49, no. 2 (1999): 84–105.

14. See Fuller, "Fixing Nancy Drew"; Eng, "Befriending Nancy Drew"; MacCann, "Nancy Drew and the Myth of White Supremacy"; and de Jesús, "Fictions of Assimilation."

15. Phillip Altbach, *Publishing in India* (New Delhi: Oxford University Press, 1975); Shamanna Kesavan, *History of Printing and Publishing in India: A Story of Cultural Re-Awakening* (New Delhi: National Book Trust, 1988); Ahmad, *In Theory*; Urvashi Butalia, "English Textbook, Indian Publisher," *Media, Culture and Society* 15, no. 2 (1993): 217–232; Vinay Dharwadker, "Print Culture and Literary Markets in Colonial India," in *Language Machines: Technologies of Literary Production*, eds. Jeffrey Masten, Peter Stallybrass, and Nancy Wickers (New York: Routledge), 108–133; Samuel Israel, "25 Years of Indian Publishing: G. R. Bhatkal Memorial Lecture," *The Indian Bookseller and Publisher* 26, no. 3 (1976): 5–15; and Priya Joshi, "Culture and Consumption: Fiction, the Reading Public, and the British Novel in Colonial India," *Book History* 1 (1998): 196–220.

16. Butalia, "English Textbook, Indian Publisher," 218.

17. Samuel Israel, "Indian Publishing: The Changing Scene," *Quest* 68 (January-February 1971): 50–58.

18. Nandy, 31–32.

19. Joshi, "Culture and Consumption," 204.

20. Joshi, "Culture and Consumption," 216.

21. Dharwadker, 123.

INDEX

ABOUT THE EDITORS AND CONTRIBUTORS

RIMA D. APPLE is Professor in the School of Human Ecology and the Women's Studies Program at the University of Wisconsin-Madison. She is the author of numerous books and articles on women's history, including *Mothers and Medicine: A Social History of Infant Feeding, 1890–1950* (1987) and a coeditor of *Mothers and Motherhood: Readings in American History* (1997).

KATHLEEN CHAMBERLAIN is Associate Professor of English and Associate Dean of the Faculty at Emory & Henry College. Her articles on juvenile series fiction have appeared in *Children's Literature Quarterly*, *The Lion and the Unicorn*, *Nancy Drew and Company* (1997), and *Scorned Literature* (2002).

ANNE LUNDIN is Associate Professor in the School of Library and Information Studies at the University of Wisconsin-Madison. She is a specialist in the reception of children's literature in history, and the author of numerous articles and *Victorian Horizons: The Reception of the Picture Books of Walter Crane, Randolph Caldecott, and Kate Greenaway* (2001).

LESLIE R. MILLER is a Ph.D. candidate in the History Department at the University of Georgia. In her dissertation, she is examining the dissemination of patriotic values to children between the end of Reconstruction and the 1920s.

PAUL C. MISHLER is the author of *Raising Reds: The Young Pioneers, Radical Summer Camps, and Communist Political Culture in the United States* (1999). He is Assistant Professor of Labor Studies at Indiana University at South Bend, and is also on the editorial board of *Science and Society*.

RADHIKA PARAMESWARAN is Assistant Professor of Journalism at Indiana University. She is the author of several publications on gender and media culture that have appeared in *Journal of Communication, Journalism & Communication Monographs, Communication Theory, Qualitative Inquiry*, and *Journal of Communication Inquiry*.

JOANNE PASSET is Assistant Professor of History at Indiana University East. She is the author of *Cultural Crusaders: Women Librarians in the American West, 1900–1917* (1994) and *Sex Radicals and the Quest for Women's Equality, 1853–1909* (2003).

LOUISE S. ROBBINS is Director and Professor in the School of Library and Information Studies at the University of Wisconsin-Madison. She is the author of *The Dismissal of Miss Ruth Brown: Civil Rights, Censorship, and the American Library* (2000) and other books and articles.

BONNIE JAMES SHAKER is an independent scholar who has served as Assistant Professor of Journalism at Youngstown State University. She is a former television news bureau chief, and the author of *Coloring Locals: Racial Formation in Kate Chopin's Youth's Companion Stories* (2003).

CAROL E. J. TRONE is a Ph.D. candidate in the Department of Educational Policy Studies at the University of Wisconsin-Madison. Her dissertation, "Image Making, Public Relations, and the Public Schools, 1890–1960," examines the changing role of communications between educators and the public since the late nineteenth century.

SUSAN TUCKER is Curator of Books and Records, Newcomb College Archives, Newcomb Center for Research on Women, Tulane University. She is the author of *Telling Memories Among Southern Women* (1988) and a coeditor of *Layered History: Scrapbooks and Their History* (2004).

CATHERINE VAN HORN received her Ph.D. in Mass Communications from the University of Washington in 1994. Her dissertation analyzed the international news flow between nineteenth-century Fiji and the West (Tonga, Australia, England, and the United States). She is currently working with the Oregon State Office of Energy.

WAYNE A. WIEGAND is F. William Summers Professor of Library and Information Studies at Florida State University and former Codirector of the Center for the History of Print Culture in Modern America. He is the author of *Irrepressible Reformer: A Biography of Melvil Dewey* (1996) and a coeditor of *Print Culture in a Diverse America* (1998).